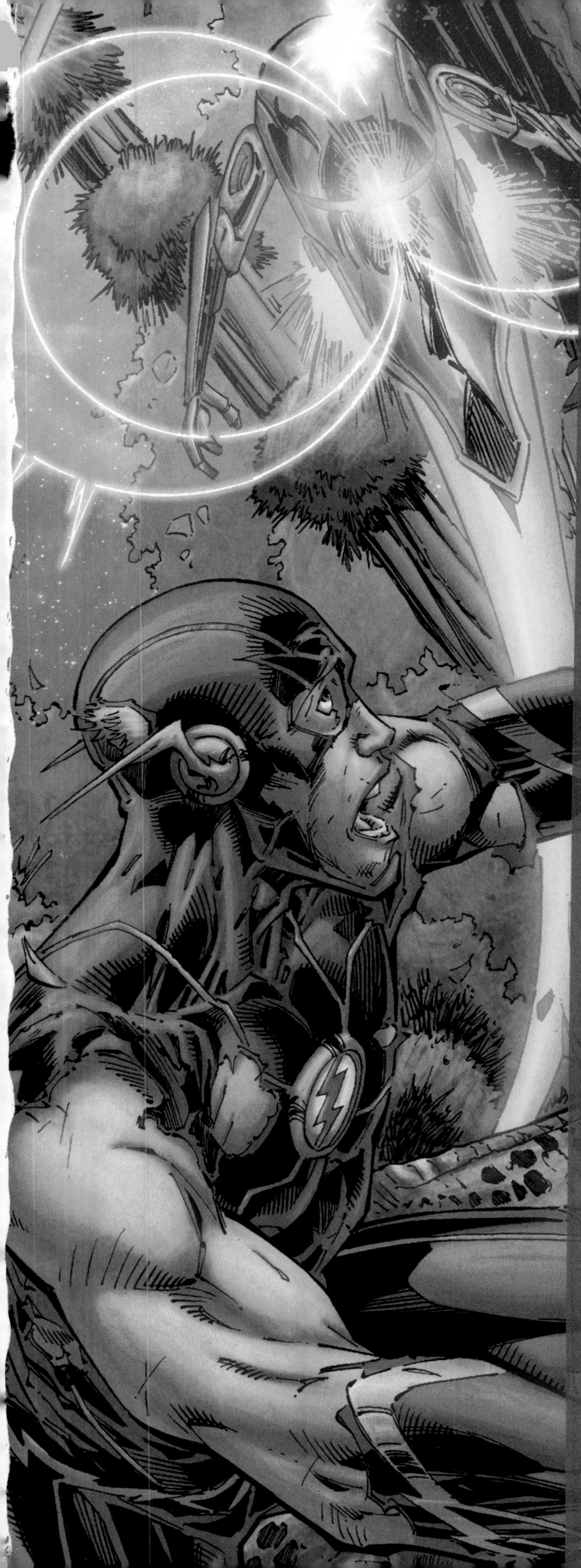

THE FLASH

VOLUME 7
SAVAGE WORLD

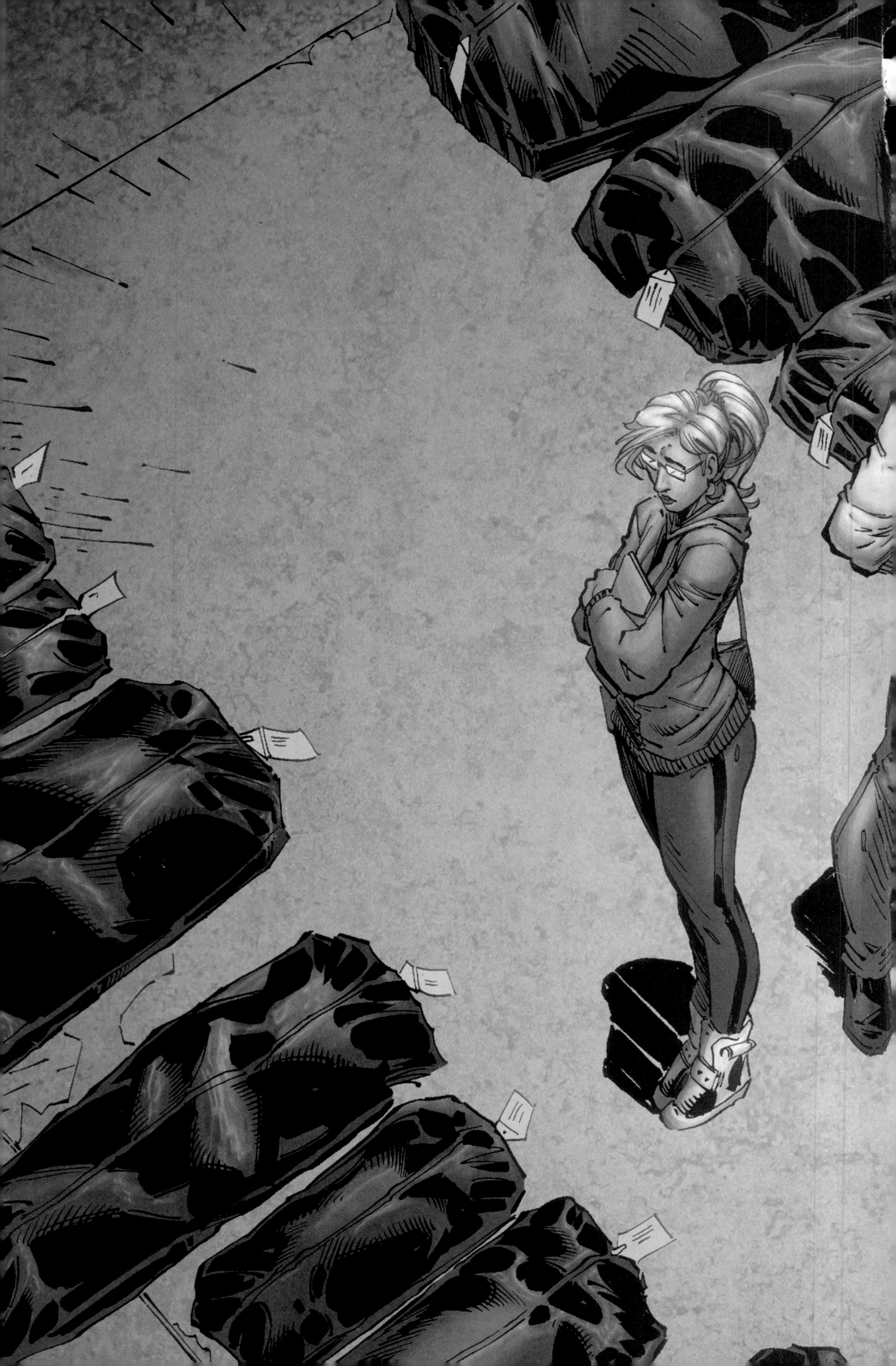

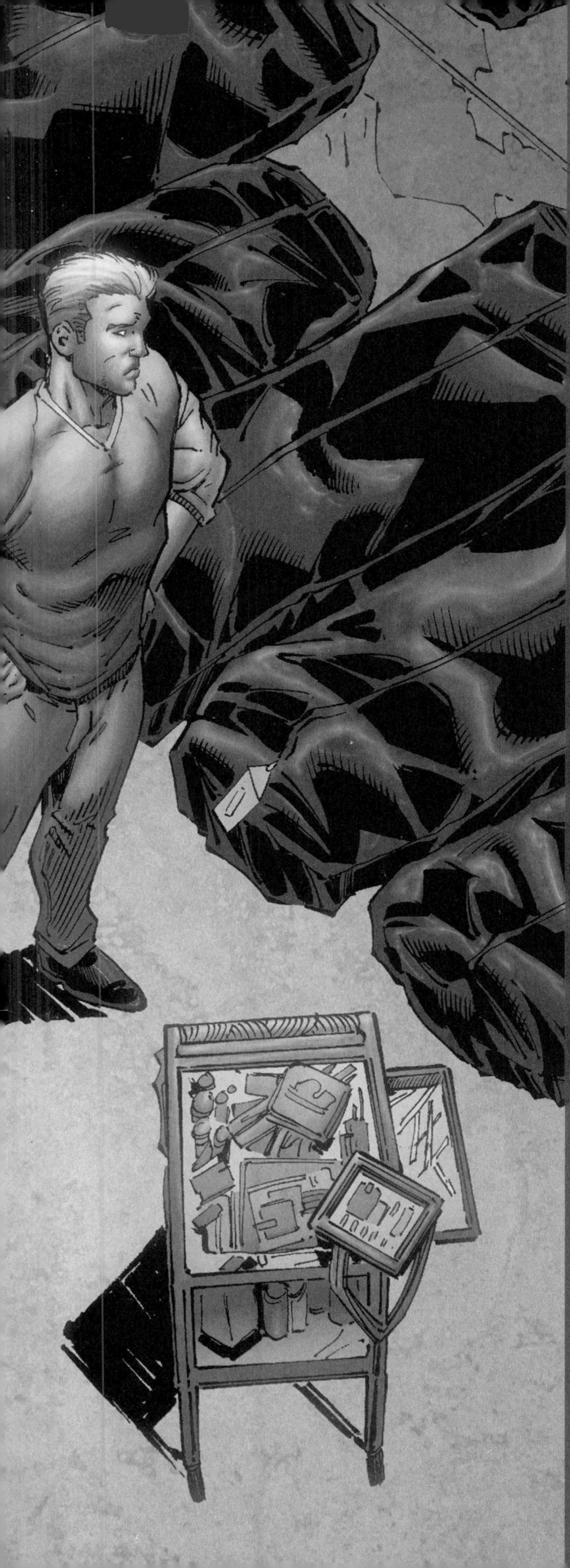

THE FLASH

VOLUME 7
SAVAGE WORLD

WRITTEN BY
ROBERT VENDITTI
VAN JENSEN

PENCILS BY
BRETT BOOTH
ANDRÉ COELHO
MIGUEL SEPULVEDA

INKS BY
NORM RAPMUND
SCOTT HANNA

COLOR BY
ANDREW DALHOUSE

LETTERS BY
TAYLOR ESPOSITO
DEZI SIENTY
PAT BROSSEAU

COLLECTION COVER ART BY
BRETT BOOTH,
NORM RAPMUND
& ANDREW DALHOUSE

BRIAN CUNNINGHAM Editor – Original Series
AMEDEO TURTURRO Assistant Editor – Original Series
JEB WOODARD Group Editor – Collected Editions
DAMIAN RYLAND Publication Design

BOB HARRAS Senior VP – Editor-in-Chief, DC Comics

DIANE NELSON President
DAN DIDIO and JIM LEE Co-Publishers
GEOFF JOHNS Chief Creative Officer
AMIT DESAI Senior VP – Marketing & Global Franchise Management
NAIRI GARDINER Senior VP – Finance
SAM ADES VP – Digital Marketing
BOBBIE CHASE VP –Talent Development
MARK CHIARELLO Senior VP – Art, Design & Collected Editions
JOHN CUNNINGHAM VP – Content Strategy
ANNE DEPIES VP – Strategy Planning & Reporting
DON FALLETTI VP – Manufacturing Operations
LAWRENCE GANEM VP – Editorial Administration & Talent Relations
ALISON GILL Senior VP – Manufacturing & Operations
HANK KANALZ Senior VP – Editorial Strategy & Administration
JAY KOGAN VP – Legal Affairs
DEREK MADDALENA Senior VP – Sales & Business Development
JACK MAHAN VP – Business Affairs
DAN MIRON VP – Sales Planning & Trade Development
NICK NAPOLITANO VP – Manufacturing Administration
CAROL ROEDER VP – Marketing
EDDIE SCANNELL VP – Mass Account & Digital Sales
COURTNEY SIMMONS Senior VP – Publicity & Communications
JIM (SKI) SOKOLOWSKI VP – Comic Book Specialty & Newsstand Sales
SANDY YI Senior VP – Global Franchise Management

THE FLASH VOL. 7: SAVAGE WORLD

DC Comics, 2900 West Alameda Ave., Burbank, CA 91505
Printed by RR Donnelley, Salem, VA, USA. 12/11/15. First Printing.
ISBN: 978-1-4012-5875-7

Library of Congress Cataloging-in-Publication Data

Venditti, Robert, author.
The Flash. Volume 7 / Robert Venditti, Van Jensen, writers ; Brett Booth, artist.
pages cm — (The New 52!)
ISBN 978-1-4012-5875-7 (hardback)
1. Graphic novels. I. Jensen, Van, author.. II. Booth, Brett, illustrator. III. Title.
PN6728.F53V46 2016
741.5'973—dc23
                            2015033156

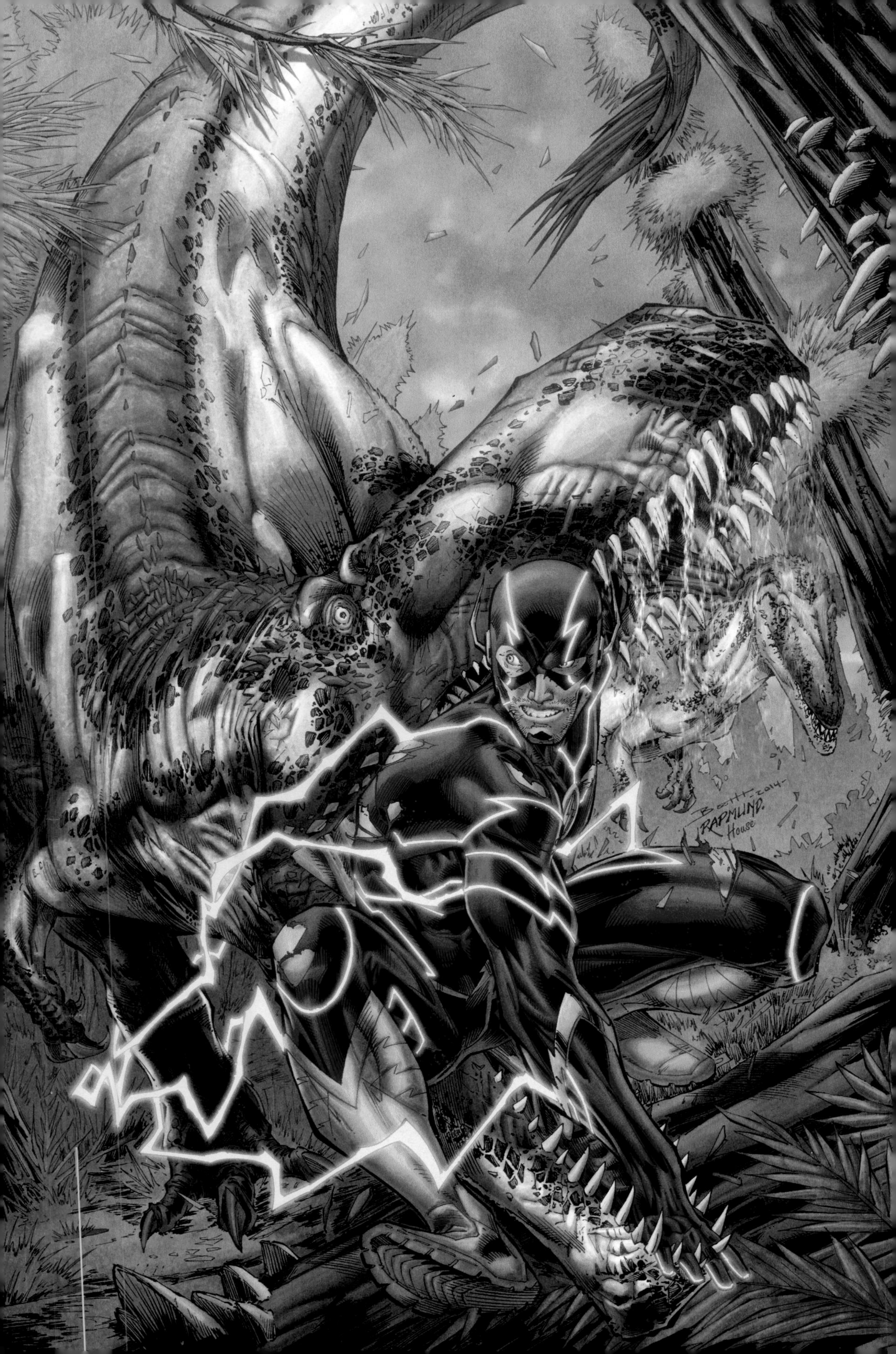
Booth 2014
RAPMUND
House

CASTAWAYS

ROBERT VENDITTI & VAN JENSEN writers BRETT BOOTH & ANDRÉ COELHO pencillers NORM RAPMUND inker ANDREW DALHOUSE colorist TAYLOR ESPOSITO letterer
cover by BRETT BOOTH, NORM RAPMUND & ANDREW DALHOUSE

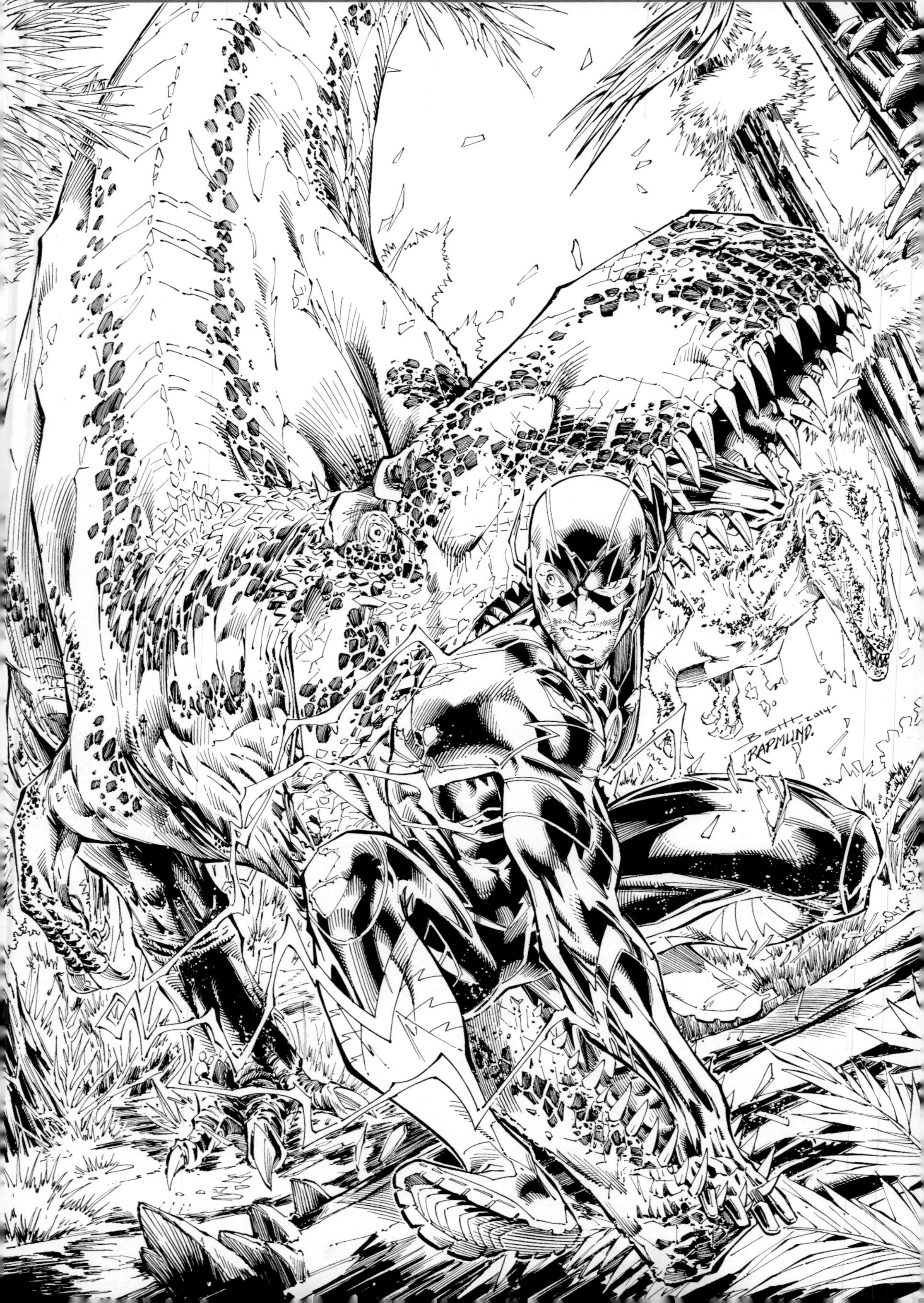

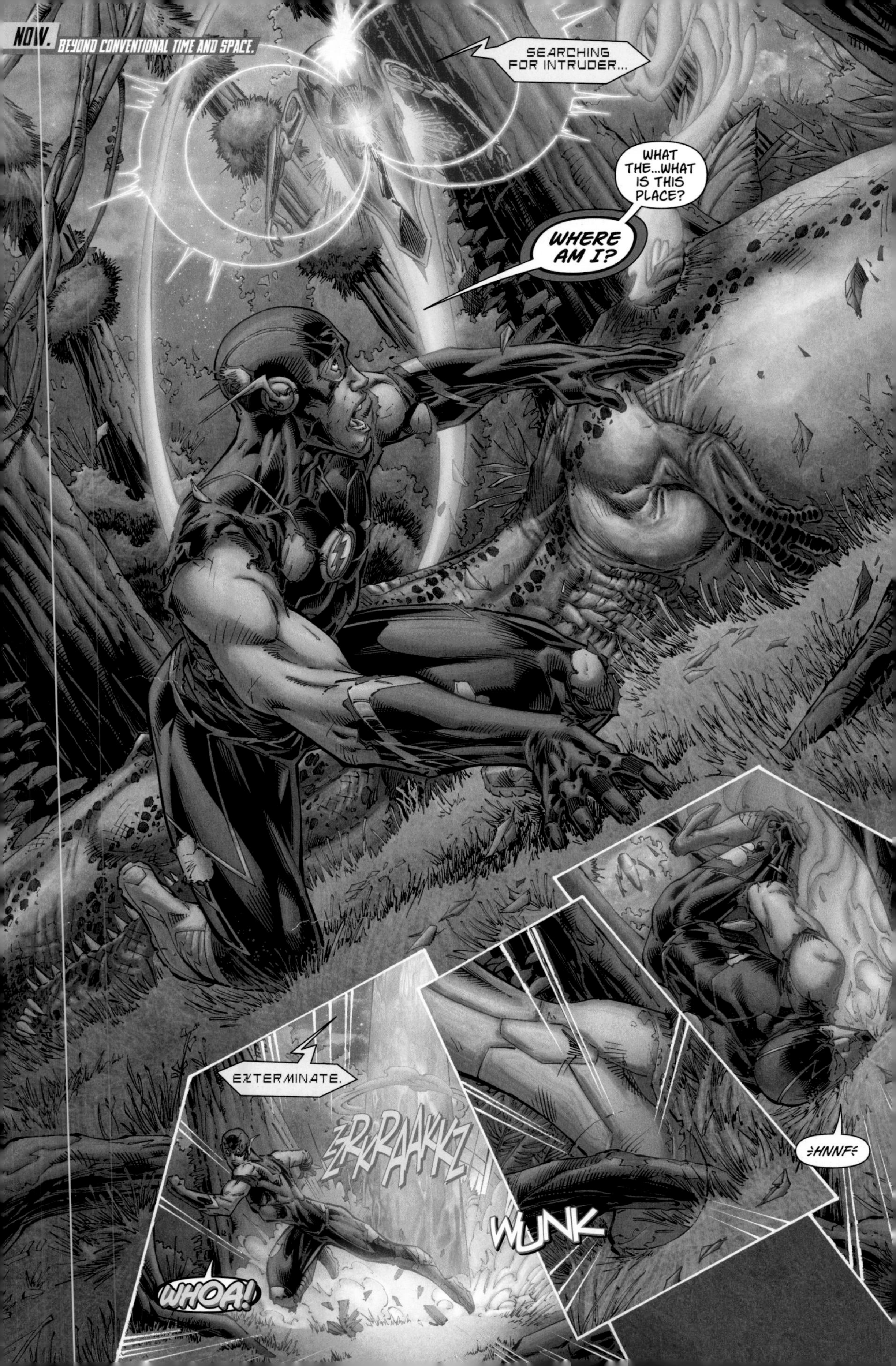
NOW. BEYOND CONVENTIONAL TIME AND SPACE.
SEARCHING FOR INTRUDER...
WHAT THE...WHAT IS THIS PLACE?
WHERE AM I?
EXTERMINATE.
ZZRRRAAKKZ
WHOA!
WUNK
HNNF

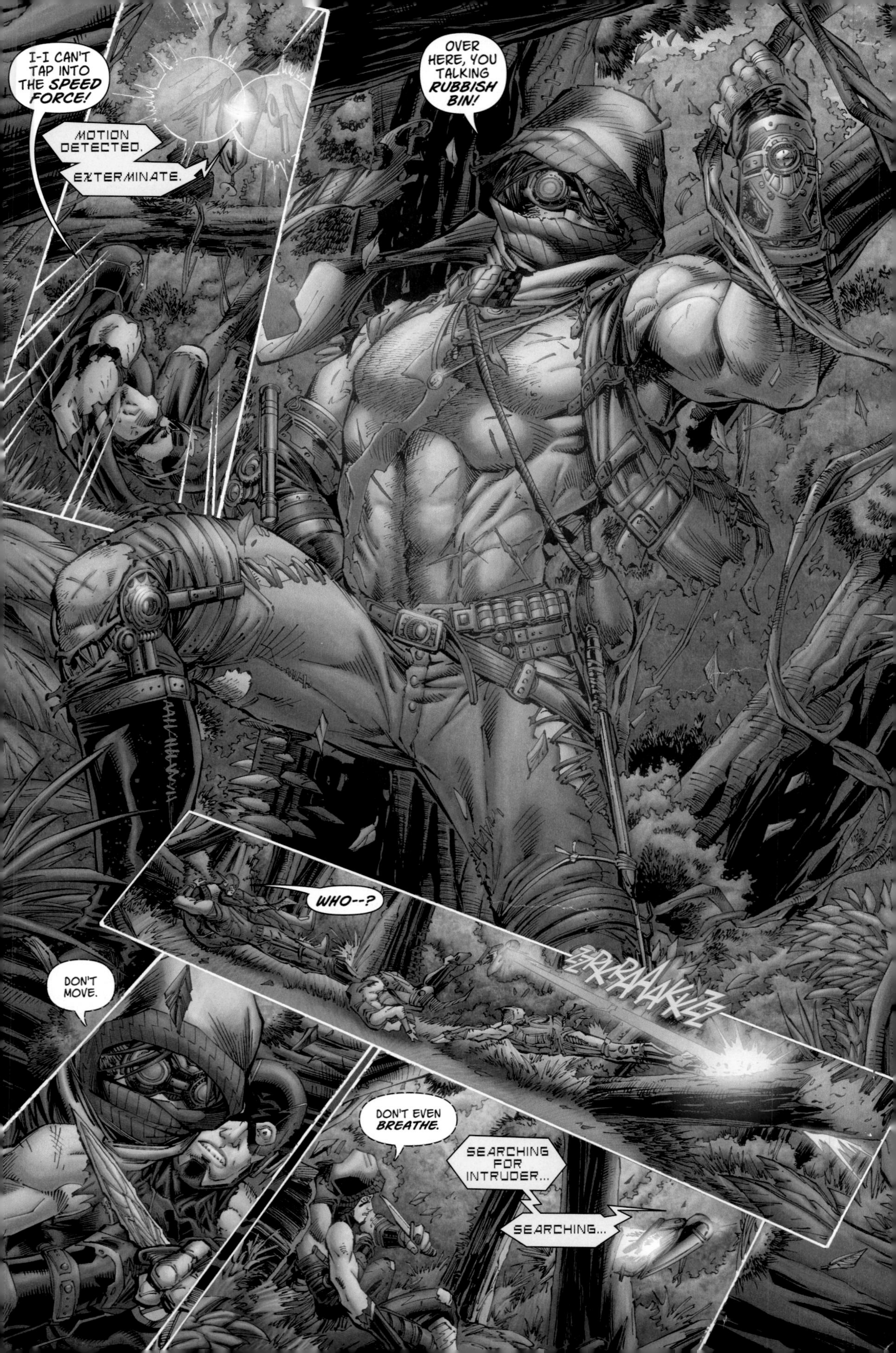
I-I CAN'T TAP INTO THE SPEED FORCE!
MOTION DETECTED.
EXTERMINATE.
OVER HERE, YOU TALKING RUBBISH BIN!
WHO--?
ZZRRRAAKKZZ
DON'T MOVE.
DON'T EVEN BREATHE.
SEARCHING FOR INTRUDER...
SEARCHING...

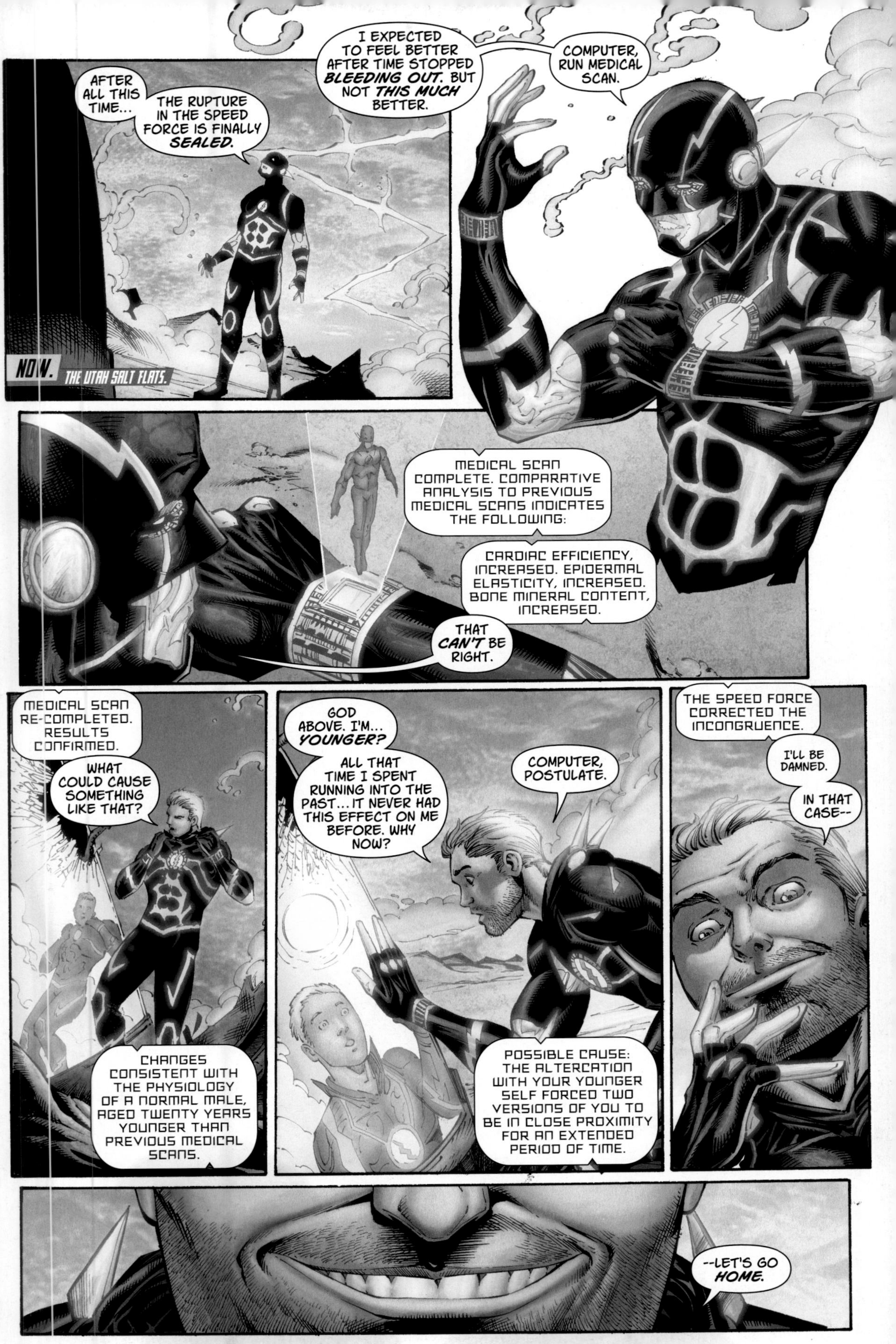

AFTER ALL THIS TIME...
THE RUPTURE IN THE SPEED FORCE IS FINALLY SEALED.
NOW. THE UTAH SALT FLATS.
I EXPECTED TO FEEL BETTER AFTER TIME STOPPED BLEEDING OUT. BUT NOT THIS MUCH BETTER.
COMPUTER, RUN MEDICAL SCAN.
MEDICAL SCAN COMPLETE. COMPARATIVE ANALYSIS TO PREVIOUS MEDICAL SCANS INDICATES THE FOLLOWING:
CARDIAC EFFICIENCY, INCREASED. EPIDERMAL ELASTICITY, INCREASED. BONE MINERAL CONTENT, INCREASED.
THAT CAN'T BE RIGHT.
MEDICAL SCAN RE-COMPLETED. RESULTS CONFIRMED.
WHAT COULD CAUSE SOMETHING LIKE THAT?
CHANGES CONSISTENT WITH THE PHYSIOLOGY OF A NORMAL MALE, AGED TWENTY YEARS YOUNGER THAN PREVIOUS MEDICAL SCANS.
GOD ABOVE. I'M... YOUNGER?
ALL THAT TIME I SPENT RUNNING INTO THE PAST... IT NEVER HAD THIS EFFECT ON ME BEFORE. WHY NOW?
COMPUTER, POSTULATE.
POSSIBLE CAUSE: THE ALTERCATION WITH YOUR YOUNGER SELF FORCED TWO VERSIONS OF YOU TO BE IN CLOSE PROXIMITY FOR AN EXTENDED PERIOD OF TIME.
THE SPEED FORCE CORRECTED THE INCONGRUENCE.
I'LL BE DAMNED.
IN THAT CASE--
--LET'S GO HOME.

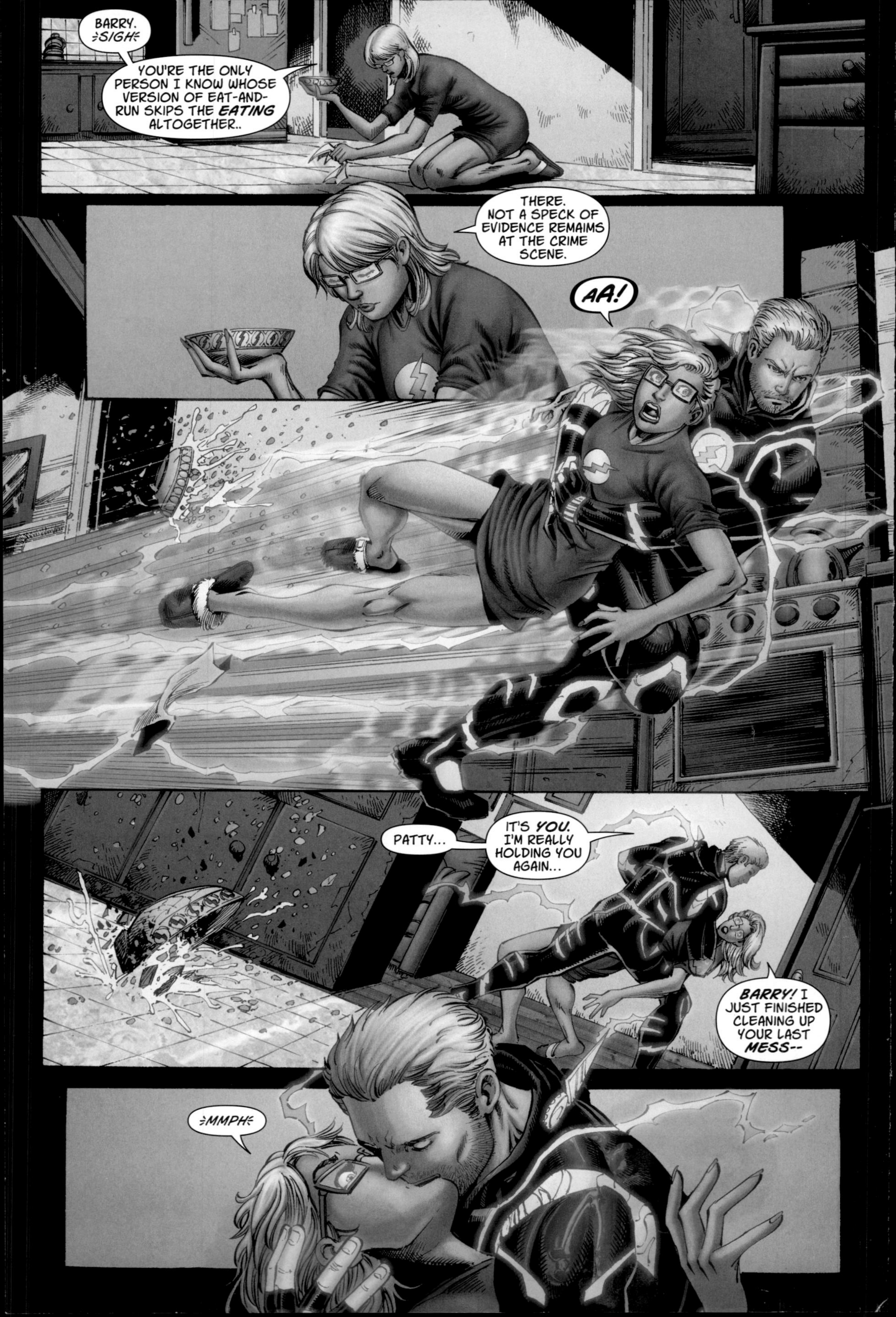

BARRY. *SIGH*
YOU'RE THE ONLY PERSON I KNOW WHOSE VERSION OF EAT-AND-RUN SKIPS THE *EATING* ALTOGETHER..
THERE. NOT A SPECK OF EVIDENCE REMAIMS AT THE CRIME SCENE.
AA!
PATTY...
IT'S *YOU.* I'M REALLY HOLDING YOU AGAIN...
BARRY! I JUST FINISHED CLEANING UP YOUR LAST *MESS--*
MMPH

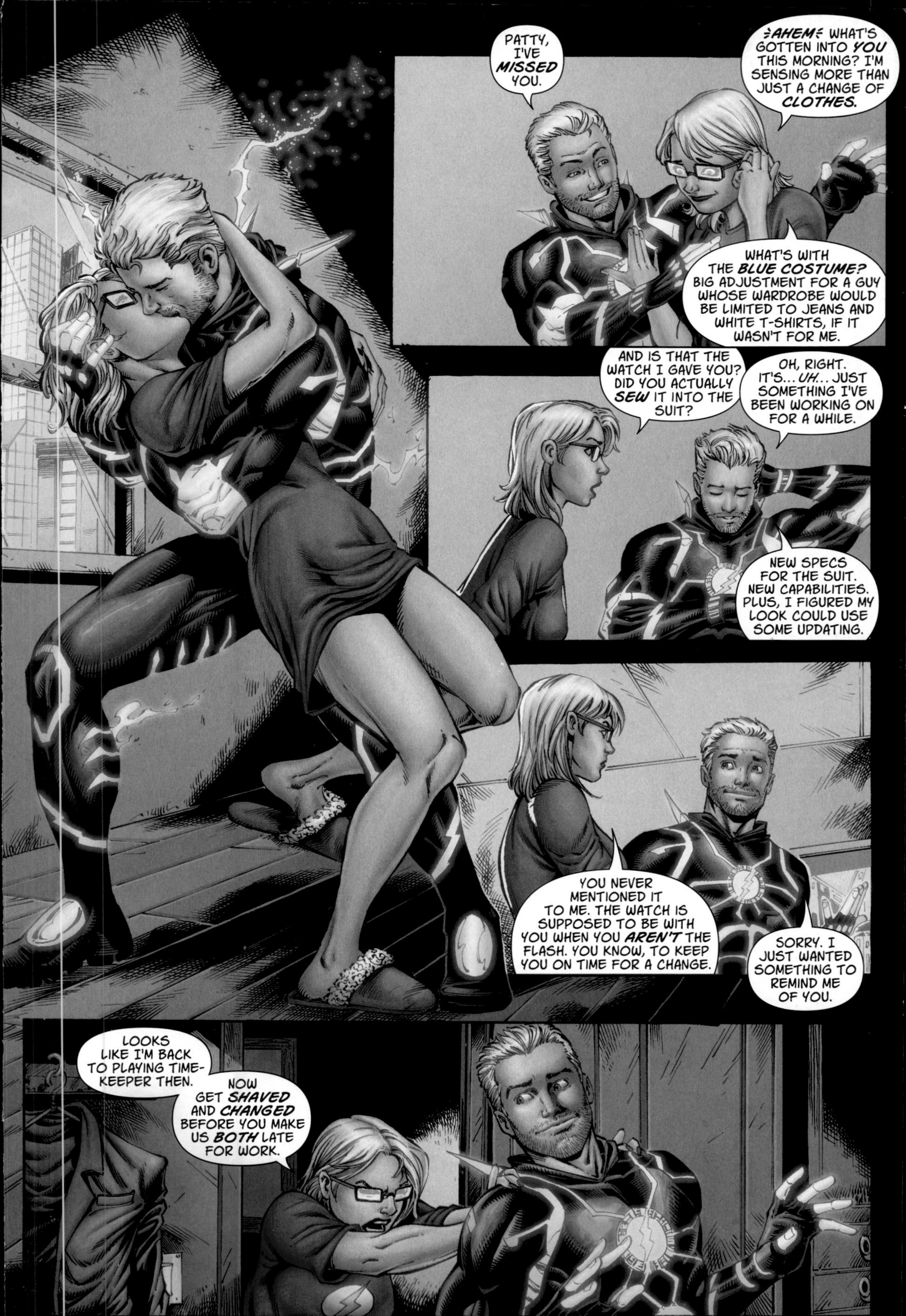
PATTY, I'VE MISSED YOU.
:AHEM: WHAT'S GOTTEN INTO YOU THIS MORNING? I'M SENSING MORE THAN JUST A CHANGE OF CLOTHES.
WHAT'S WITH THE BLUE COSTUME? BIG ADJUSTMENT FOR A GUY WHOSE WARDROBE WOULD BE LIMITED TO JEANS AND WHITE T-SHIRTS, IF IT WASN'T FOR ME.
AND IS THAT THE WATCH I GAVE YOU? DID YOU ACTUALLY SEW IT INTO THE SUIT?
OH, RIGHT. IT'S... UH... JUST SOMETHING I'VE BEEN WORKING ON FOR A WHILE.
NEW SPECS FOR THE SUIT. NEW CAPABILITIES. PLUS, I FIGURED MY LOOK COULD USE SOME UPDATING.
YOU NEVER MENTIONED IT TO ME. THE WATCH IS SUPPOSED TO BE WITH YOU WHEN YOU AREN'T THE FLASH. YOU KNOW, TO KEEP YOU ON TIME FOR A CHANGE.
SORRY. I JUST WANTED SOMETHING TO REMIND ME OF YOU.
LOOKS LIKE I'M BACK TO PLAYING TIME-KEEPER THEN.
NOW GET SHAVED AND CHANGED BEFORE YOU MAKE US BOTH LATE FOR WORK.

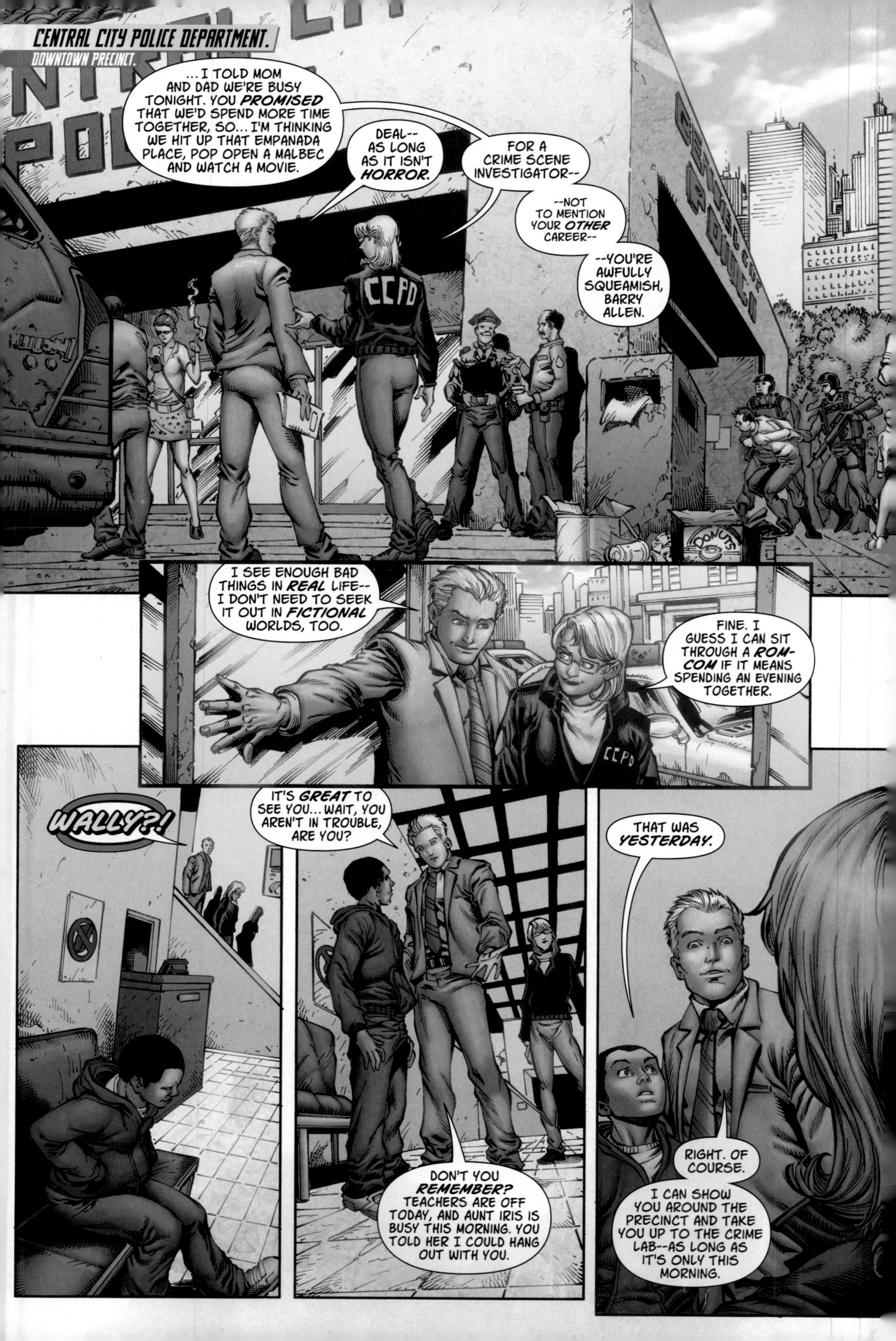
CENTRAL CITY POLICE DEPARTMENT.
DOWNTOWN PRECINCT.
...I TOLD MOM AND DAD WE'RE BUSY TONIGHT. YOU PROMISED THAT WE'D SPEND MORE TIME TOGETHER, SO... I'M THINKING WE HIT UP THAT EMPANADA PLACE, POP OPEN A MALBEC AND WATCH A MOVIE.
DEAL-- AS LONG AS IT ISN'T HORROR.
FOR A CRIME SCENE INVESTIGATOR--
--NOT TO MENTION YOUR OTHER CAREER--
--YOU'RE AWFULLY SQUEAMISH, BARRY ALLEN.
DONUTS
I SEE ENOUGH BAD THINGS IN REAL LIFE-- I DON'T NEED TO SEEK IT OUT IN FICTIONAL WORLDS, TOO.
FINE. I GUESS I CAN SIT THROUGH A ROM-COM IF IT MEANS SPENDING AN EVENING TOGETHER.
CCPD
WALLY?!
IT'S GREAT TO SEE YOU... WAIT, YOU AREN'T IN TROUBLE, ARE YOU?
DON'T YOU REMEMBER? TEACHERS ARE OFF TODAY, AND AUNT IRIS IS BUSY THIS MORNING. YOU TOLD HER I COULD HANG OUT WITH YOU.
THAT WAS YESTERDAY.
RIGHT. OF COURSE.
I CAN SHOW YOU AROUND THE PRECINCT AND TAKE YOU UP TO THE CRIME LAB--AS LONG AS IT'S ONLY THIS MORNING.

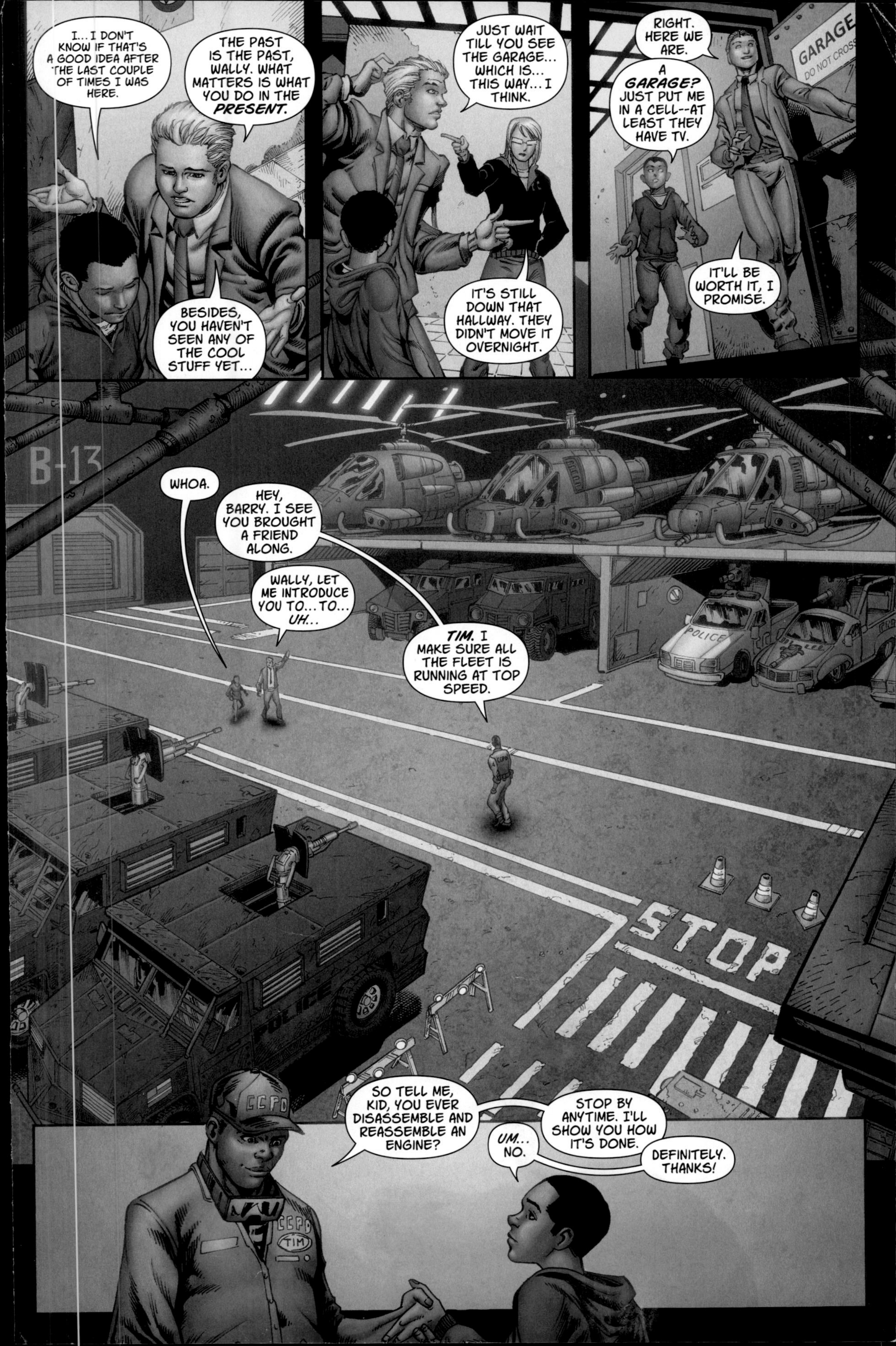
I... I DON'T KNOW IF THAT'S A GOOD IDEA AFTER THE LAST COUPLE OF TIMES I WAS HERE.
THE PAST IS THE PAST, WALLY. WHAT MATTERS IS WHAT YOU DO IN THE *PRESENT.*
BESIDES, YOU HAVEN'T SEEN ANY OF THE COOL STUFF YET...
JUST WAIT TILL YOU SEE THE GARAGE... WHICH IS... THIS WAY... I THINK.
IT'S STILL DOWN THAT HALLWAY. THEY DIDN'T MOVE IT OVERNIGHT.
RIGHT. HERE WE ARE.
GARAGE
DO NOT CROSS
A *GARAGE?* JUST PUT ME IN A CELL--AT LEAST THEY HAVE TV.
IT'LL BE WORTH IT, I PROMISE.
B-13
WHOA.
HEY, BARRY. I SEE YOU BROUGHT A FRIEND ALONG.
WALLY, LET ME INTRODUCE YOU TO... TO... *UH...*
TIM. I MAKE SURE ALL THE FLEET IS RUNNING AT TOP SPEED.
POLICE
STOP
POLICE
CCPD
SO TELL ME, KID, YOU EVER DISASSEMBLE AND REASSEMBLE AN ENGINE?
UM... NO.
STOP BY ANYTIME. I'LL SHOW YOU HOW IT'S DONE.
DEFINITELY. THANKS!
CCPD
TIM

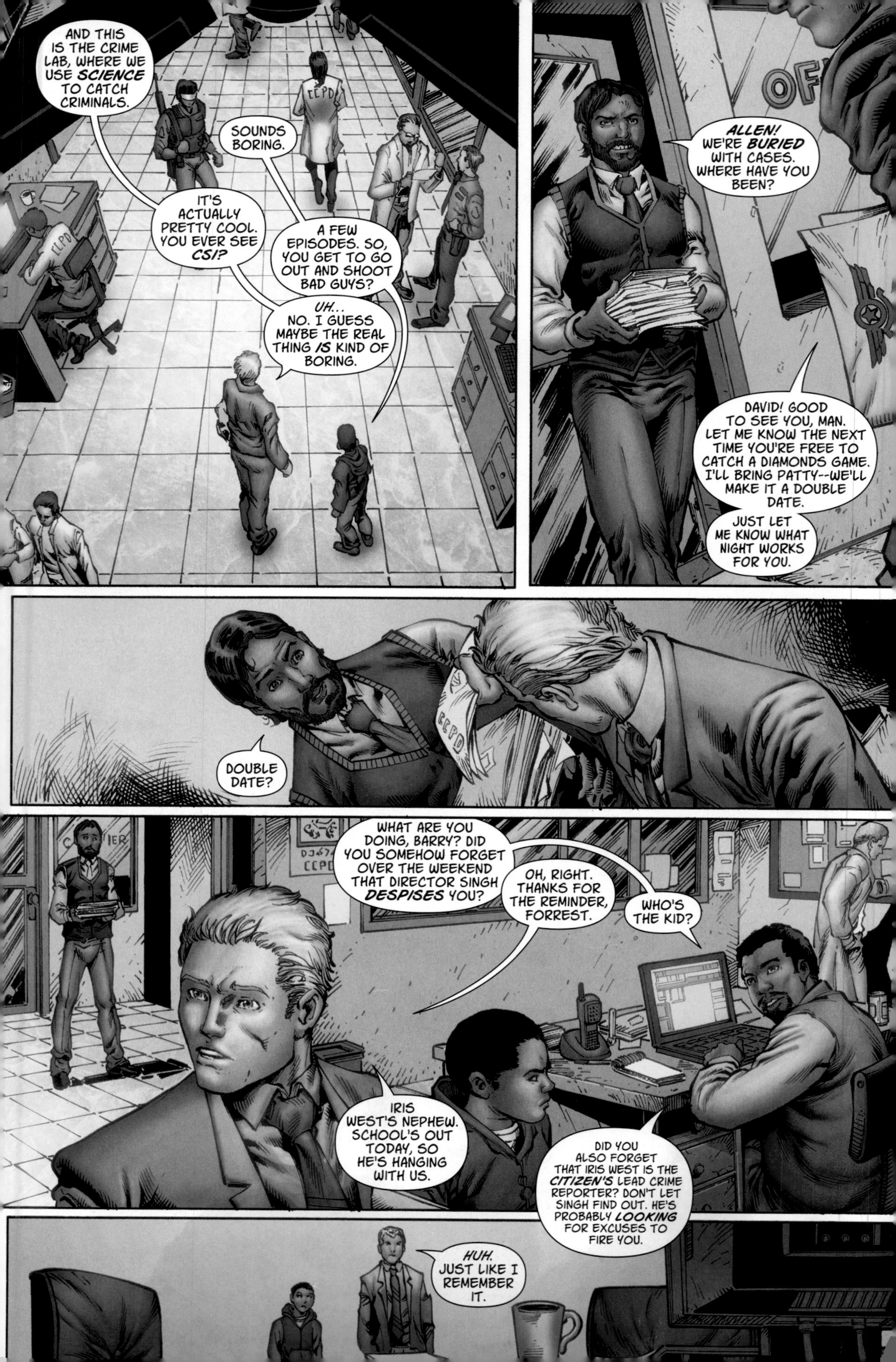
AND THIS IS THE CRIME LAB, WHERE WE USE SCIENCE TO CATCH CRIMINALS.
SOUNDS BORING.
IT'S ACTUALLY PRETTY COOL. YOU EVER SEE CSI?
A FEW EPISODES. SO, YOU GET TO GO OUT AND SHOOT BAD GUYS?
UH... NO. I GUESS MAYBE THE REAL THING IS KIND OF BORING.
ALLEN! WE'RE BURIED WITH CASES. WHERE HAVE YOU BEEN?
DAVID! GOOD TO SEE YOU, MAN. LET ME KNOW THE NEXT TIME YOU'RE FREE TO CATCH A DIAMONDS GAME. I'LL BRING PATTY--WE'LL MAKE IT A DOUBLE DATE.
JUST LET ME KNOW WHAT NIGHT WORKS FOR YOU.
DOUBLE DATE?
WHAT ARE YOU DOING, BARRY? DID YOU SOMEHOW FORGET OVER THE WEEKEND THAT DIRECTOR SINGH DESPISES YOU?
OH, RIGHT. THANKS FOR THE REMINDER, FORREST.
WHO'S THE KID?
IRIS WEST'S NEPHEW. SCHOOL'S OUT TODAY, SO HE'S HANGING WITH US.
DID YOU ALSO FORGET THAT IRIS WEST IS THE CITIZEN'S LEAD CRIME REPORTER? DON'T LET SINGH FIND OUT. HE'S PROBABLY LOOKING FOR EXCUSES TO FIRE YOU.
HUH. JUST LIKE I REMEMBER IT.

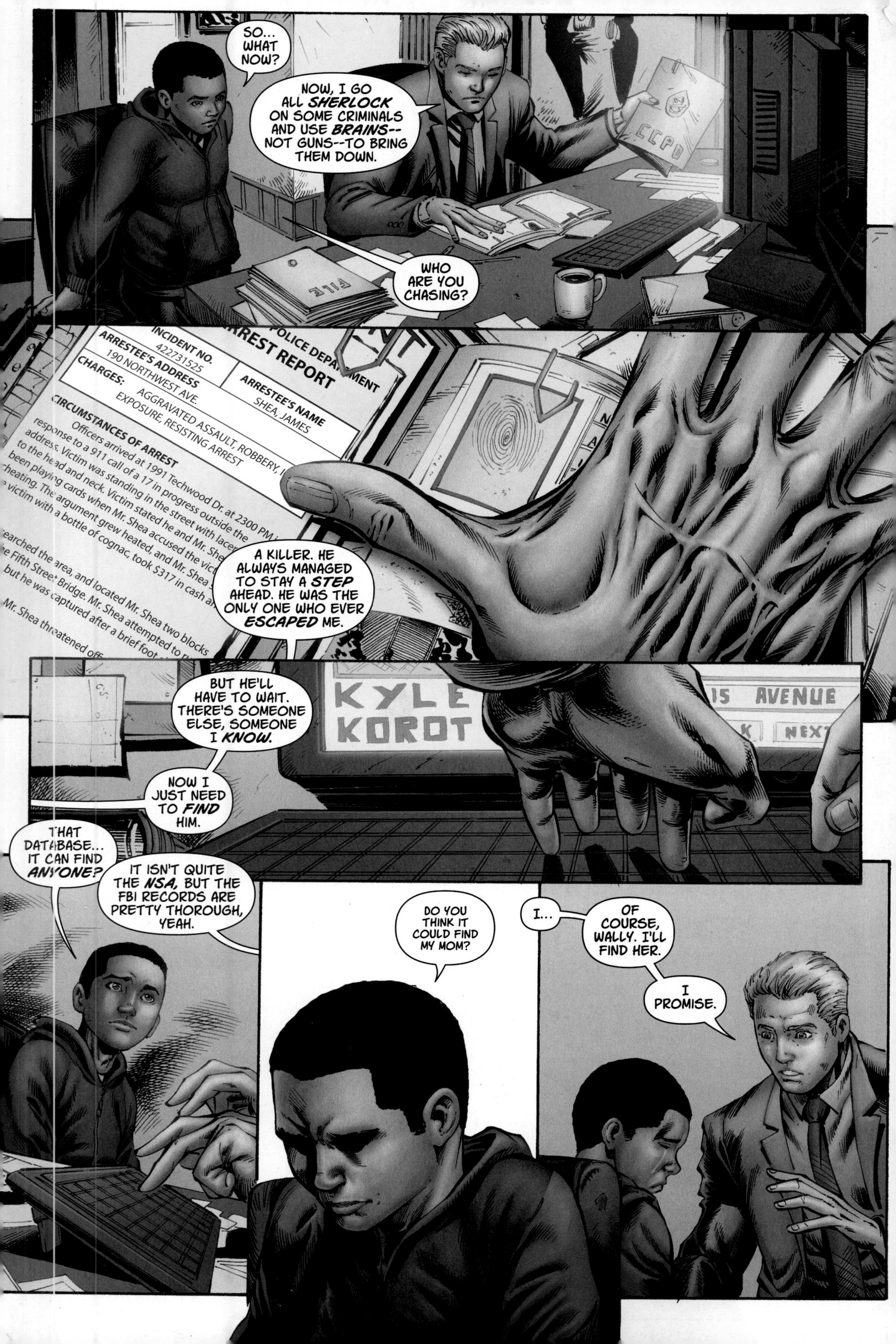
SO... WHAT NOW?
NOW, I GO ALL SHERLOCK ON SOME CRIMINALS AND USE BRAINS--NOT GUNS--TO BRING THEM DOWN.
CCPD
FILE
WHO ARE YOU CHASING?
POLICE DEPARTMENT
ARREST REPORT
INCIDENT NO.
422731525
ARRESTEE'S NAME
SHEA, JAMES
ARRESTEE'S ADDRESS
190 NORTHWEST AVE.
CHARGES:
AGGRAVATED ASSAULT, ROBBERY,
EXPOSURE, RESISTING ARREST
CIRCUMSTANCES OF ARREST
A KILLER. HE ALWAYS MANAGED TO STAY A STEP AHEAD. HE WAS THE ONLY ONE WHO EVER ESCAPED ME.
KYLE KOROT
AVENUE
NEXT
BUT HE'LL HAVE TO WAIT. THERE'S SOMEONE ELSE, SOMEONE I KNOW.
NOW I JUST NEED TO FIND HIM.
THAT DATABASE... IT CAN FIND ANYONE?
IT ISN'T QUITE THE NSA, BUT THE FBI RECORDS ARE PRETTY THOROUGH, YEAH.
DO YOU THINK IT COULD FIND MY MOM?
I...
OF COURSE, WALLY. I'LL FIND HER.
I PROMISE.

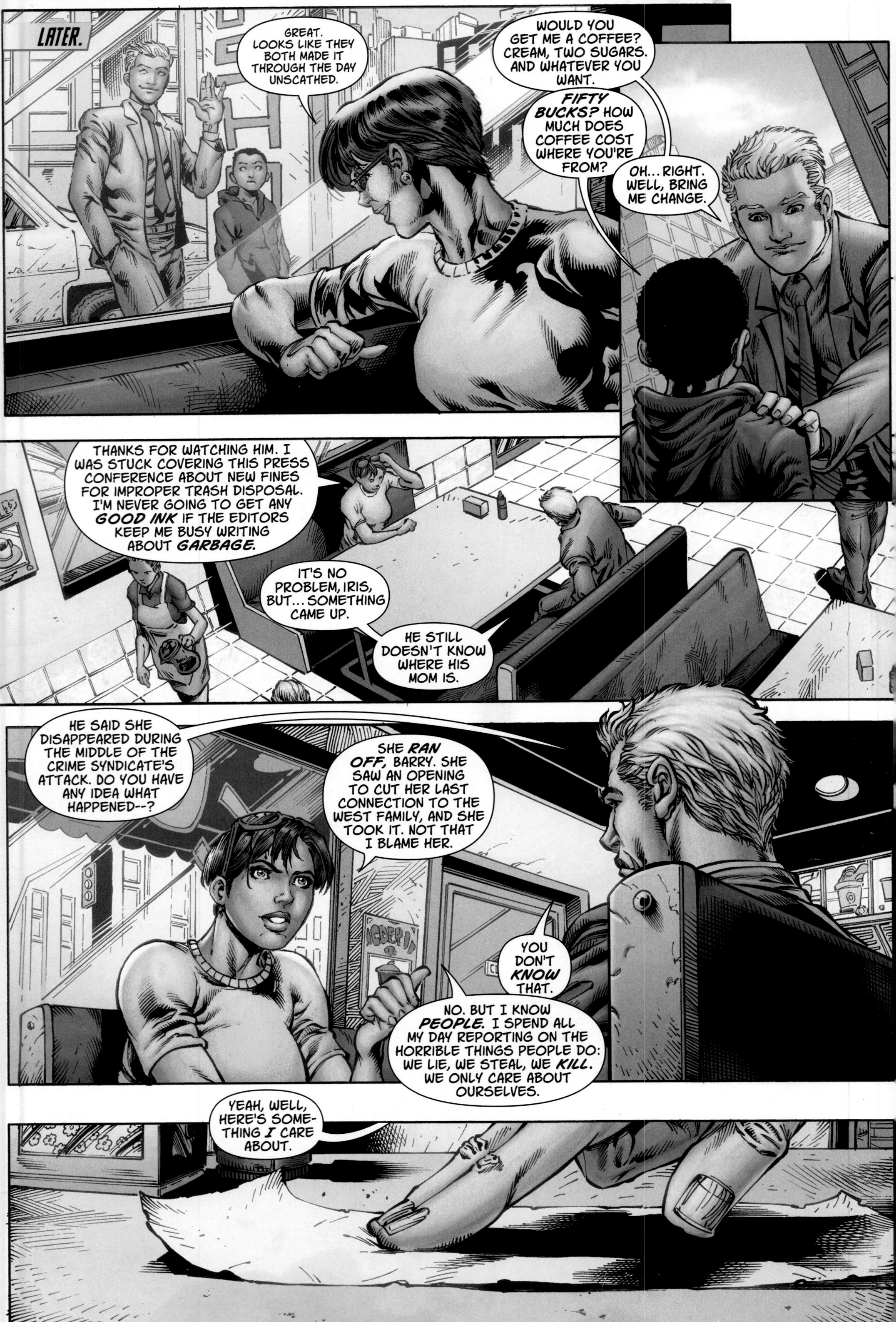
LATER.
GREAT. LOOKS LIKE THEY BOTH MADE IT THROUGH THE DAY UNSCATHED.
WOULD YOU GET ME A COFFEE? CREAM, TWO SUGARS. AND WHATEVER YOU WANT.
FIFTY BUCKS? HOW MUCH DOES COFFEE COST WHERE YOU'RE FROM?
OH... RIGHT. WELL, BRING ME CHANGE.
THANKS FOR WATCHING HIM. I WAS STUCK COVERING THIS PRESS CONFERENCE ABOUT NEW FINES FOR IMPROPER TRASH DISPOSAL. I'M NEVER GOING TO GET ANY GOOD INK IF THE EDITORS KEEP ME BUSY WRITING ABOUT GARBAGE.
IT'S NO PROBLEM, IRIS, BUT... SOMETHING CAME UP.
HE STILL DOESN'T KNOW WHERE HIS MOM IS.
HE SAID SHE DISAPPEARED DURING THE MIDDLE OF THE CRIME SYNDICATE'S ATTACK. DO YOU HAVE ANY IDEA WHAT HAPPENED--?
SHE RAN OFF, BARRY. SHE SAW AN OPENING TO CUT HER LAST CONNECTION TO THE WEST FAMILY, AND SHE TOOK IT. NOT THAT I BLAME HER.
YOU DON'T KNOW THAT.
NO. BUT I KNOW PEOPLE. I SPEND ALL MY DAY REPORTING ON THE HORRIBLE THINGS PEOPLE DO: WE LIE, WE STEAL, WE KILL. WE ONLY CARE ABOUT OURSELVES.
YEAH, WELL, HERE'S SOMETHING I CARE ABOUT.

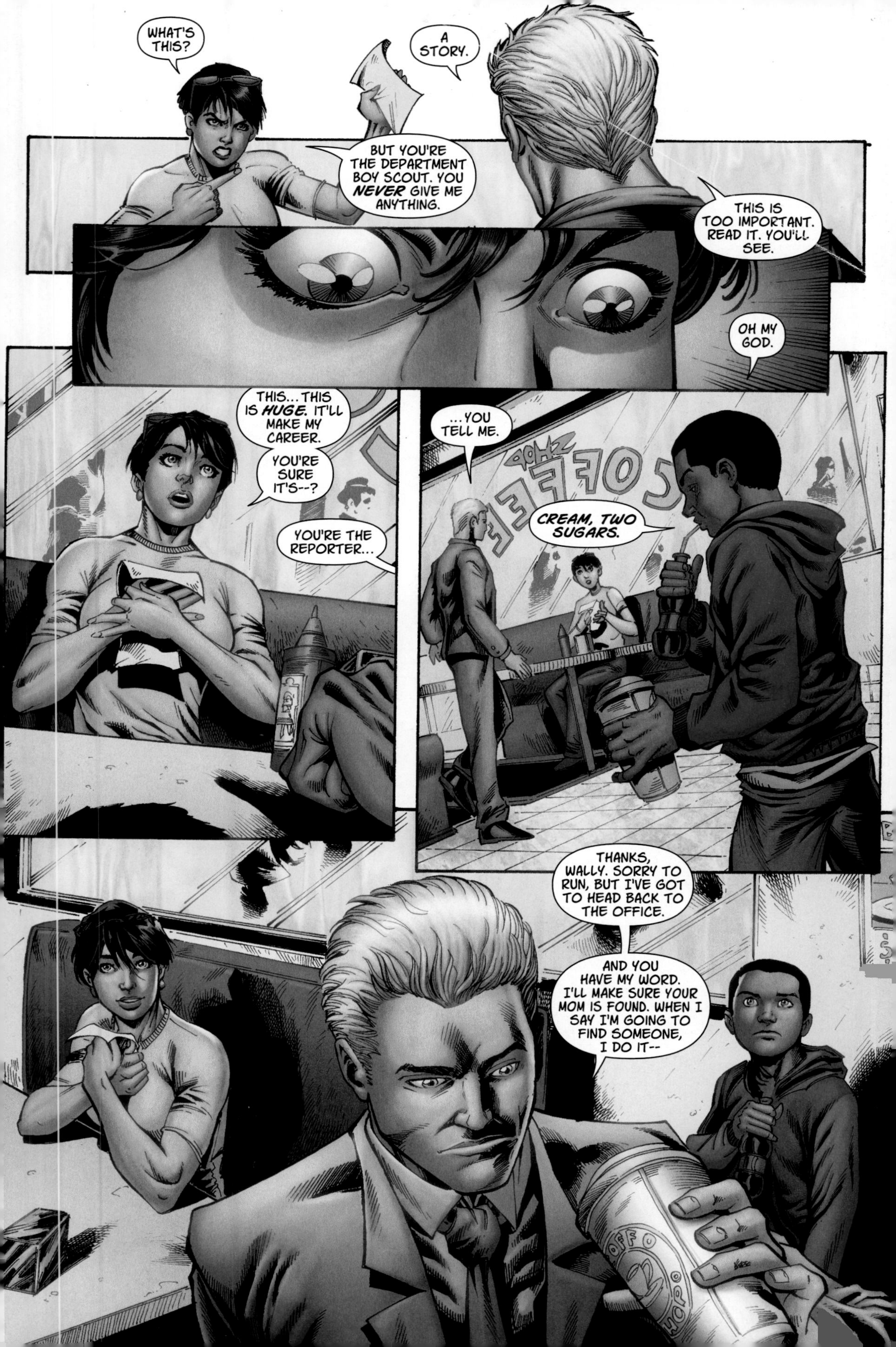
WHAT'S THIS?
A STORY.
BUT YOU'RE THE DEPARTMENT BOY SCOUT. YOU NEVER GIVE ME ANYTHING.
THIS IS TOO IMPORTANT. READ IT. YOU'LL SEE.
OH MY GOD.
THIS... THIS IS HUGE. IT'LL MAKE MY CAREER.
YOU'RE SURE IT'S--?
YOU'RE THE REPORTER...
...YOU TELL ME.
CREAM, TWO SUGARS.
THANKS, WALLY. SORRY TO RUN, BUT I'VE GOT TO HEAD BACK TO THE OFFICE.
AND YOU HAVE MY WORD. I'LL MAKE SURE YOUR MOM IS FOUND. WHEN I SAY I'M GOING TO FIND SOMEONE, I DO IT--

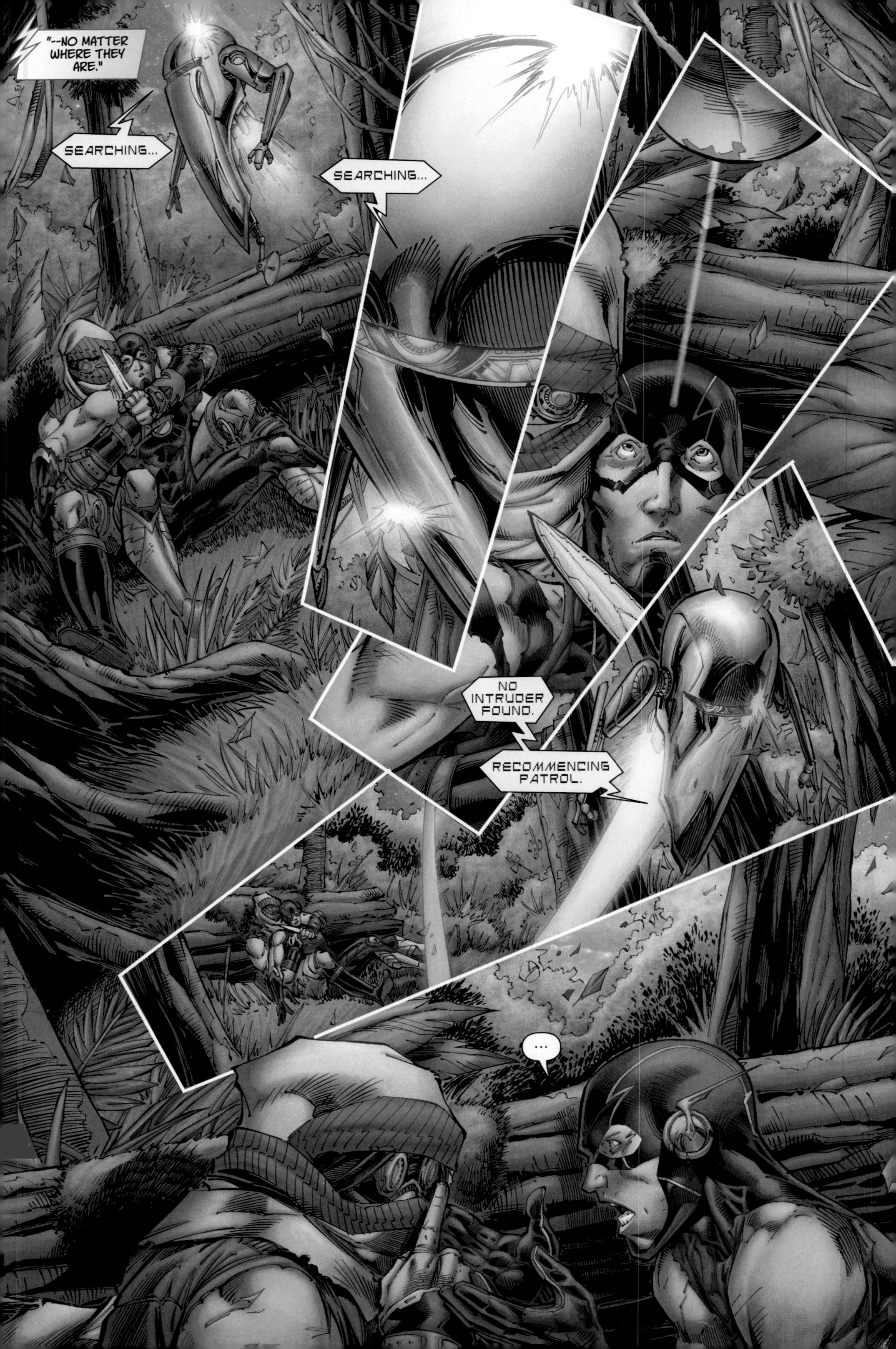
"--NO MATTER WHERE THEY ARE."
SEARCHING...
SEARCHING...
NO INTRUDER FOUND.
RECOMMENCING PATROL.
...

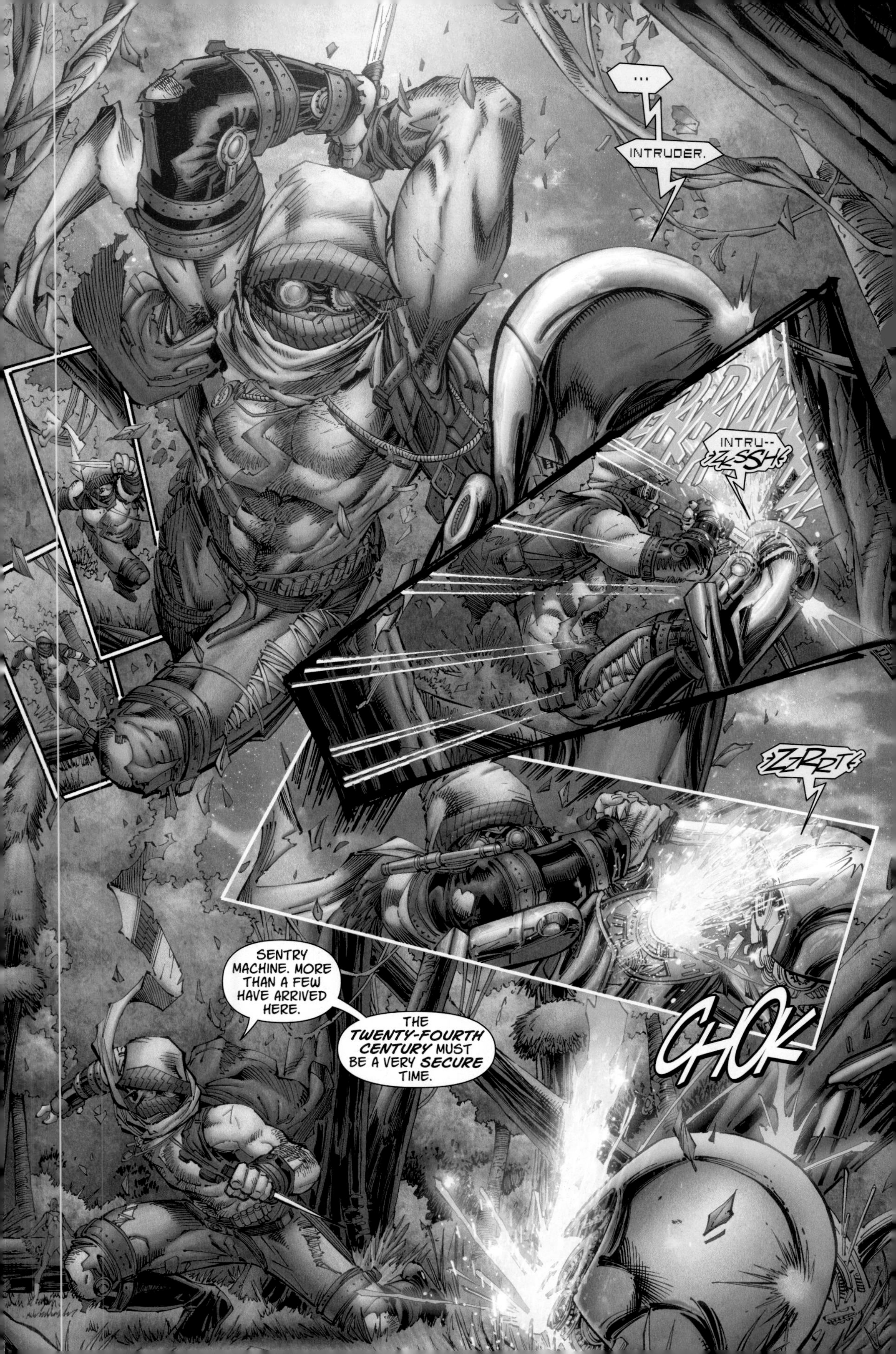
...
INTRUDER.
INTRU--
ZZSSH
ZZRRT
SENTRY MACHINE. MORE THAN A FEW HAVE ARRIVED HERE.
THE *TWENTY-FOURTH CENTURY* MUST BE A VERY *SECURE* TIME.
CHOK

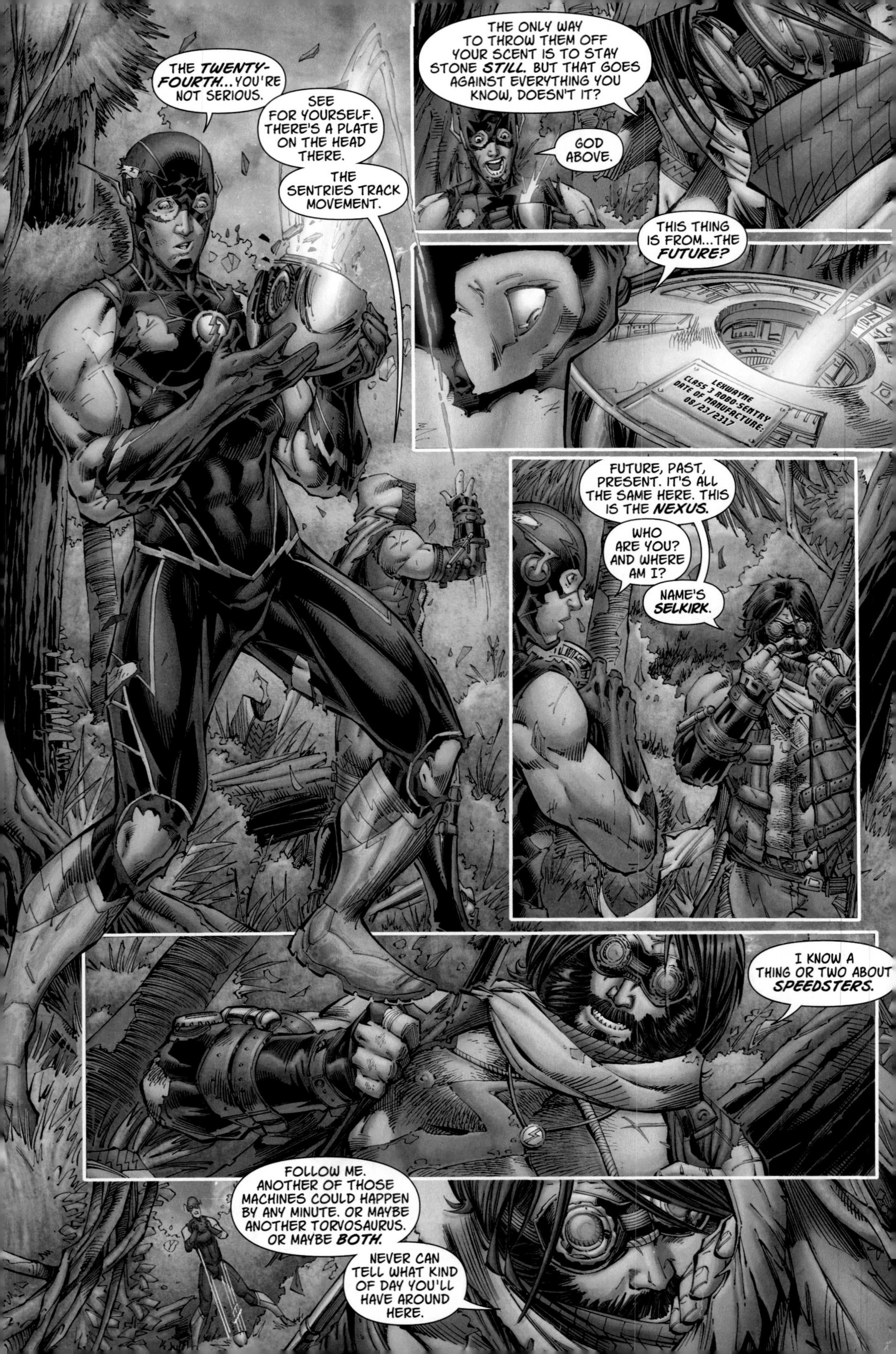
THE TWENTY-FOURTH...YOU'RE NOT SERIOUS.
SEE FOR YOURSELF. THERE'S A PLATE ON THE HEAD THERE.
THE SENTRIES TRACK MOVEMENT.
THE ONLY WAY TO THROW THEM OFF YOUR SCENT IS TO STAY STONE STILL. BUT THAT GOES AGAINST EVERYTHING YOU KNOW, DOESN'T IT?
GOD ABOVE.
THIS THING IS FROM...THE FUTURE?
LEXWAYNE CLASS 3 ROBO-SENTRY DATE OF MANUFACTURE: 08/23/2317
FUTURE, PAST, PRESENT. IT'S ALL THE SAME HERE. THIS IS THE NEXUS.
WHO ARE YOU? AND WHERE AM I?
NAME'S SELKIRK.
I KNOW A THING OR TWO ABOUT SPEEDSTERS.
FOLLOW ME. ANOTHER OF THOSE MACHINES COULD HAPPEN BY ANY MINUTE. OR MAYBE ANOTHER TORVOSAURUS. OR MAYBE BOTH.
NEVER CAN TELL WHAT KIND OF DAY YOU'LL HAVE AROUND HERE.

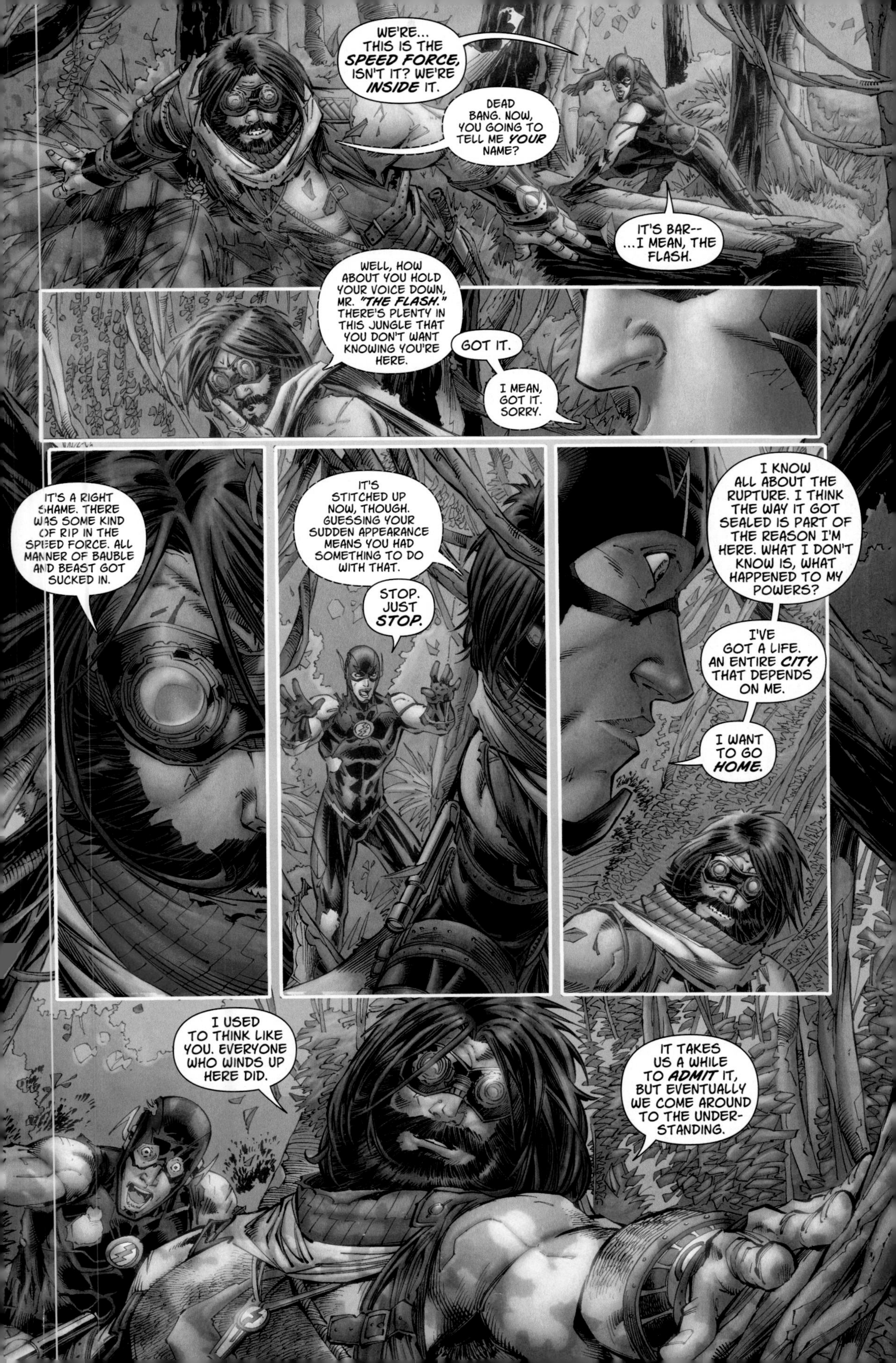

WE'RE... THIS IS THE SPEED FORCE, ISN'T IT? WE'RE INSIDE IT.
DEAD BANG. NOW, YOU GOING TO TELL ME YOUR NAME?
IT'S BAR-- ...I MEAN, THE FLASH.
WELL, HOW ABOUT YOU HOLD YOUR VOICE DOWN, MR. "THE FLASH." THERE'S PLENTY IN THIS JUNGLE THAT YOU DON'T WANT KNOWING YOU'RE HERE.
GOT IT.
I MEAN, GOT IT. SORRY.
IT'S A RIGHT SHAME. THERE WAS SOME KIND OF RIP IN THE SPEED FORCE. ALL MANNER OF BAUBLE AND BEAST GOT SUCKED IN.
IT'S STITCHED UP NOW, THOUGH. GUESSING YOUR SUDDEN APPEARANCE MEANS YOU HAD SOMETHING TO DO WITH THAT.
STOP. JUST STOP.
I KNOW ALL ABOUT THE RUPTURE. I THINK THE WAY IT GOT SEALED IS PART OF THE REASON I'M HERE. WHAT I DON'T KNOW IS, WHAT HAPPENED TO MY POWERS?
I'VE GOT A LIFE. AN ENTIRE CITY THAT DEPENDS ON ME.
I WANT TO GO HOME.
I USED TO THINK LIKE YOU. EVERYONE WHO WINDS UP HERE DID.
IT TAKES US A WHILE TO ADMIT IT, BUT EVENTUALLY WE COME AROUND TO THE UNDER-STANDING.

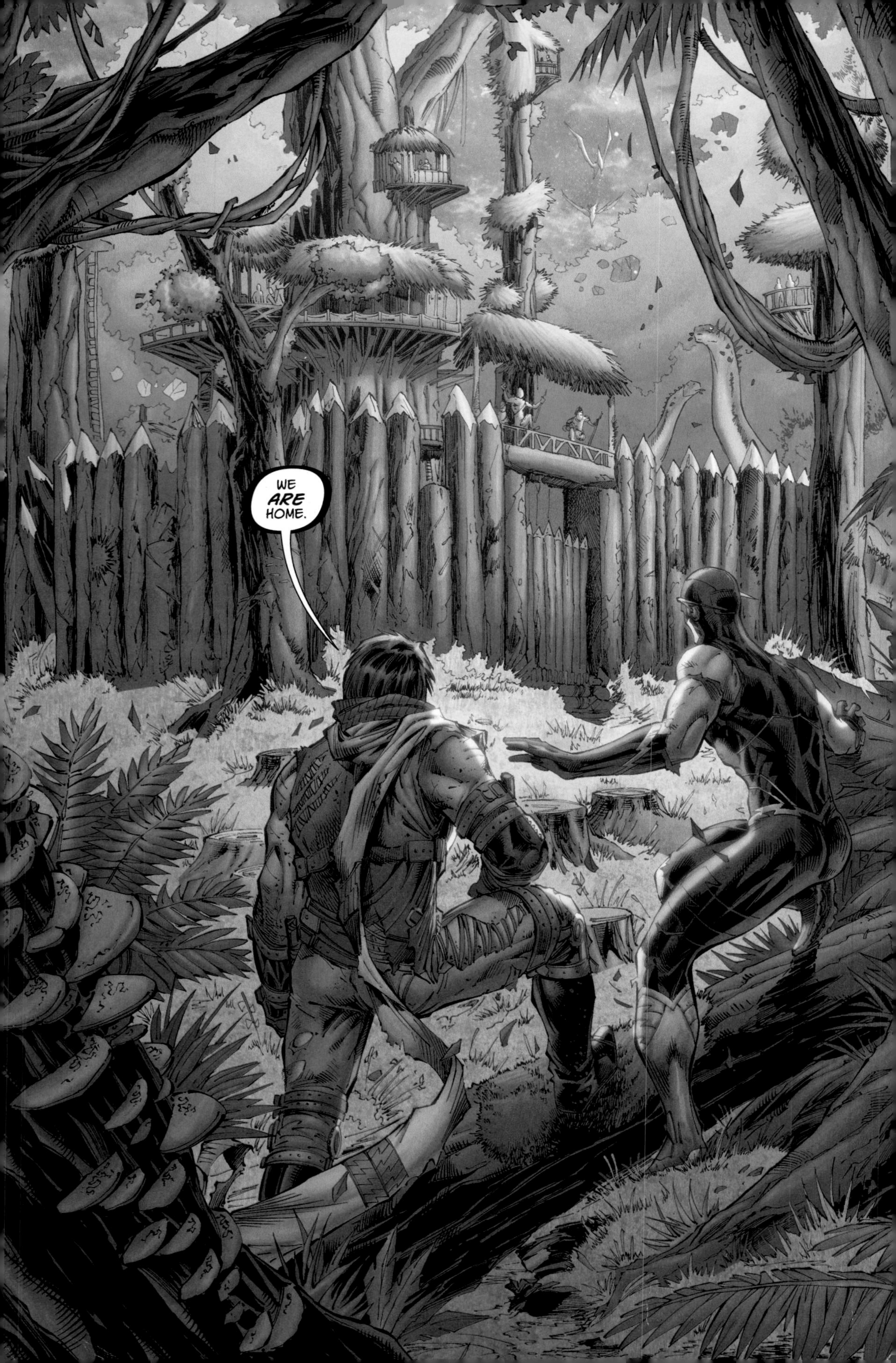
WE *ARE* HOME.

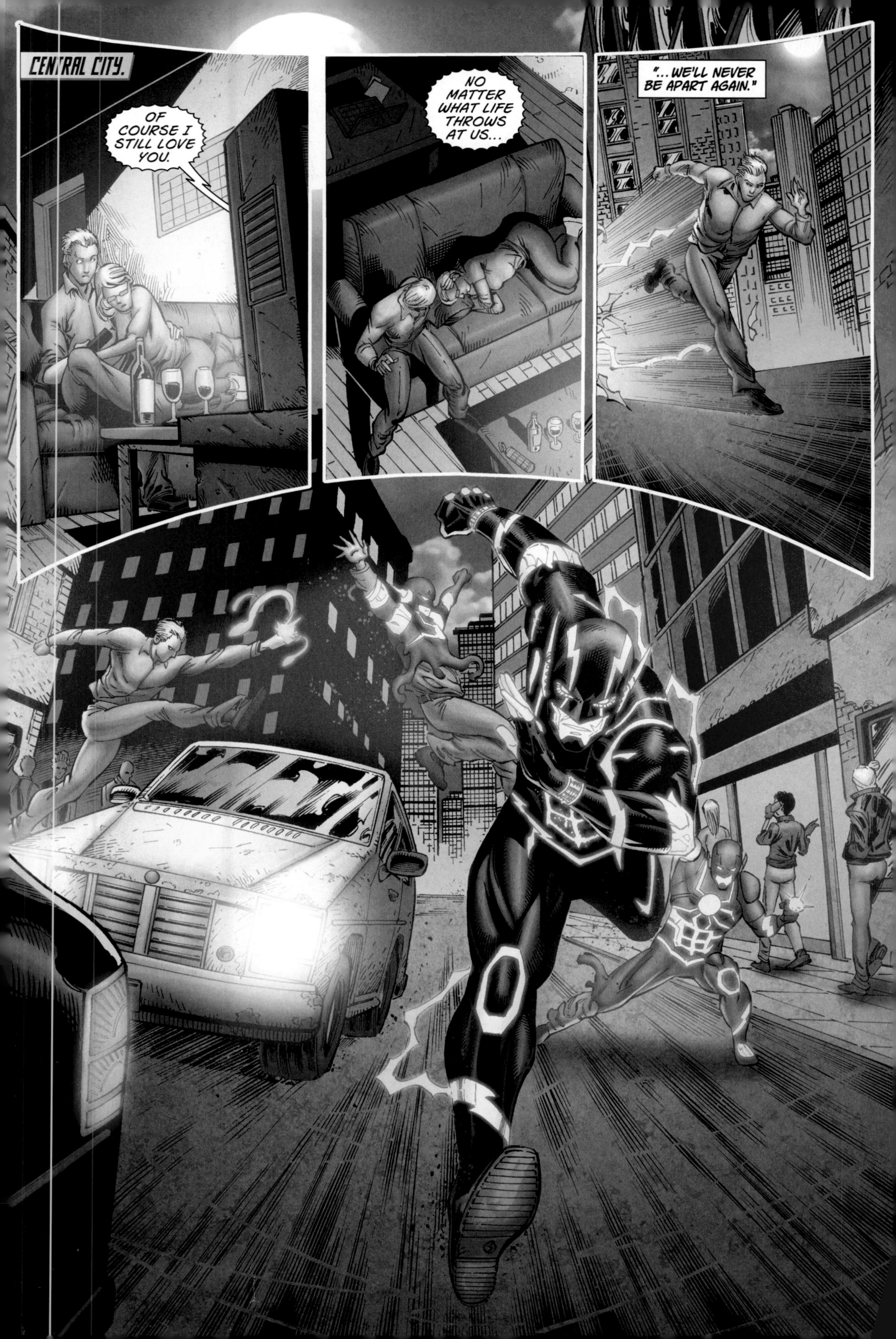
CENTRAL CITY.
OF COURSE I STILL LOVE YOU.
NO MATTER WHAT LIFE THROWS AT US...
"...WE'LL NEVER BE APART AGAIN."

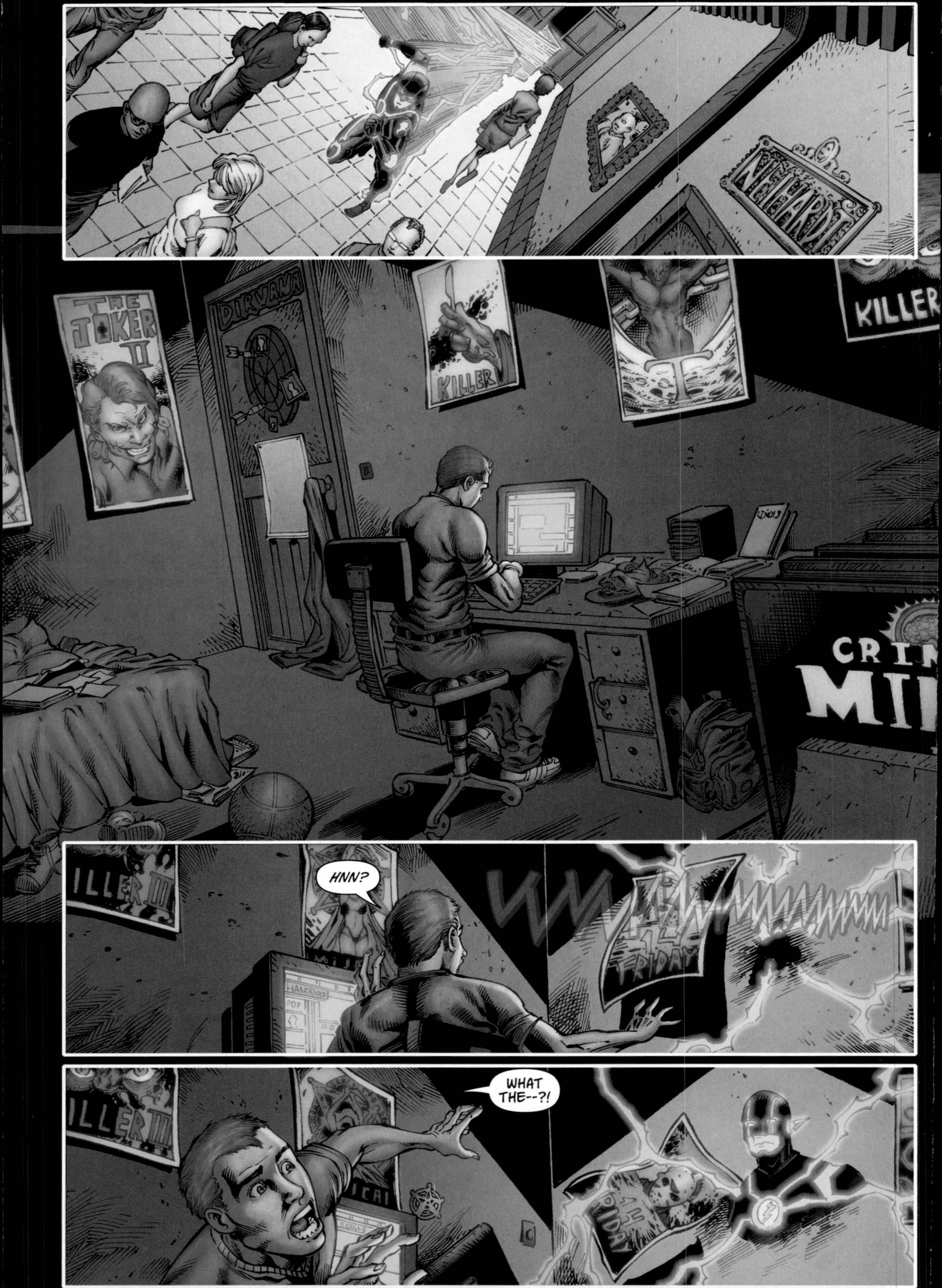
THE JOKER II
KILLER
KILLER
HNN?
WHAT THE--?!

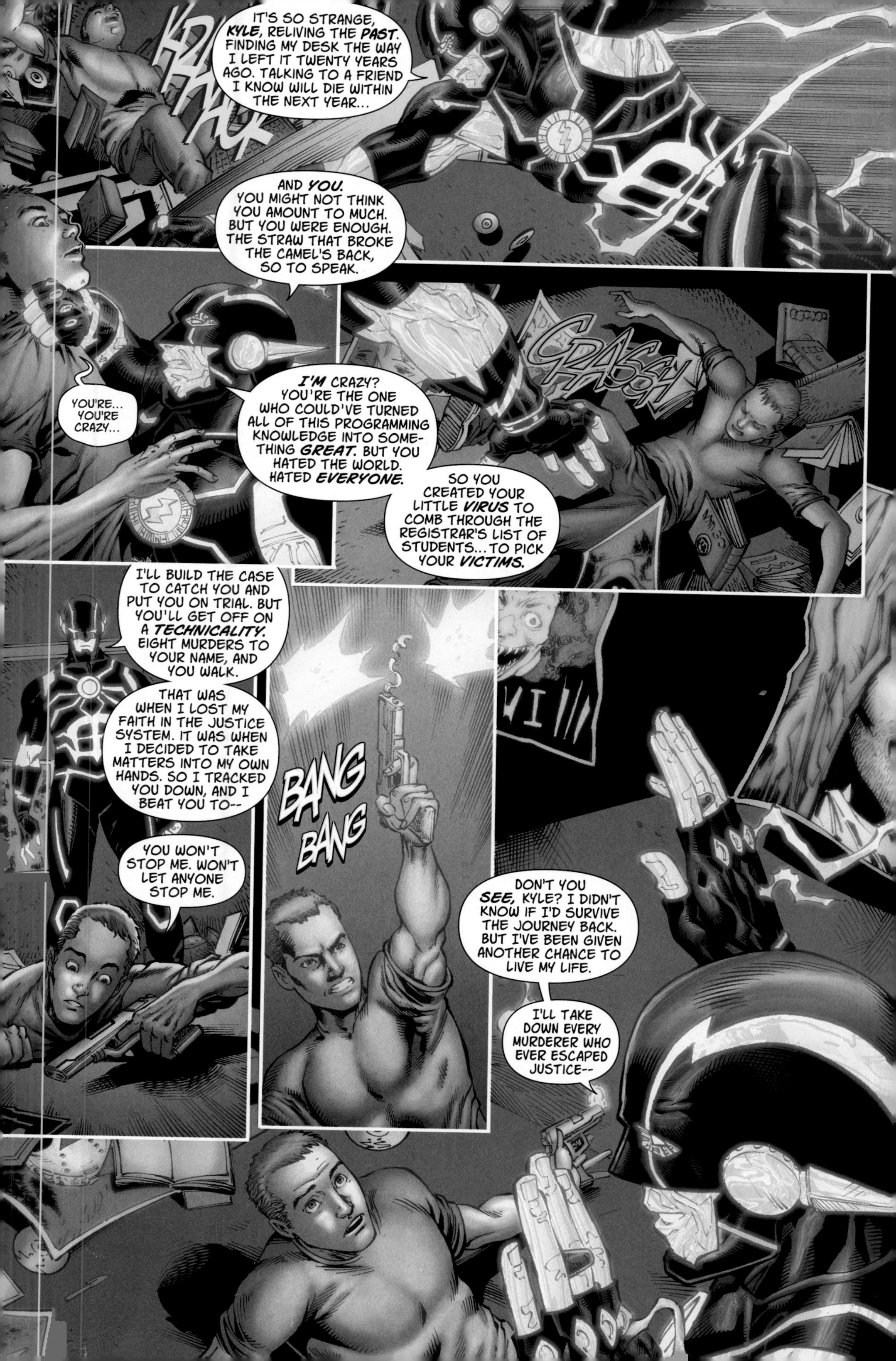

KRAKK
IT'S SO STRANGE, KYLE, RELIVING THE PAST. FINDING MY DESK THE WAY I LEFT IT TWENTY YEARS AGO. TALKING TO A FRIEND I KNOW WILL DIE WITHIN THE NEXT YEAR...
AND YOU. YOU MIGHT NOT THINK YOU AMOUNT TO MUCH. BUT YOU WERE ENOUGH. THE STRAW THAT BROKE THE CAMEL'S BACK, SO TO SPEAK.
YOU'RE... YOU'RE CRAZY...
I'M CRAZY? YOU'RE THE ONE WHO COULD'VE TURNED ALL OF THIS PROGRAMMING KNOWLEDGE INTO SOMETHING GREAT. BUT YOU HATED THE WORLD. HATED EVERYONE.
CRASSH
SO YOU CREATED YOUR LITTLE VIRUS TO COMB THROUGH THE REGISTRAR'S LIST OF STUDENTS...TO PICK YOUR VICTIMS.
I'LL BUILD THE CASE TO CATCH YOU AND PUT YOU ON TRIAL. BUT YOU'LL GET OFF ON A TECHNICALITY. EIGHT MURDERS TO YOUR NAME, AND YOU WALK.
THAT WAS WHEN I LOST MY FAITH IN THE JUSTICE SYSTEM. IT WAS WHEN I DECIDED TO TAKE MATTERS INTO MY OWN HANDS. SO I TRACKED YOU DOWN, AND I BEAT YOU TO--
YOU WON'T STOP ME. WON'T LET ANYONE STOP ME.
BANG
BANG
DON'T YOU SEE, KYLE? I DIDN'T KNOW IF I'D SURVIVE THE JOURNEY BACK. BUT I'VE BEEN GIVEN ANOTHER CHANCE TO LIVE MY LIFE.
I'LL TAKE DOWN EVERY MURDERER WHO EVER ESCAPED JUSTICE--

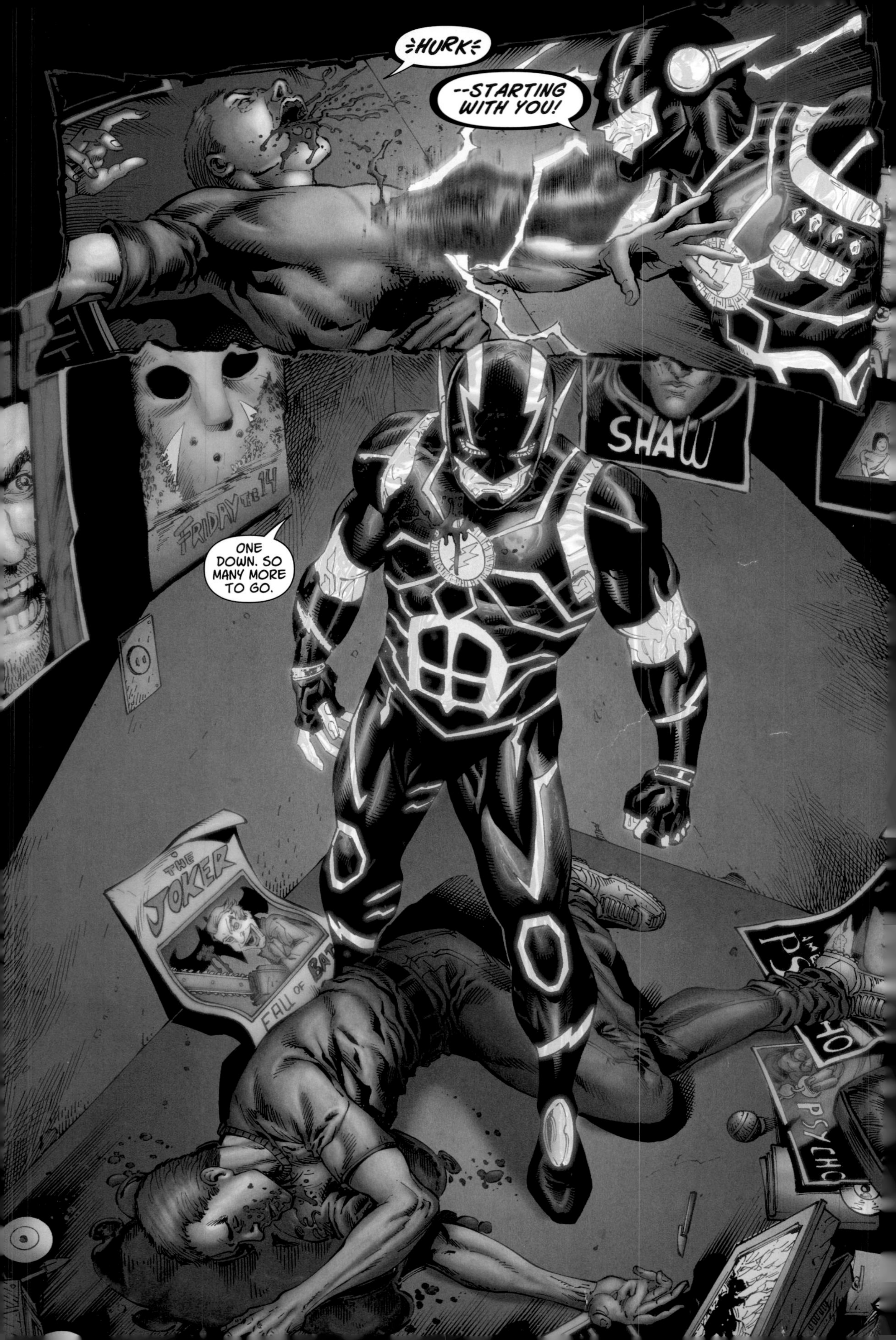

HURK
--STARTING WITH YOU!
ONE DOWN. SO MANY MORE TO GO.
SHAW
FRIDAY THE 14
THE JOKER
FALL OF BAT
PSYCHO
PSYCHO

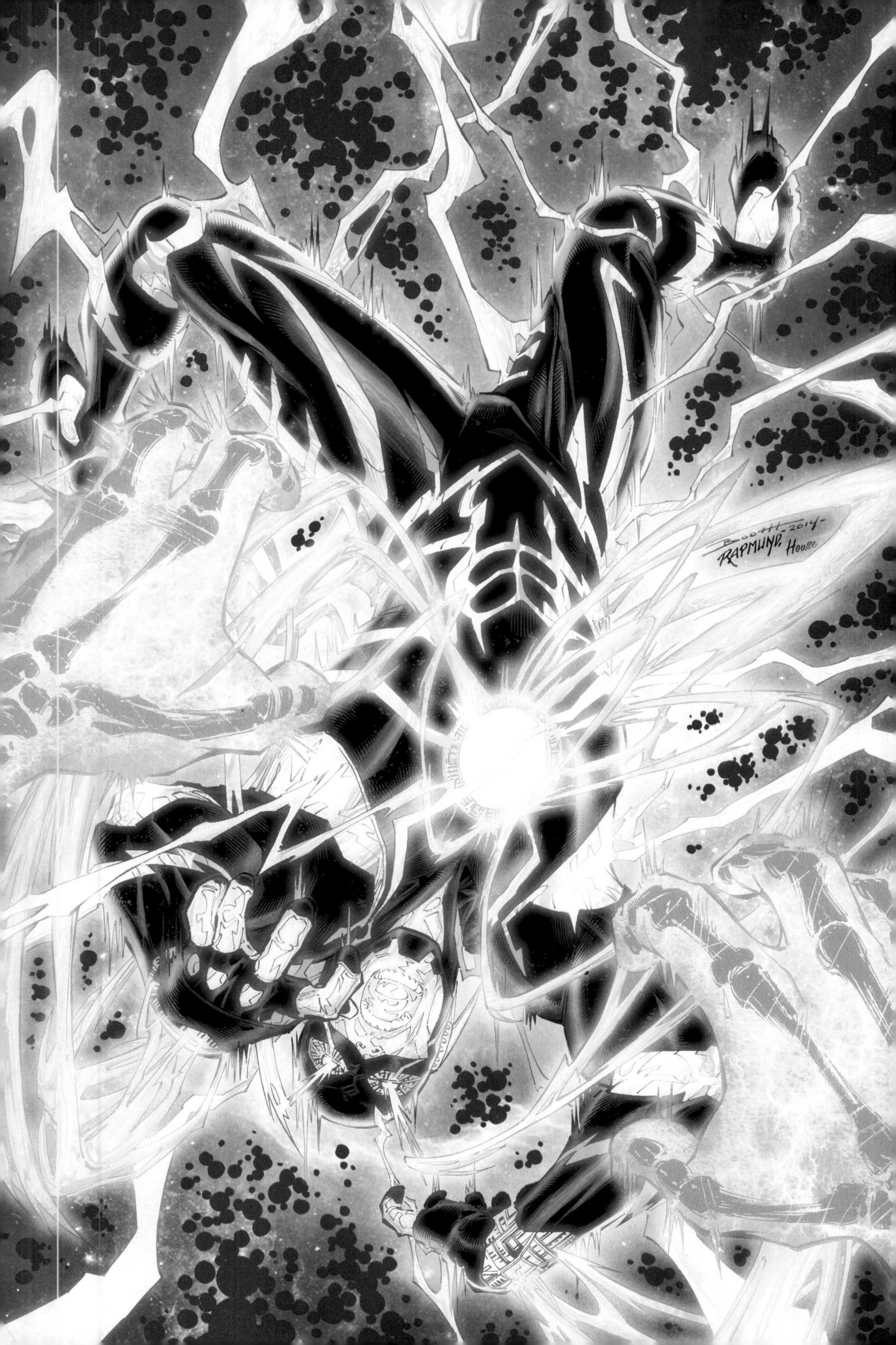
RAPMUND
House

THE SAVAGE WORLD OF THE SPEED FORCE

ROBERT VENDITTI & VAN JENSEN writers BRETT BOOTH penciller NORM RAPMUND inker ANDREW DALHOUSE colorist DEZI SIENTY letterer
cover by BRETT BOOTH, NORM RAPMUND & ANDREW DALHOUSE

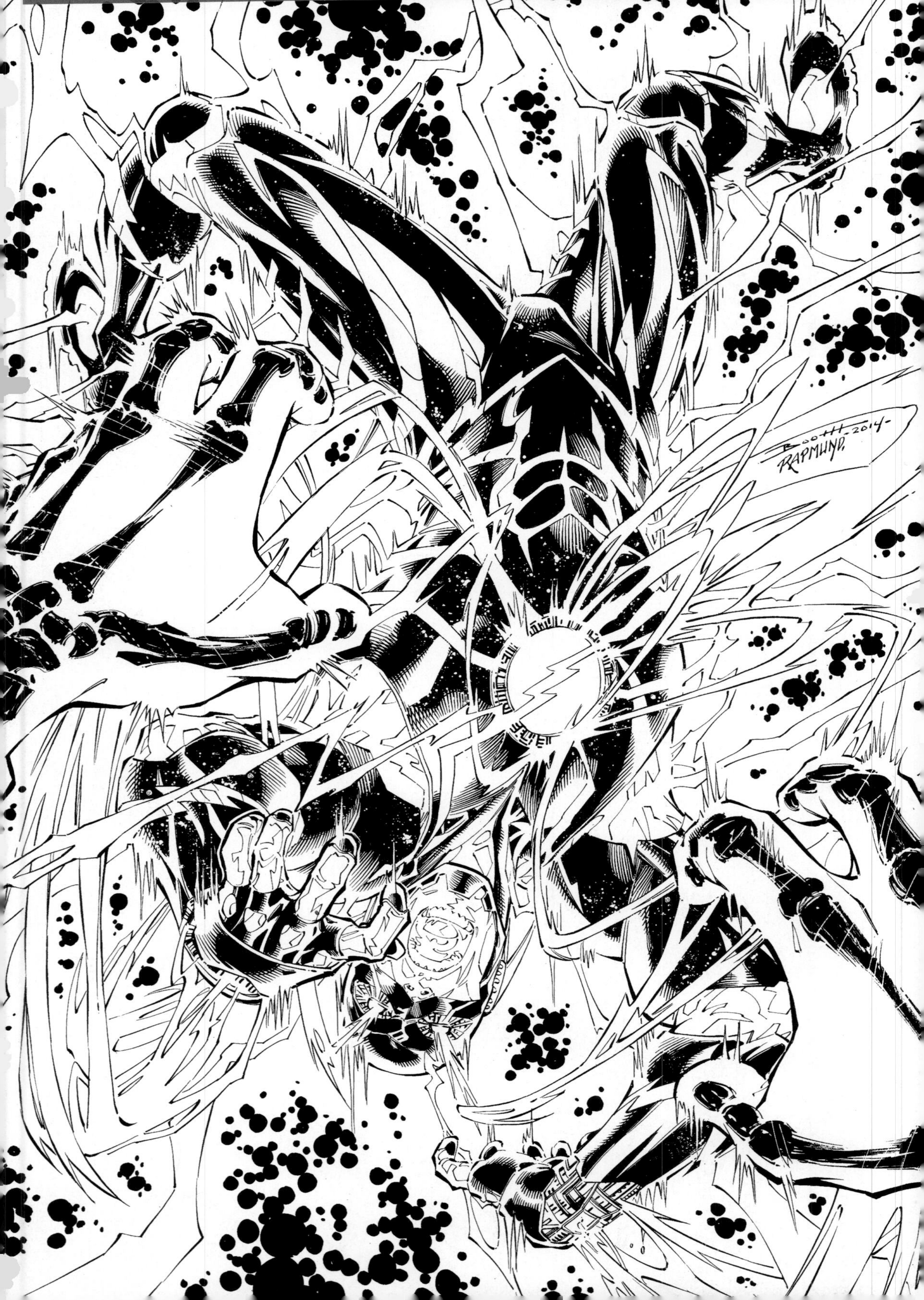
BOOTH -2014-
RAPMUND

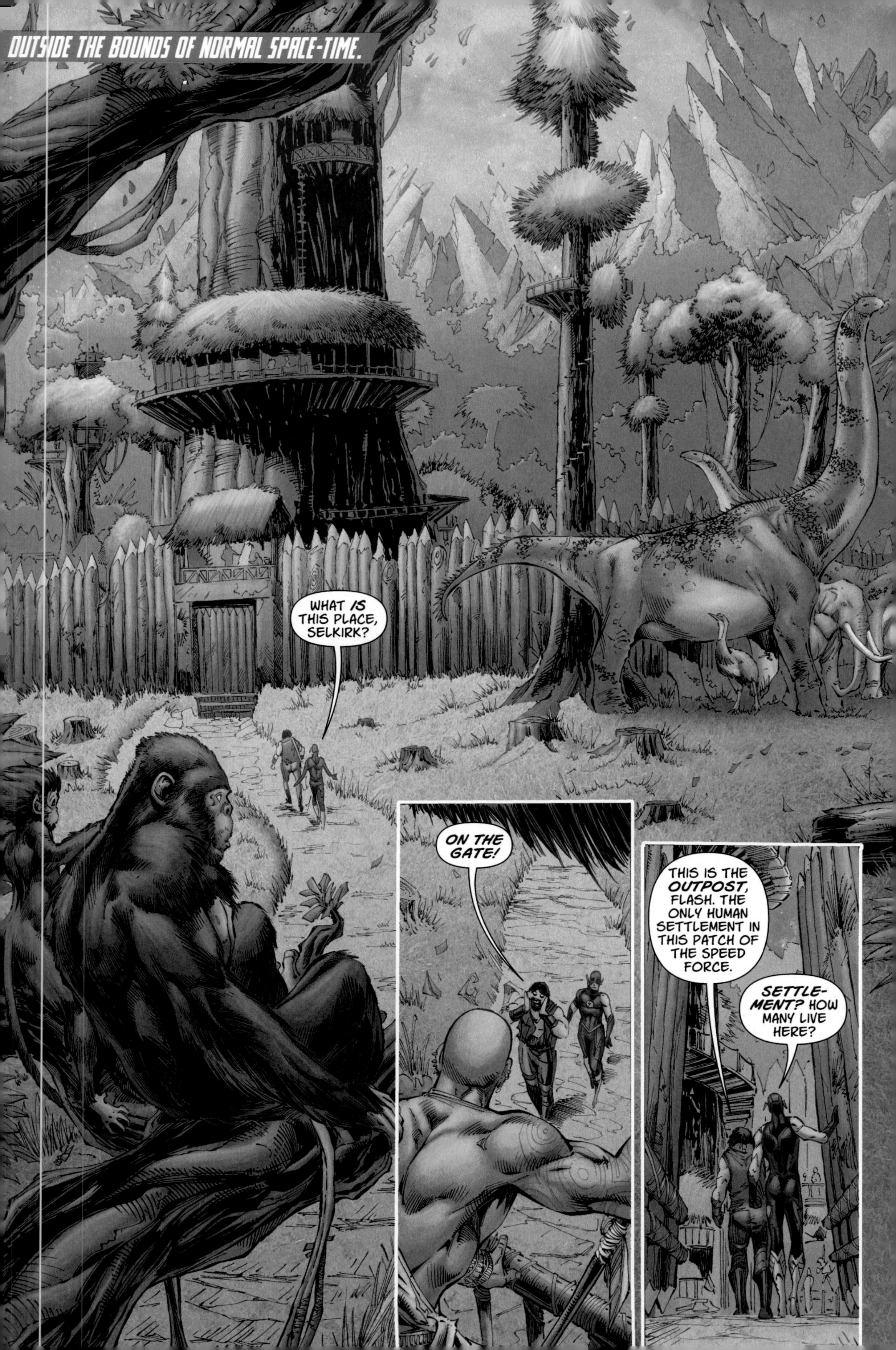
OUTSIDE THE BOUNDS OF NORMAL SPACE-TIME.
WHAT *IS* THIS PLACE, SELKIRK?
ON THE GATE!
THIS IS THE ***OUTPOST,*** FLASH. THE ONLY HUMAN SETTLEMENT IN THIS PATCH OF THE SPEED FORCE.
SETTLE-MENT? HOW MANY LIVE HERE?

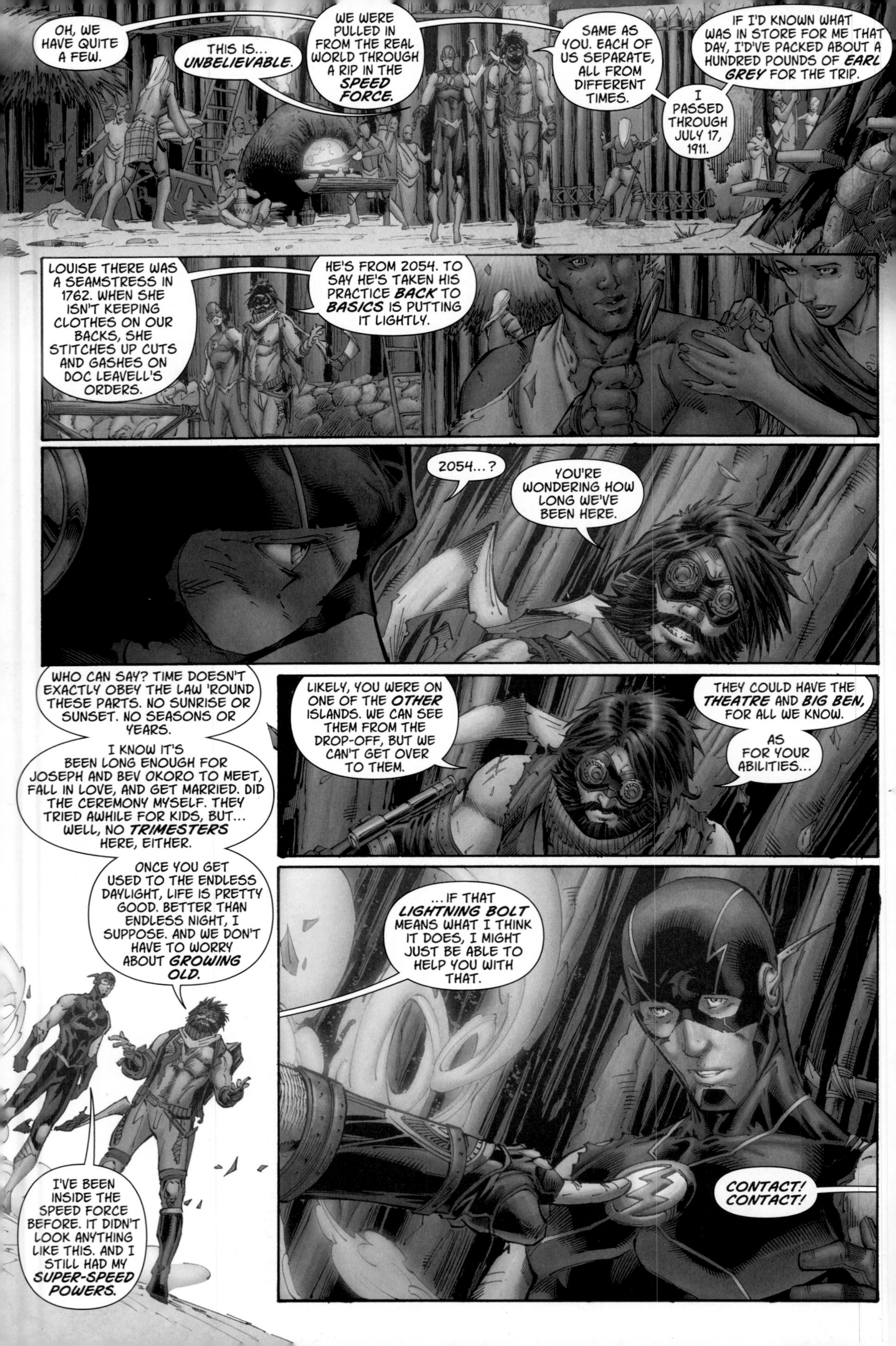
OH, WE HAVE QUITE A FEW.
THIS IS... UNBELIEVABLE.
WE WERE PULLED IN FROM THE REAL WORLD THROUGH A RIP IN THE SPEED FORCE.
SAME AS YOU. EACH OF US SEPARATE, ALL FROM DIFFERENT TIMES.
I PASSED THROUGH JULY 17, 1911.
IF I'D KNOWN WHAT WAS IN STORE FOR ME THAT DAY, I'D'VE PACKED ABOUT A HUNDRED POUNDS OF EARL GREY FOR THE TRIP.
LOUISE THERE WAS A SEAMSTRESS IN 1762. WHEN SHE ISN'T KEEPING CLOTHES ON OUR BACKS, SHE STITCHES UP CUTS AND GASHES ON DOC LEAVELL'S ORDERS.
HE'S FROM 2054. TO SAY HE'S TAKEN HIS PRACTICE BACK TO BASICS IS PUTTING IT LIGHTLY.
2054...?
YOU'RE WONDERING HOW LONG WE'VE BEEN HERE.
WHO CAN SAY? TIME DOESN'T EXACTLY OBEY THE LAW 'ROUND THESE PARTS. NO SUNRISE OR SUNSET. NO SEASONS OR YEARS.
I KNOW IT'S BEEN LONG ENOUGH FOR JOSEPH AND BEV OKORO TO MEET, FALL IN LOVE, AND GET MARRIED. DID THE CEREMONY MYSELF. THEY TRIED AWHILE FOR KIDS, BUT... WELL, NO TRIMESTERS HERE, EITHER.
ONCE YOU GET USED TO THE ENDLESS DAYLIGHT, LIFE IS PRETTY GOOD. BETTER THAN ENDLESS NIGHT, I SUPPOSE. AND WE DON'T HAVE TO WORRY ABOUT GROWING OLD.
I'VE BEEN INSIDE THE SPEED FORCE BEFORE. IT DIDN'T LOOK ANYTHING LIKE THIS. AND I STILL HAD MY SUPER-SPEED POWERS.
LIKELY, YOU WERE ON ONE OF THE OTHER ISLANDS. WE CAN SEE THEM FROM THE DROP-OFF, BUT WE CAN'T GET OVER TO THEM.
THEY COULD HAVE THE THEATRE AND BIG BEN, FOR ALL WE KNOW.
AS FOR YOUR ABILITIES...
...IF THAT LIGHTNING BOLT MEANS WHAT I THINK IT DOES, I MIGHT JUST BE ABLE TO HELP YOU WITH THAT.
CONTACT! CONTACT!

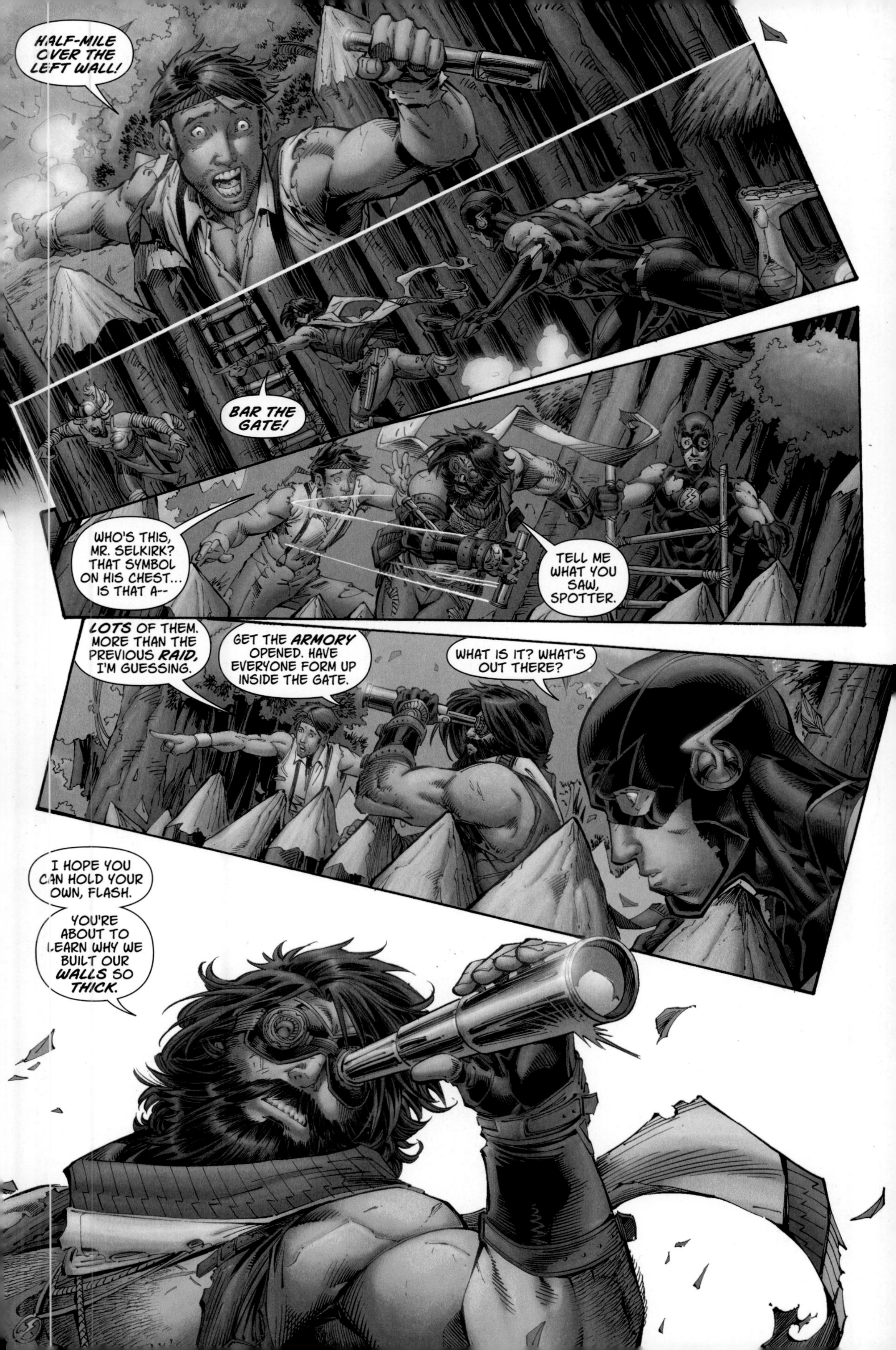
HALF-MILE OVER THE LEFT WALL!
BAR THE GATE!
WHO'S THIS, MR. SELKIRK? THAT SYMBOL ON HIS CHEST... IS THAT A--
TELL ME WHAT YOU SAW, SPOTTER.
LOTS OF THEM. MORE THAN THE PREVIOUS RAID, I'M GUESSING.
GET THE ARMORY OPENED. HAVE EVERYONE FORM UP INSIDE THE GATE.
WHAT IS IT? WHAT'S OUT THERE?
I HOPE YOU CAN HOLD YOUR OWN, FLASH.
YOU'RE ABOUT TO LEARN WHY WE BUILT OUR WALLS SO THICK.

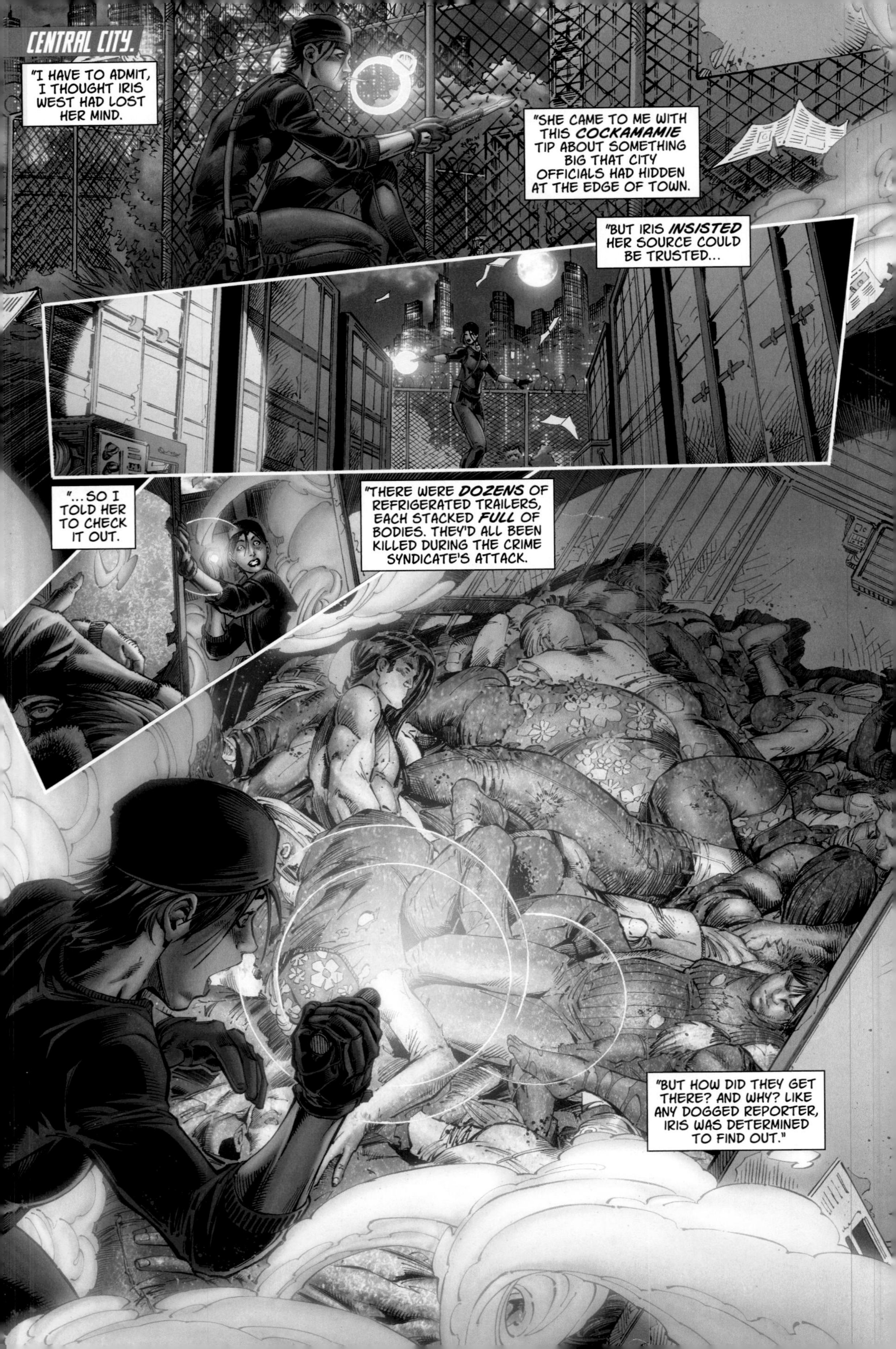
CENTRAL CITY.
"I HAVE TO ADMIT, I THOUGHT IRIS WEST HAD LOST HER MIND.
"SHE CAME TO ME WITH THIS COCKAMAMIE TIP ABOUT SOMETHING BIG THAT CITY OFFICIALS HAD HIDDEN AT THE EDGE OF TOWN.
"BUT IRIS INSISTED HER SOURCE COULD BE TRUSTED...
"...SO I TOLD HER TO CHECK IT OUT.
"THERE WERE DOZENS OF REFRIGERATED TRAILERS, EACH STACKED FULL OF BODIES. THEY'D ALL BEEN KILLED DURING THE CRIME SYNDICATE'S ATTACK.
"BUT HOW DID THEY GET THERE? AND WHY? LIKE ANY DOGGED REPORTER, IRIS WAS DETERMINED TO FIND OUT."

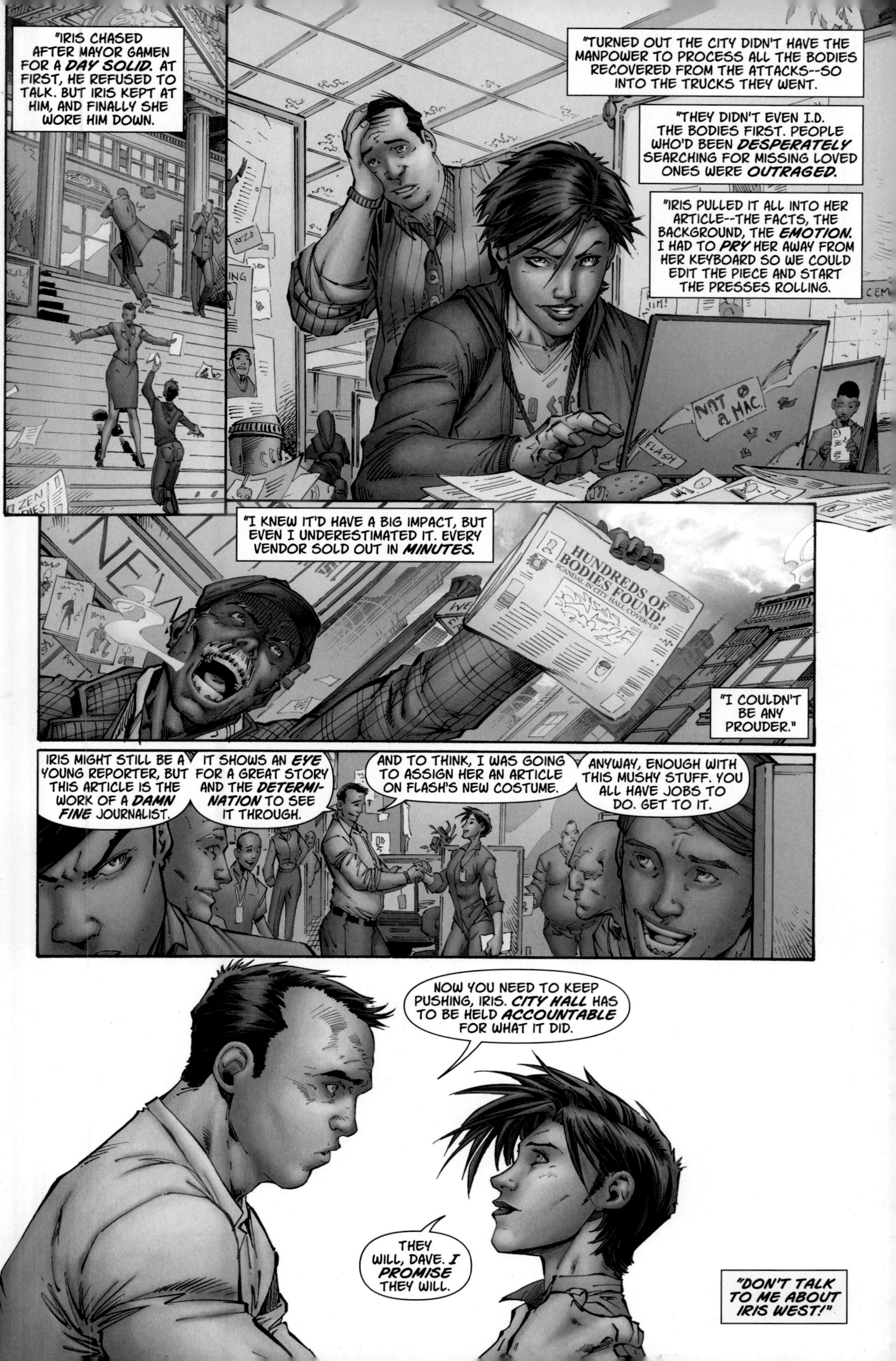
"IRIS CHASED AFTER MAYOR GAMEN FOR A DAY SOLID. AT FIRST, HE REFUSED TO TALK. BUT IRIS KEPT AT HIM, AND FINALLY SHE WORE HIM DOWN.
"TURNED OUT THE CITY DIDN'T HAVE THE MANPOWER TO PROCESS ALL THE BODIES RECOVERED FROM THE ATTACKS--SO INTO THE TRUCKS THEY WENT.
"THEY DIDN'T EVEN I.D. THE BODIES FIRST. PEOPLE WHO'D BEEN DESPERATELY SEARCHING FOR MISSING LOVED ONES WERE OUTRAGED.
"IRIS PULLED IT ALL INTO HER ARTICLE--THE FACTS, THE BACKGROUND, THE EMOTION. I HAD TO PRY HER AWAY FROM HER KEYBOARD SO WE COULD EDIT THE PIECE AND START THE PRESSES ROLLING.
NOT A MAC
FLASH
"I KNEW IT'D HAVE A BIG IMPACT, BUT EVEN I UNDERESTIMATED IT. EVERY VENDOR SOLD OUT IN MINUTES.
HUNDREDS OF BODIES FOUND!
SCANDAL IN CITY HALL COVER-UP
"I COULDN'T BE ANY PROUDER."
IRIS MIGHT STILL BE A YOUNG REPORTER, BUT THIS ARTICLE IS THE WORK OF A DAMN FINE JOURNALIST.
IT SHOWS AN EYE FOR A GREAT STORY AND THE DETERMINATION TO SEE IT THROUGH.
AND TO THINK, I WAS GOING TO ASSIGN HER AN ARTICLE ON FLASH'S NEW COSTUME.
ANYWAY, ENOUGH WITH THIS MUSHY STUFF. YOU ALL HAVE JOBS TO DO. GET TO IT.
NOW YOU NEED TO KEEP PUSHING, IRIS. CITY HALL HAS TO BE HELD ACCOUNTABLE FOR WHAT IT DID.
THEY WILL, DAVE. I PROMISE THEY WILL.
"DON'T TALK TO ME ABOUT IRIS WEST!"

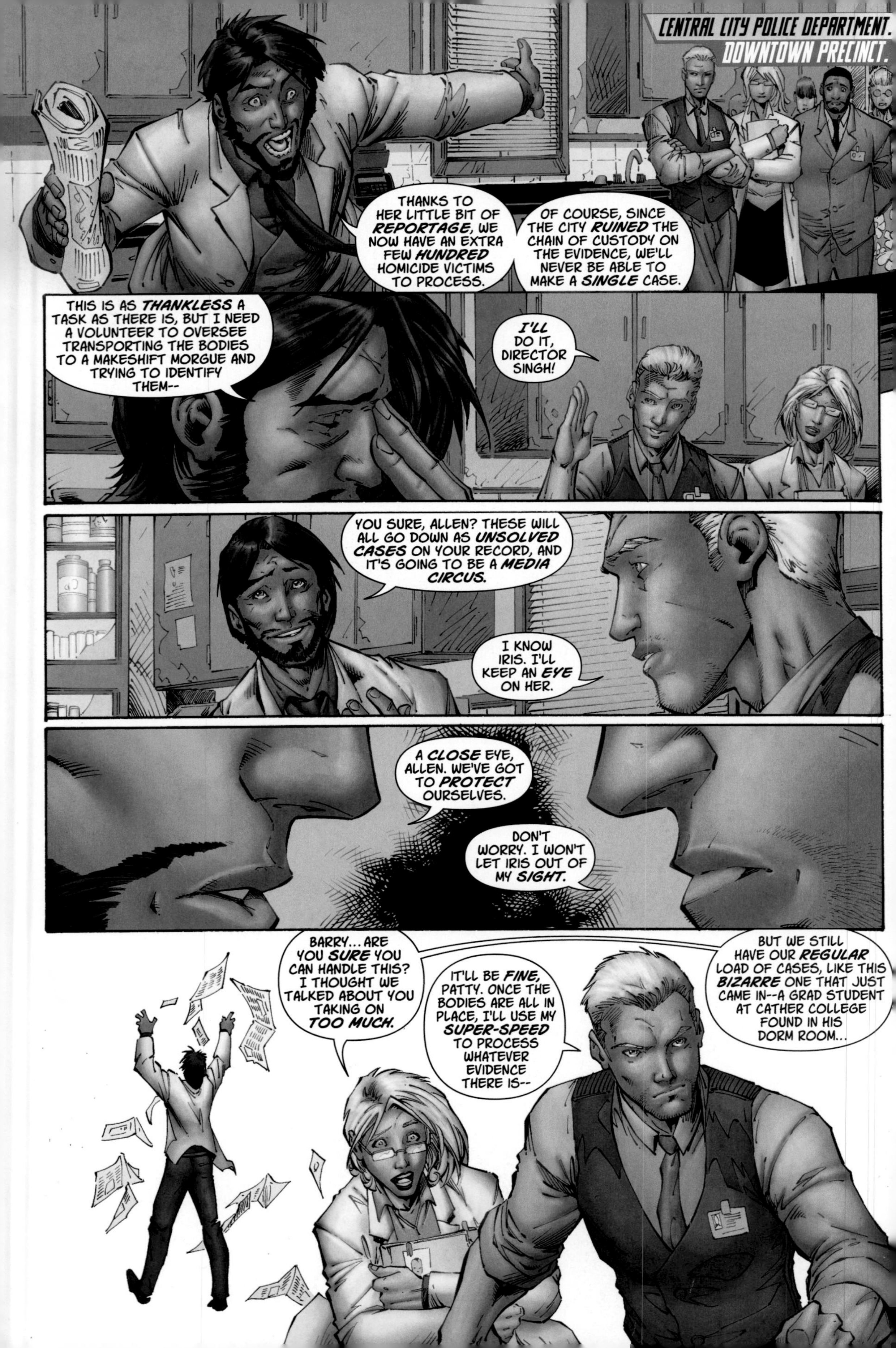
CENTRAL CITY POLICE DEPARTMENT.
DOWNTOWN PRECINCT.
THANKS TO HER LITTLE BIT OF REPORTAGE, WE NOW HAVE AN EXTRA FEW HUNDRED HOMICIDE VICTIMS TO PROCESS.
OF COURSE, SINCE THE CITY RUINED THE CHAIN OF CUSTODY ON THE EVIDENCE, WE'LL NEVER BE ABLE TO MAKE A SINGLE CASE.
THIS IS AS THANKLESS A TASK AS THERE IS, BUT I NEED A VOLUNTEER TO OVERSEE TRANSPORTING THE BODIES TO A MAKESHIFT MORGUE AND TRYING TO IDENTIFY THEM--
I'LL DO IT, DIRECTOR SINGH!
YOU SURE, ALLEN? THESE WILL ALL GO DOWN AS UNSOLVED CASES ON YOUR RECORD, AND IT'S GOING TO BE A MEDIA CIRCUS.
I KNOW IRIS. I'LL KEEP AN EYE ON HER.
A CLOSE EYE, ALLEN. WE'VE GOT TO PROTECT OURSELVES.
DON'T WORRY. I WON'T LET IRIS OUT OF MY SIGHT.
BARRY... ARE YOU SURE YOU CAN HANDLE THIS? I THOUGHT WE TALKED ABOUT YOU TAKING ON TOO MUCH.
IT'LL BE FINE, PATTY. ONCE THE BODIES ARE ALL IN PLACE, I'LL USE MY SUPER-SPEED TO PROCESS WHATEVER EVIDENCE THERE IS--
BUT WE STILL HAVE OUR REGULAR LOAD OF CASES, LIKE THIS BIZARRE ONE THAT JUST CAME IN--A GRAD STUDENT AT CATHER COLLEGE FOUND IN HIS DORM ROOM...

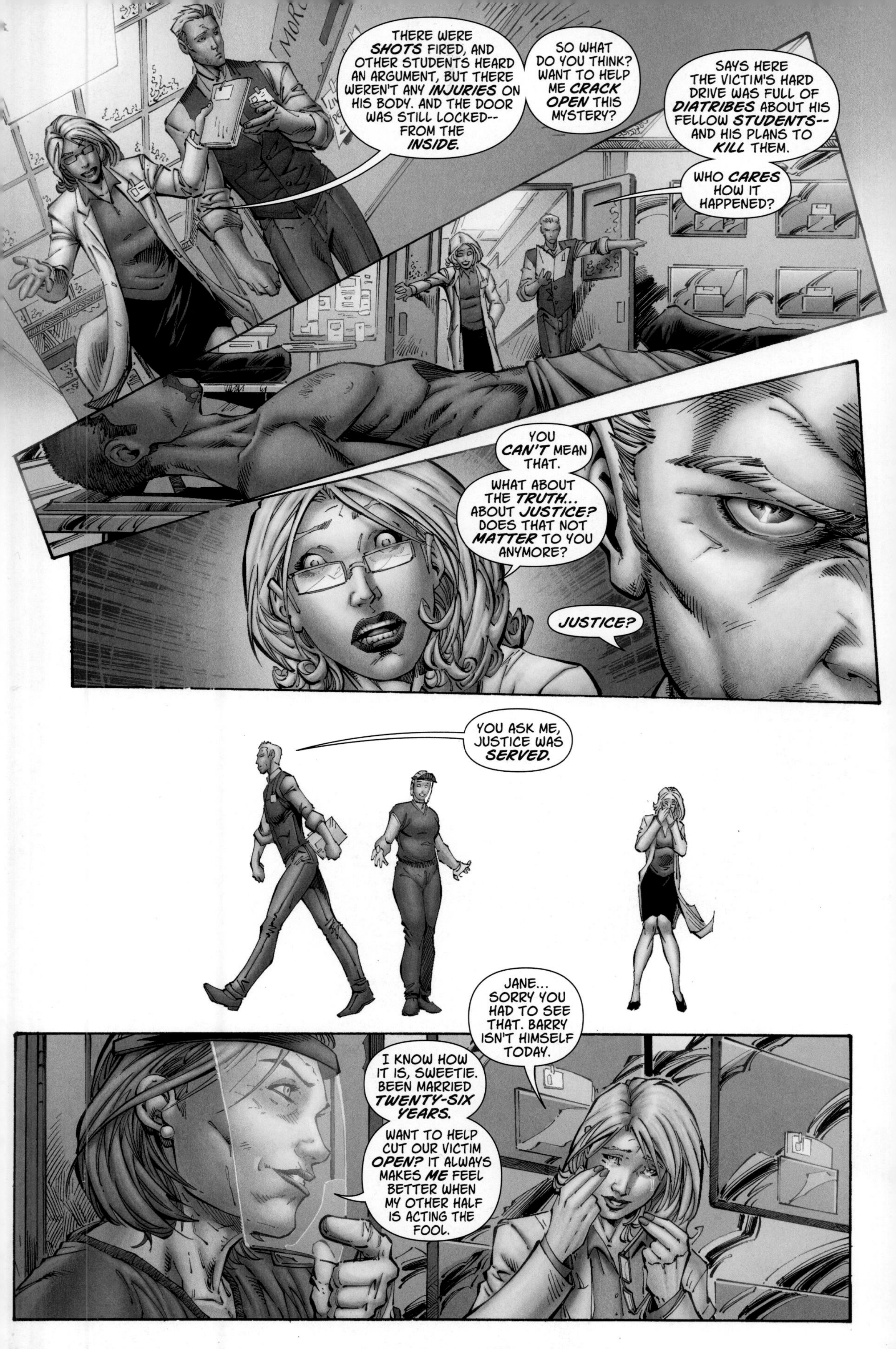
THERE WERE SHOTS FIRED, AND OTHER STUDENTS HEARD AN ARGUMENT, BUT THERE WEREN'T ANY INJURIES ON HIS BODY. AND THE DOOR WAS STILL LOCKED-- FROM THE INSIDE.
SO WHAT DO YOU THINK? WANT TO HELP ME CRACK OPEN THIS MYSTERY?
SAYS HERE THE VICTIM'S HARD DRIVE WAS FULL OF DIATRIBES ABOUT HIS FELLOW STUDENTS-- AND HIS PLANS TO KILL THEM.
WHO CARES HOW IT HAPPENED?
YOU CAN'T MEAN THAT.
WHAT ABOUT THE TRUTH... ABOUT JUSTICE? DOES THAT NOT MATTER TO YOU ANYMORE?
JUSTICE?
YOU ASK ME, JUSTICE WAS SERVED.
JANE... SORRY YOU HAD TO SEE THAT. BARRY ISN'T HIMSELF TODAY.
I KNOW HOW IT IS, SWEETIE. BEEN MARRIED TWENTY-SIX YEARS.
WANT TO HELP CUT OUR VICTIM OPEN? IT ALWAYS MAKES ME FEEL BETTER WHEN MY OTHER HALF IS ACTING THE FOOL.

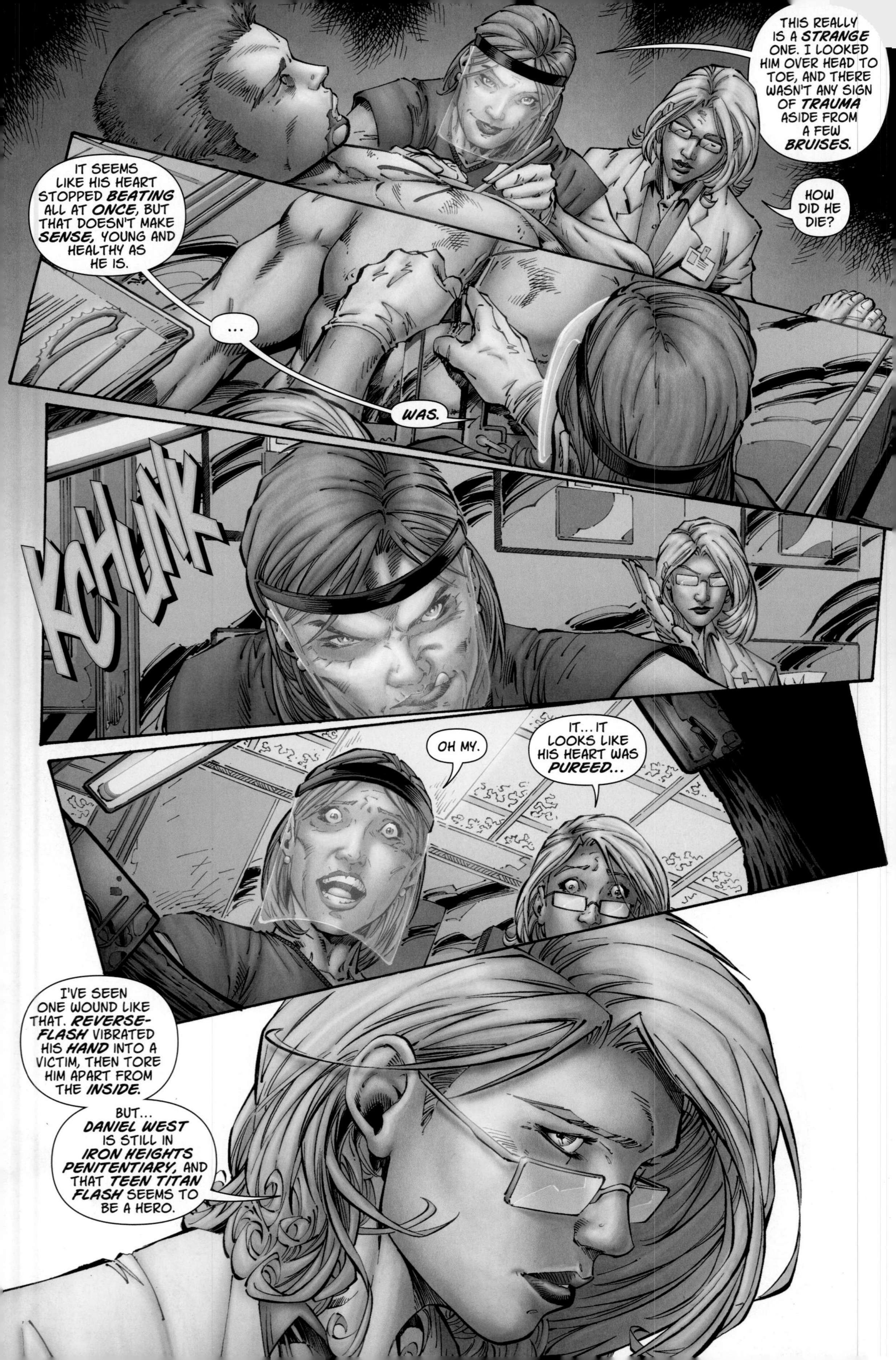
THIS REALLY IS A STRANGE ONE. I LOOKED HIM OVER HEAD TO TOE, AND THERE WASN'T ANY SIGN OF TRAUMA ASIDE FROM A FEW BRUISES.
HOW DID HE DIE?
IT SEEMS LIKE HIS HEART STOPPED BEATING ALL AT ONCE, BUT THAT DOESN'T MAKE SENSE, YOUNG AND HEALTHY AS HE IS.
...
WAS.
KCHUNK
OH MY.
IT... IT LOOKS LIKE HIS HEART WAS PUREED...
I'VE SEEN ONE WOUND LIKE THAT. REVERSE-FLASH VIBRATED HIS HAND INTO A VICTIM, THEN TORE HIM APART FROM THE INSIDE.
BUT... DANIEL WEST IS STILL IN IRON HEIGHTS PENITENTIARY, AND THAT TEEN TITAN FLASH SEEMS TO BE A HERO.

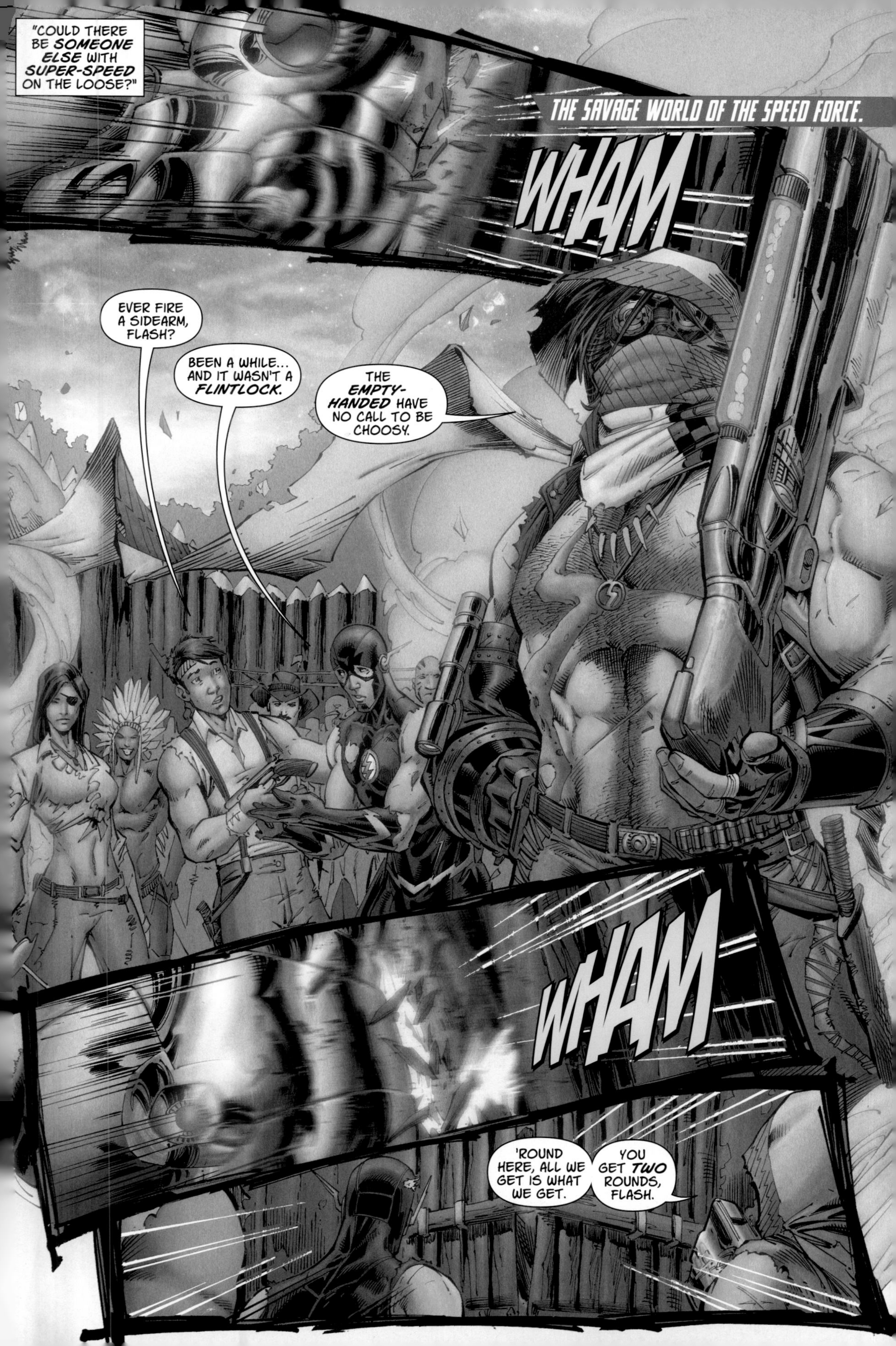
"COULD THERE BE SOMEONE ELSE WITH SUPER-SPEED ON THE LOOSE?"
THE SAVAGE WORLD OF THE SPEED FORCE.
WHAM
EVER FIRE A SIDEARM, FLASH?
BEEN A WHILE... AND IT WASN'T A FLINTLOCK.
THE EMPTY-HANDED HAVE NO CALL TO BE CHOOSY.
WHAM
'ROUND HERE, ALL WE GET IS WHAT WE GET.
YOU GET TWO ROUNDS, FLASH.

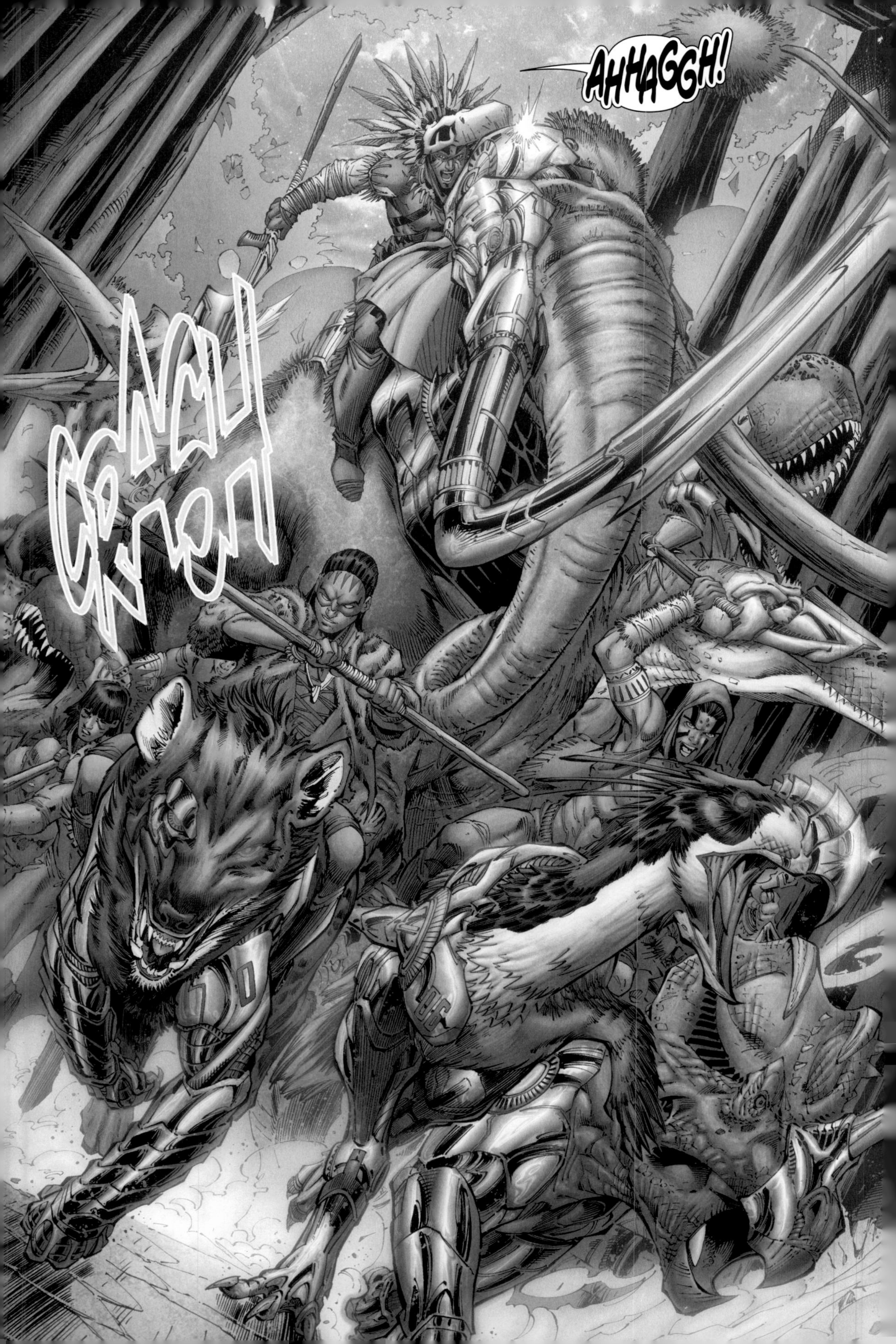
AHHAGGH!

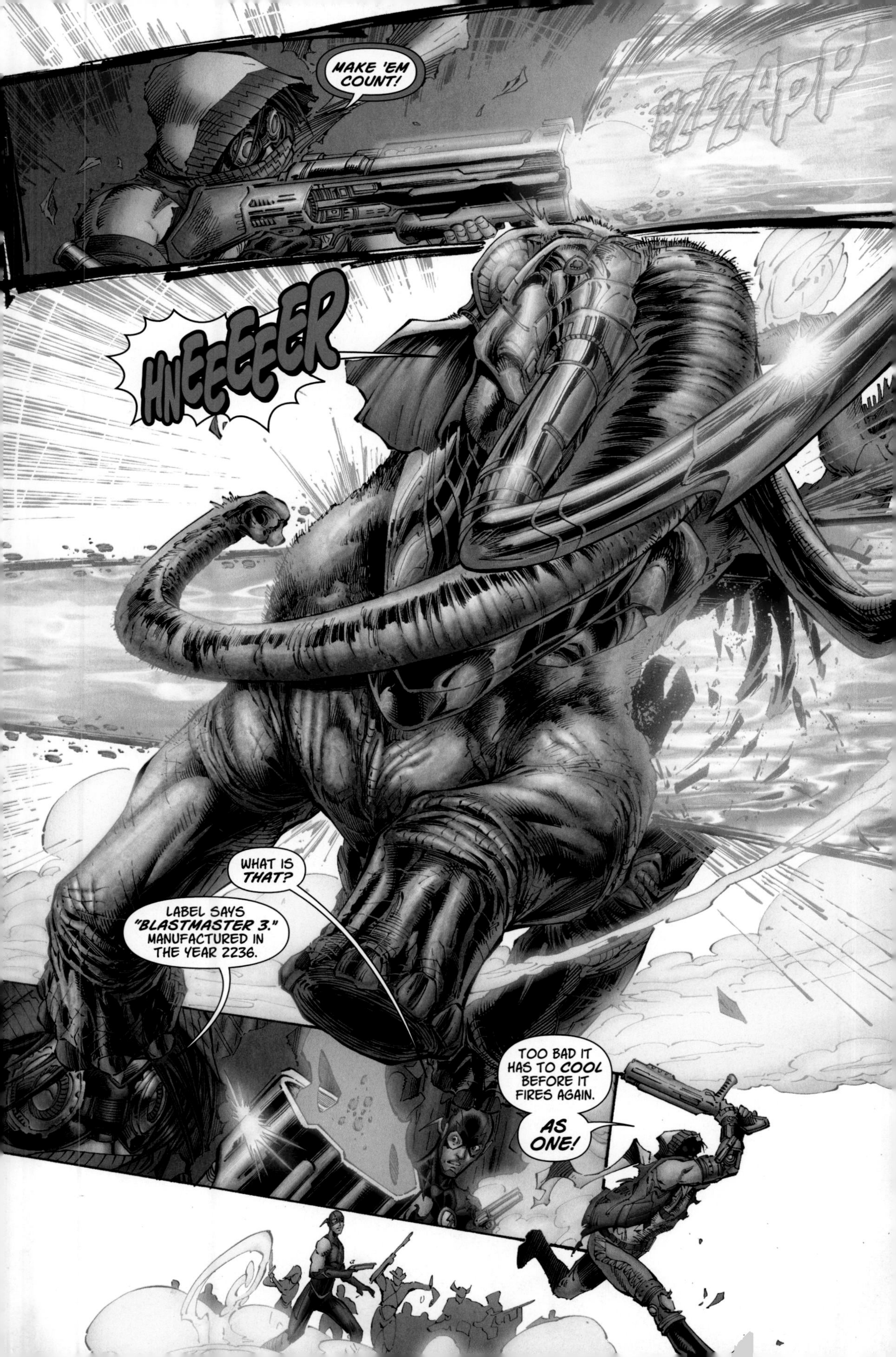
MAKE 'EM COUNT!
HNEEEEER
WHAT IS *THAT?*
LABEL SAYS *"BLASTMASTER 3."* MANUFACTURED IN THE YEAR 2236.
TOO BAD IT HAS TO *COOL* BEFORE IT FIRES AGAIN.
AS ONE!

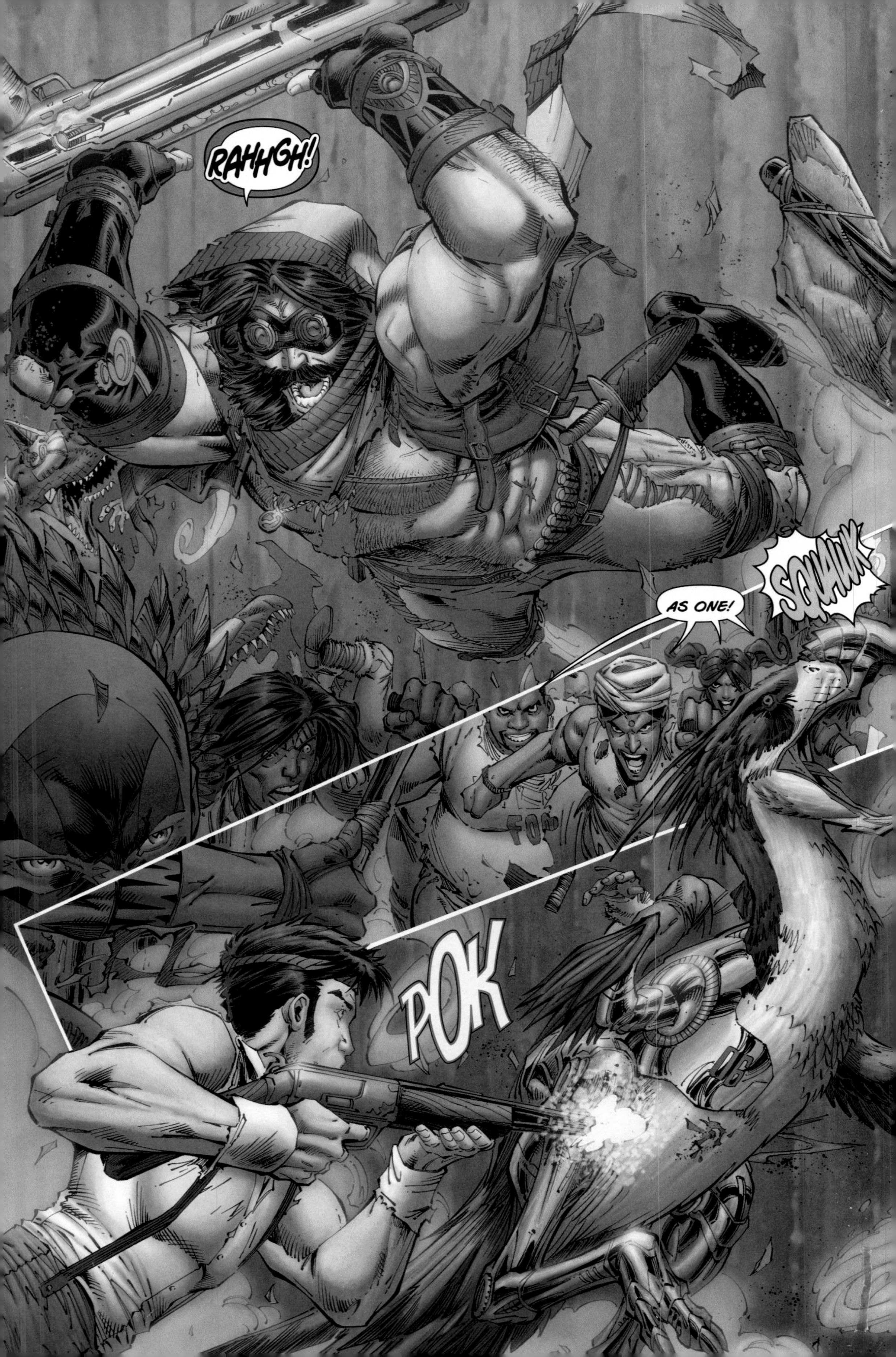
RAHHGH!
AS ONE!
SQUAWK
POK

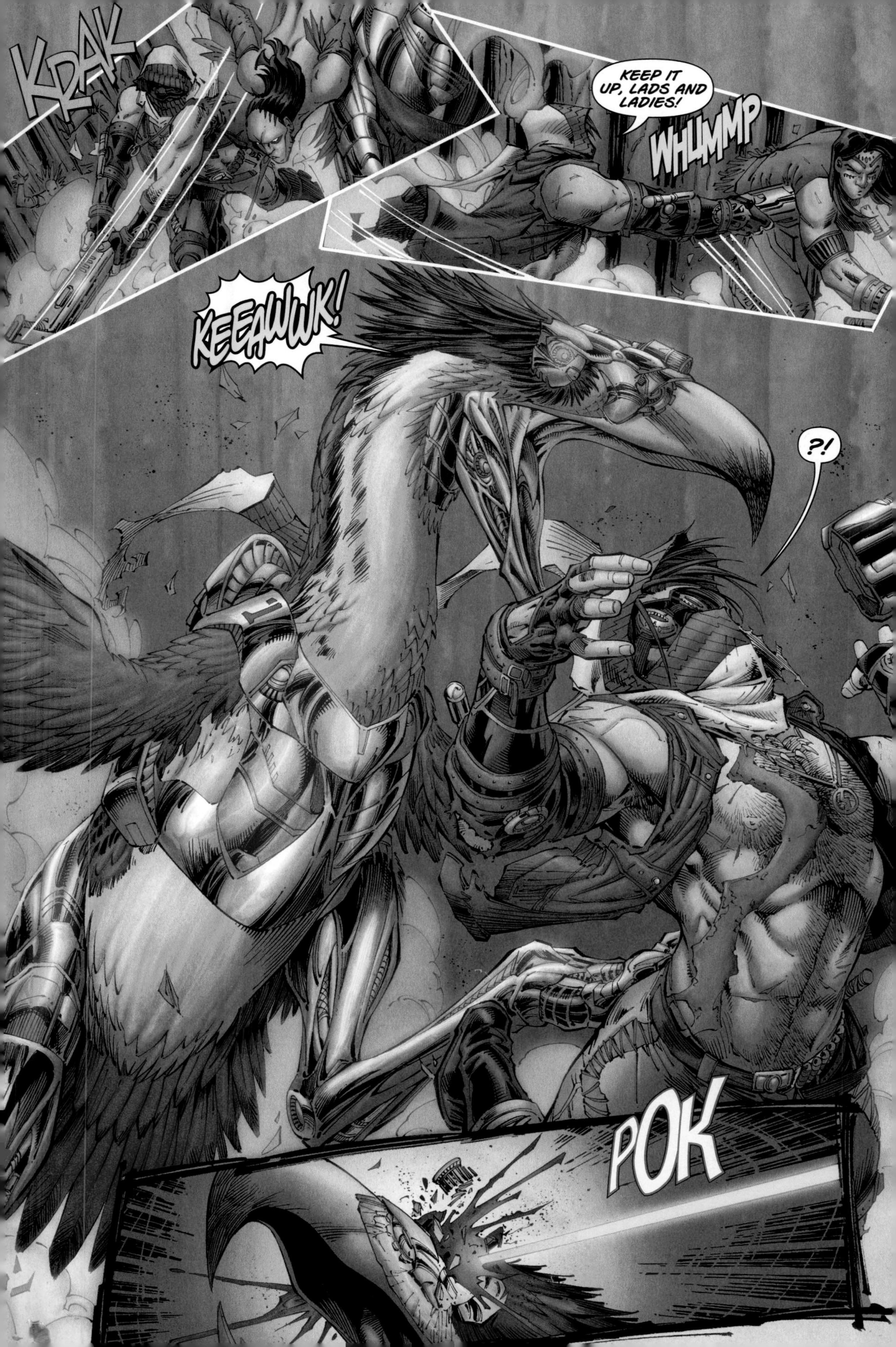
KRAK
KEEP IT UP, LADS AND LADIES!
WHUMMP
KEEAWWK!
?!
POK

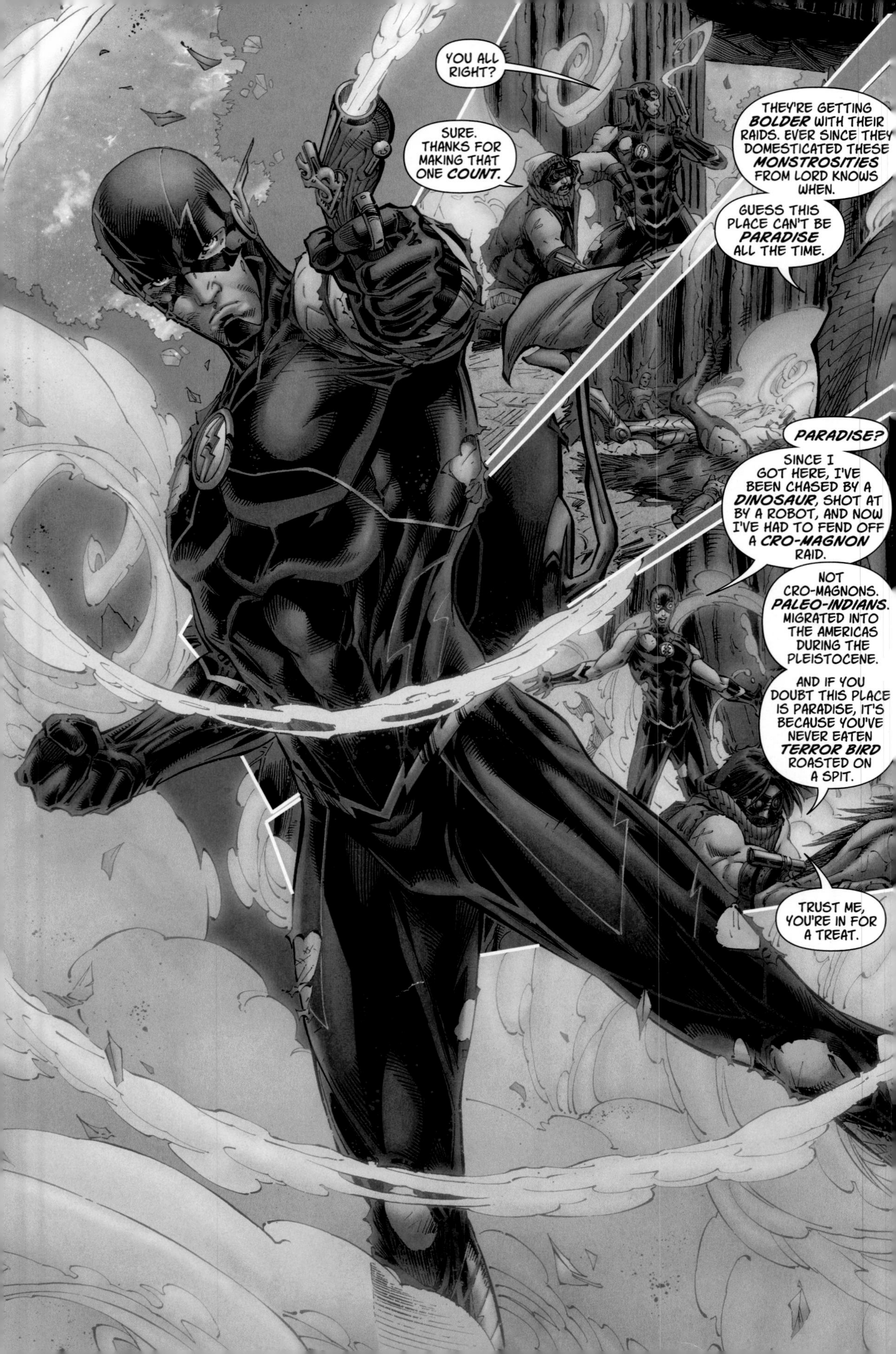
YOU ALL RIGHT?
SURE. THANKS FOR MAKING THAT ONE COUNT.
THEY'RE GETTING BOLDER WITH THEIR RAIDS. EVER SINCE THEY DOMESTICATED THESE MONSTROSITIES FROM LORD KNOWS WHEN.
GUESS THIS PLACE CAN'T BE PARADISE ALL THE TIME.
PARADISE?
SINCE I GOT HERE, I'VE BEEN CHASED BY A DINOSAUR, SHOT AT BY A ROBOT, AND NOW I'VE HAD TO FEND OFF A CRO-MAGNON RAID.
NOT CRO-MAGNONS. PALEO-INDIANS. MIGRATED INTO THE AMERICAS DURING THE PLEISTOCENE.
AND IF YOU DOUBT THIS PLACE IS PARADISE, IT'S BECAUSE YOU'VE NEVER EATEN TERROR BIRD ROASTED ON A SPIT.
TRUST ME, YOU'RE IN FOR A TREAT.

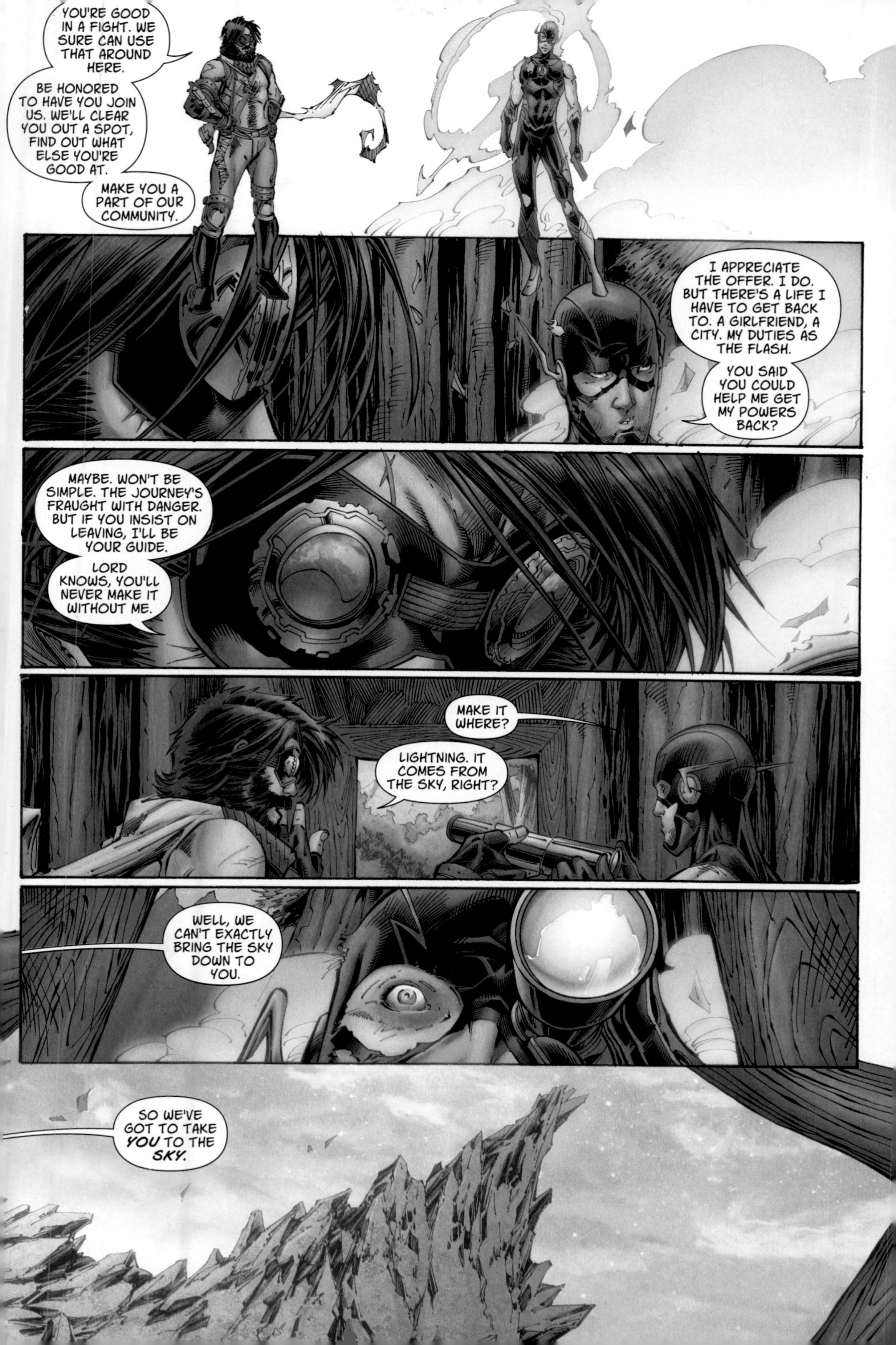
YOU'RE GOOD IN A FIGHT. WE SURE CAN USE THAT AROUND HERE.
BE HONORED TO HAVE YOU JOIN US. WE'LL CLEAR YOU OUT A SPOT, FIND OUT WHAT ELSE YOU'RE GOOD AT.
MAKE YOU A PART OF OUR COMMUNITY.
I APPRECIATE THE OFFER. I DO. BUT THERE'S A LIFE I HAVE TO GET BACK TO. A GIRLFRIEND, A CITY. MY DUTIES AS THE FLASH.
YOU SAID YOU COULD HELP ME GET MY POWERS BACK?
MAYBE. WON'T BE SIMPLE. THE JOURNEY'S FRAUGHT WITH DANGER. BUT IF YOU INSIST ON LEAVING, I'LL BE YOUR GUIDE.
LORD KNOWS, YOU'LL NEVER MAKE IT WITHOUT ME.
MAKE IT WHERE?
LIGHTNING. IT COMES FROM THE SKY, RIGHT?
WELL, WE CAN'T EXACTLY BRING THE SKY DOWN TO YOU.
SO WE'VE GOT TO TAKE YOU TO THE SKY.

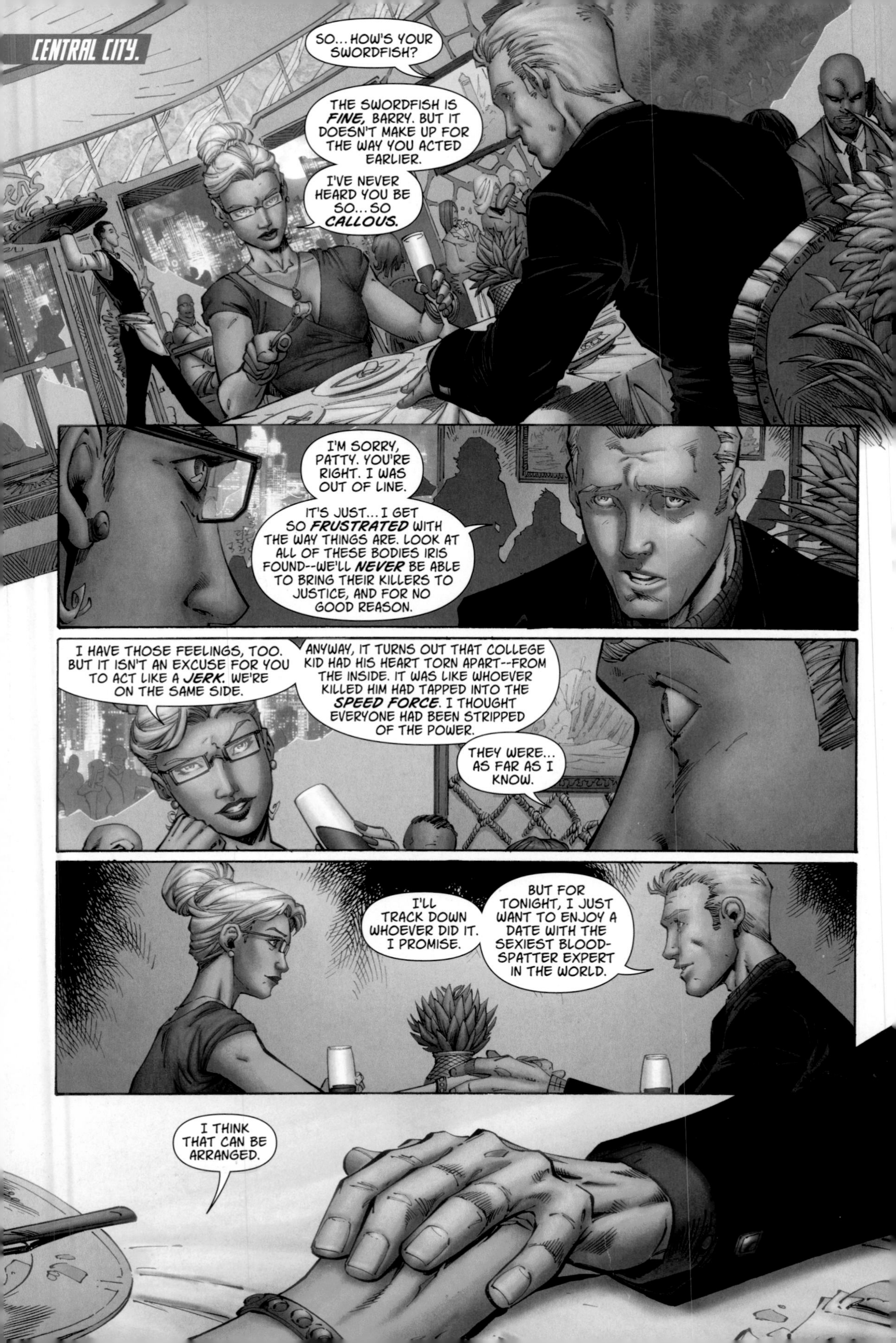
CENTRAL CITY.
SO... HOW'S YOUR SWORDFISH?
THE SWORDFISH IS FINE, BARRY. BUT IT DOESN'T MAKE UP FOR THE WAY YOU ACTED EARLIER.
I'VE NEVER HEARD YOU BE SO... SO CALLOUS.
I'M SORRY, PATTY. YOU'RE RIGHT. I WAS OUT OF LINE.
IT'S JUST... I GET SO FRUSTRATED WITH THE WAY THINGS ARE. LOOK AT ALL OF THESE BODIES IRIS FOUND--WE'LL NEVER BE ABLE TO BRING THEIR KILLERS TO JUSTICE, AND FOR NO GOOD REASON.
I HAVE THOSE FEELINGS, TOO. BUT IT ISN'T AN EXCUSE FOR YOU TO ACT LIKE A JERK. WE'RE ON THE SAME SIDE.
ANYWAY, IT TURNS OUT THAT COLLEGE KID HAD HIS HEART TORN APART--FROM THE INSIDE. IT WAS LIKE WHOEVER KILLED HIM HAD TAPPED INTO THE SPEED FORCE. I THOUGHT EVERYONE HAD BEEN STRIPPED OF THE POWER.
THEY WERE... AS FAR AS I KNOW.
I'LL TRACK DOWN WHOEVER DID IT. I PROMISE.
BUT FOR TONIGHT, I JUST WANT TO ENJOY A DATE WITH THE SEXIEST BLOOD-SPATTER EXPERT IN THE WORLD.
I THINK THAT CAN BE ARRANGED.

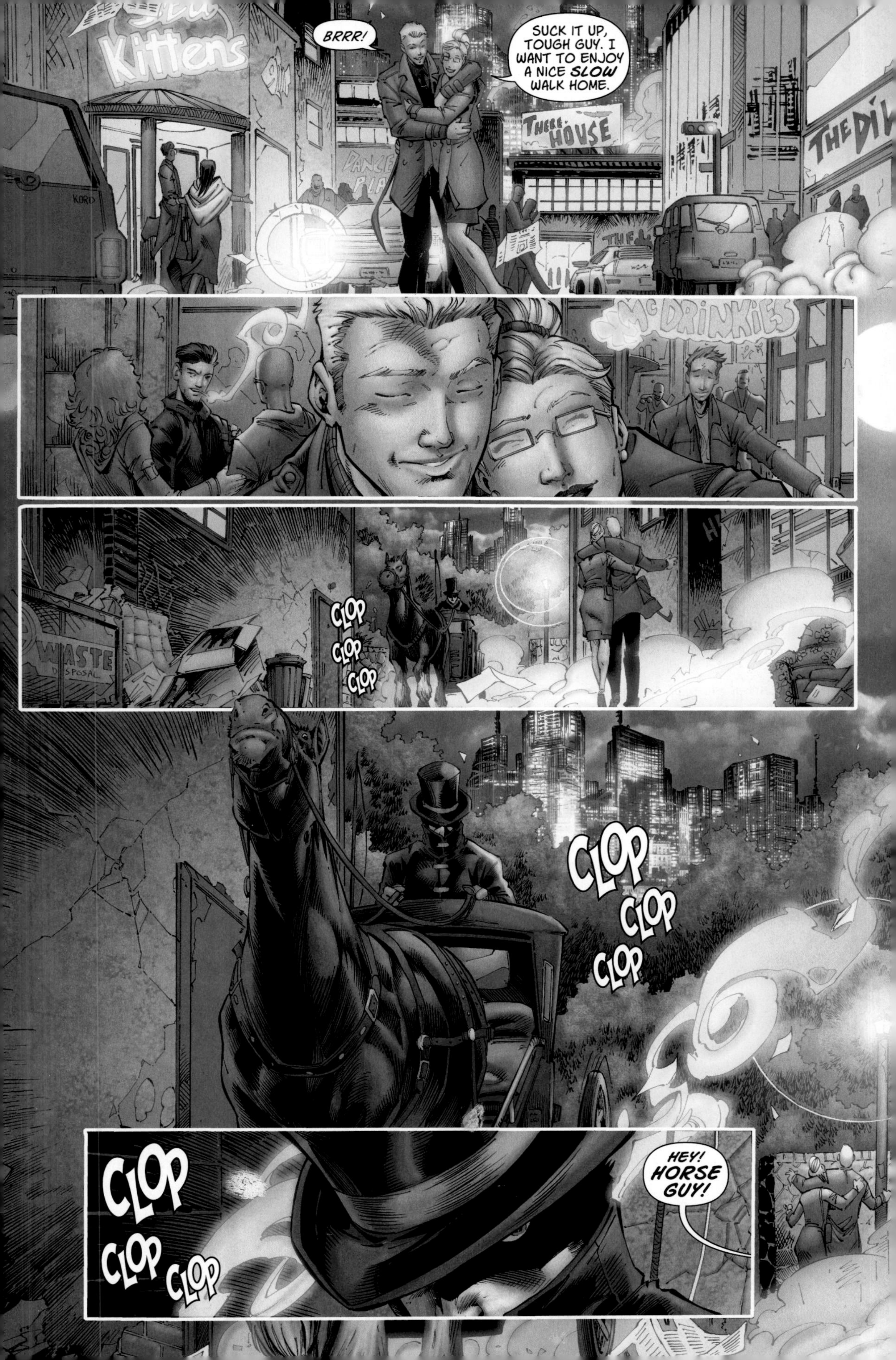
BRRR!
SUCK IT UP, TOUGH GUY. I WANT TO ENJOY A NICE SLOW WALK HOME.
Kittens
THERE-HOUSE
McDRINKIES
WASTE DISPOSAL
CLOP
CLOP
CLOP
CLOP
CLOP
CLOP
CLOP
CLOP
CLOP
HEY! HORSE GUY!

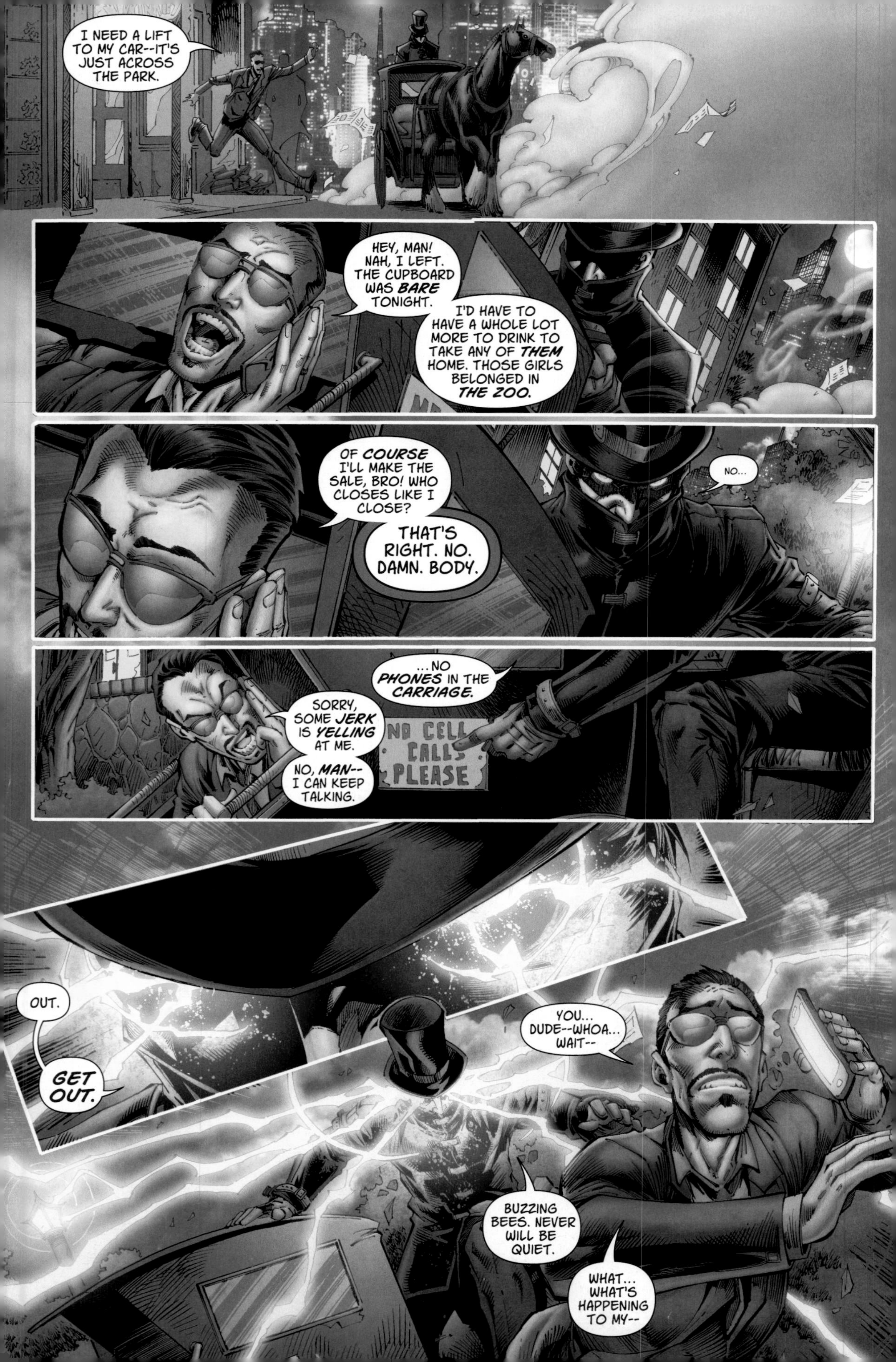

I NEED A LIFT TO MY CAR--IT'S JUST ACROSS THE PARK.
HEY, MAN! NAH, I LEFT. THE CUPBOARD WAS BARE TONIGHT.
I'D HAVE TO HAVE A WHOLE LOT MORE TO DRINK TO TAKE ANY OF THEM HOME. THOSE GIRLS BELONGED IN THE ZOO.
OF COURSE I'LL MAKE THE SALE, BRO! WHO CLOSES LIKE I CLOSE?
THAT'S RIGHT. NO. DAMN. BODY.
NO...
...NO PHONES IN THE CARRIAGE.
SORRY, SOME JERK IS YELLING AT ME.
NO, MAN-- I CAN KEEP TALKING.
NO CELL CALLS PLEASE
OUT.
GET OUT.
YOU... DUDE--WHOA... WAIT--
BUZZING BEES. NEVER WILL BE QUIET.
WHAT... WHAT'S HAPPENING TO MY--

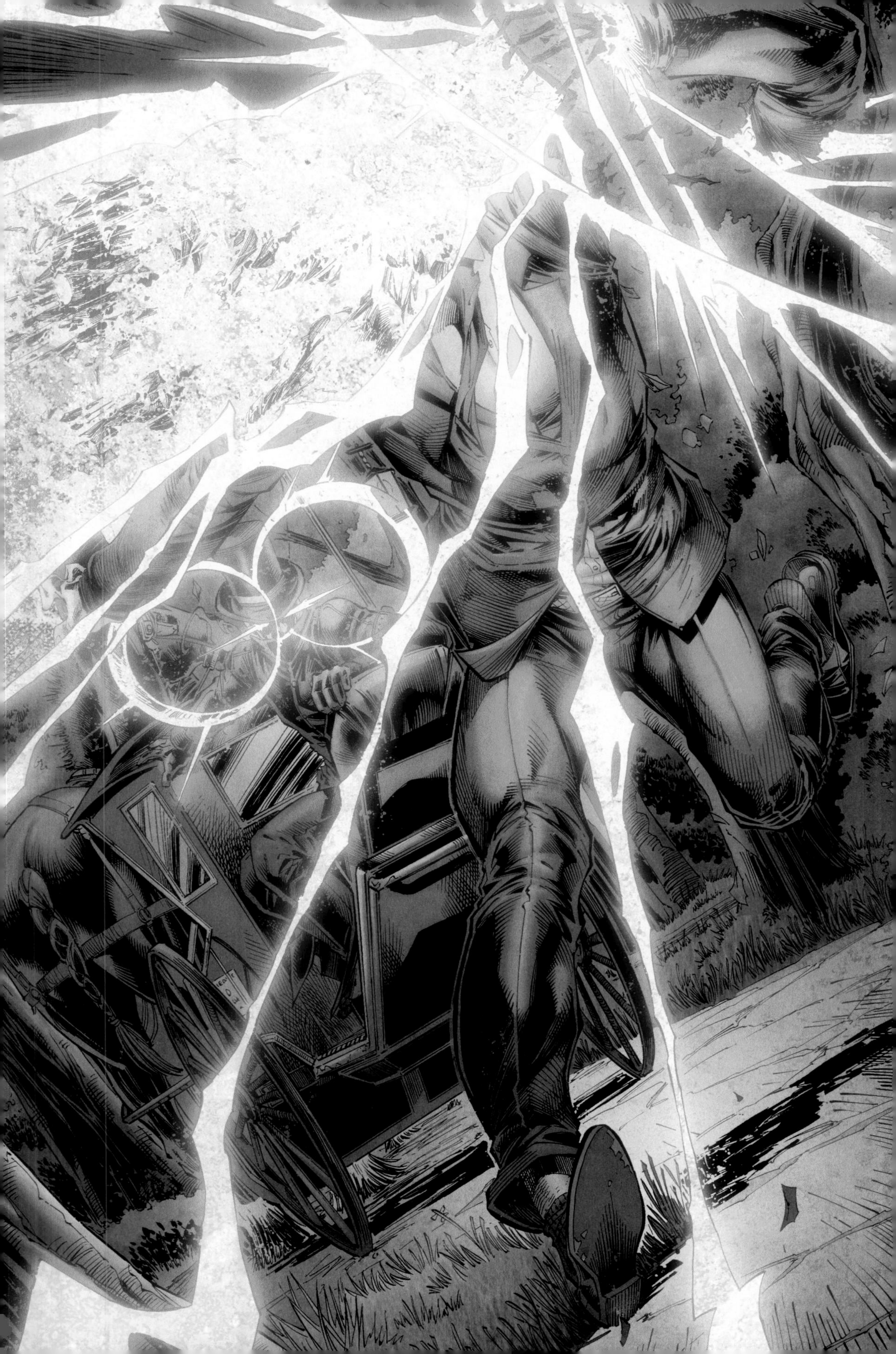

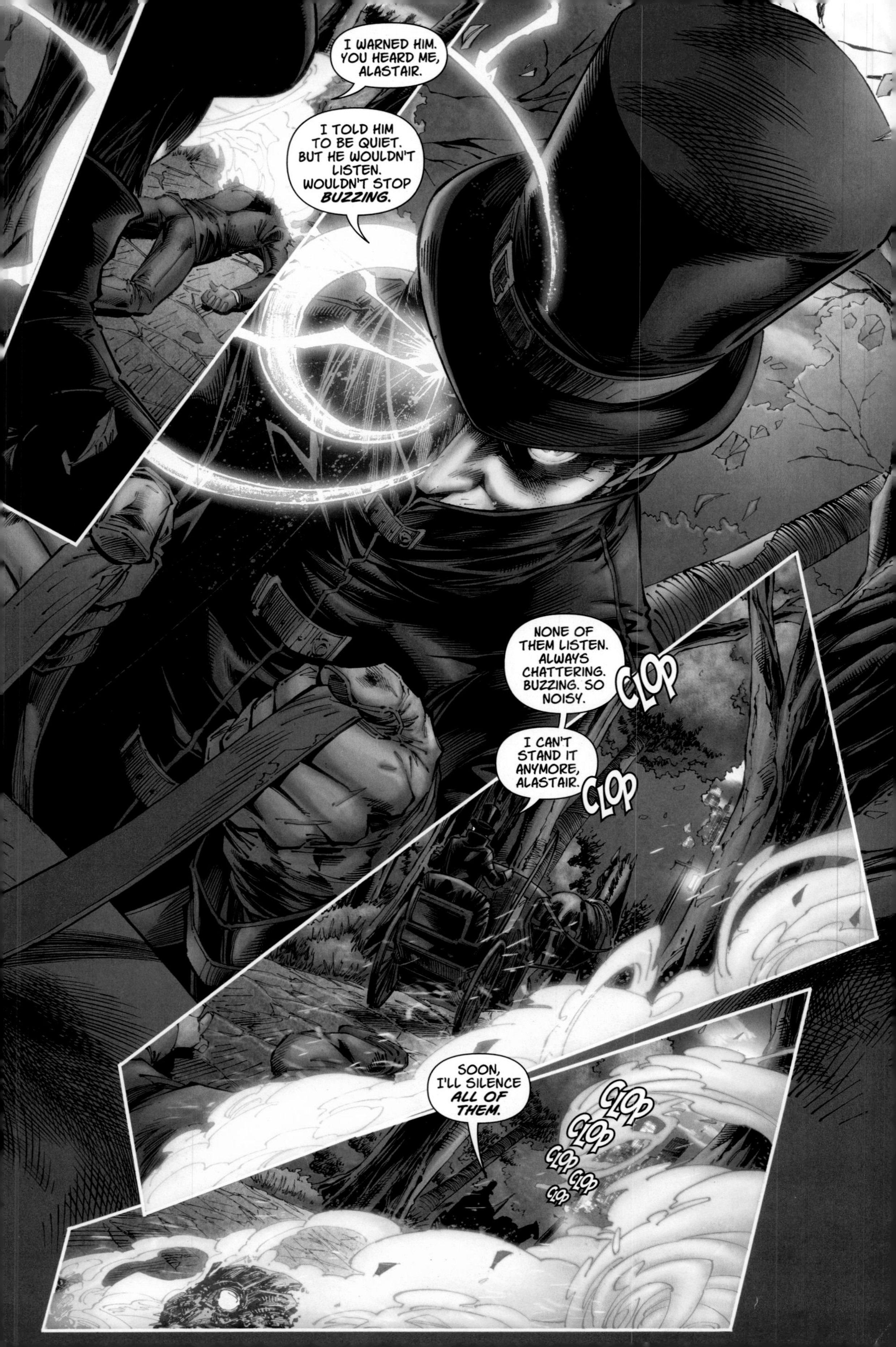
I WARNED HIM. YOU HEARD ME, ALASTAIR.
I TOLD HIM TO BE QUIET. BUT HE WOULDN'T LISTEN. WOULDN'T STOP *BUZZING*.
NONE OF THEM LISTEN. ALWAYS CHATTERING. BUZZING. SO NOISY.
CLOP
I CAN'T STAND IT ANYMORE, ALASTAIR.
CLOP
SOON, I'LL SILENCE *ALL OF THEM*.

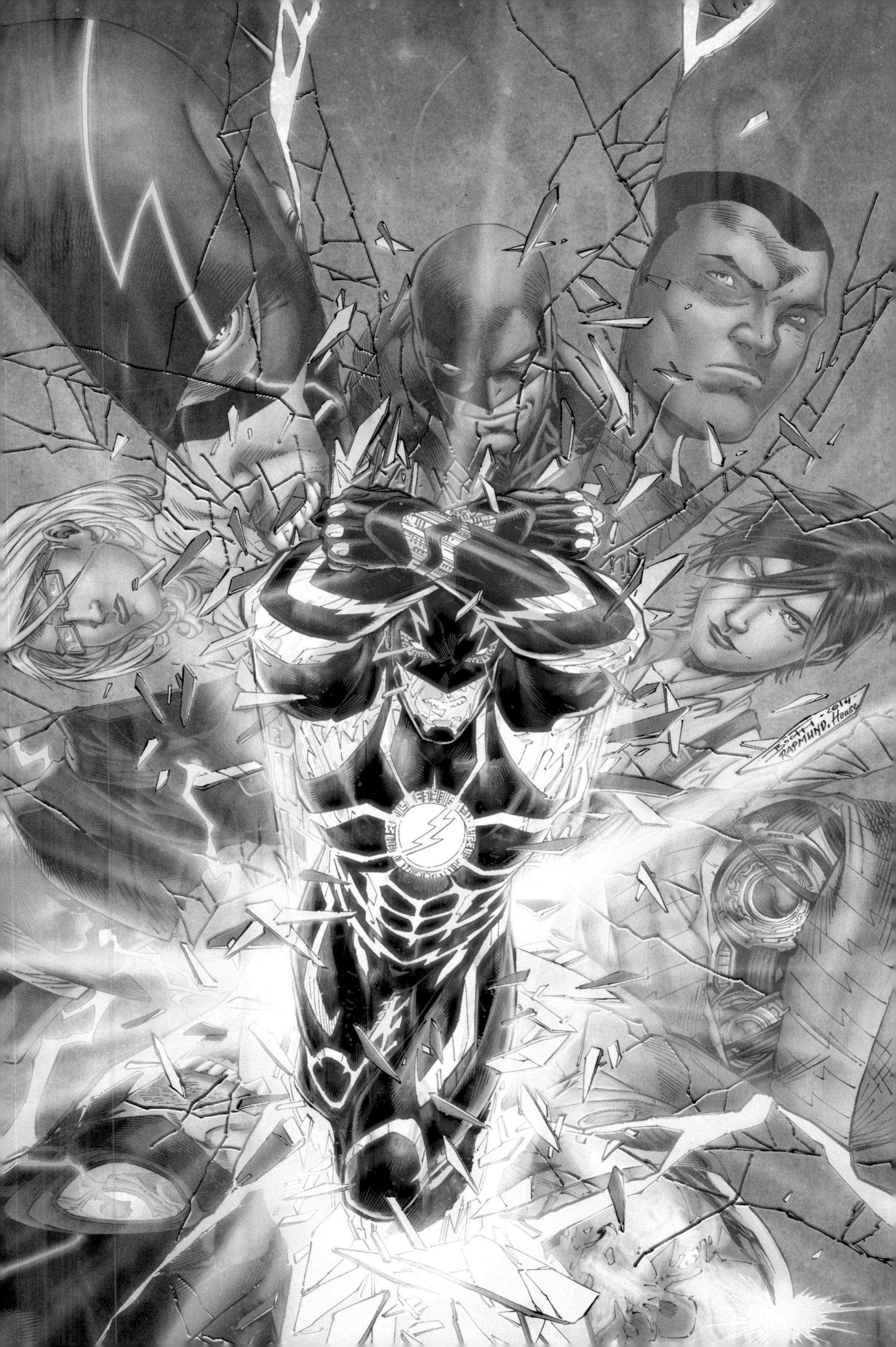
-2014-
RAPMUND. House

SKELETONS IN THE CLOSET

ROBERT VENDITTI & VAN JENSEN writers BRETT BOOTH penciller NORM RAPMUND inker ANDREW DALHOUSE colorist PAT BROSSEAU letterer
cover by BRETT BOOTH, NORM RAPMUND & ANDREW DALHOUSE

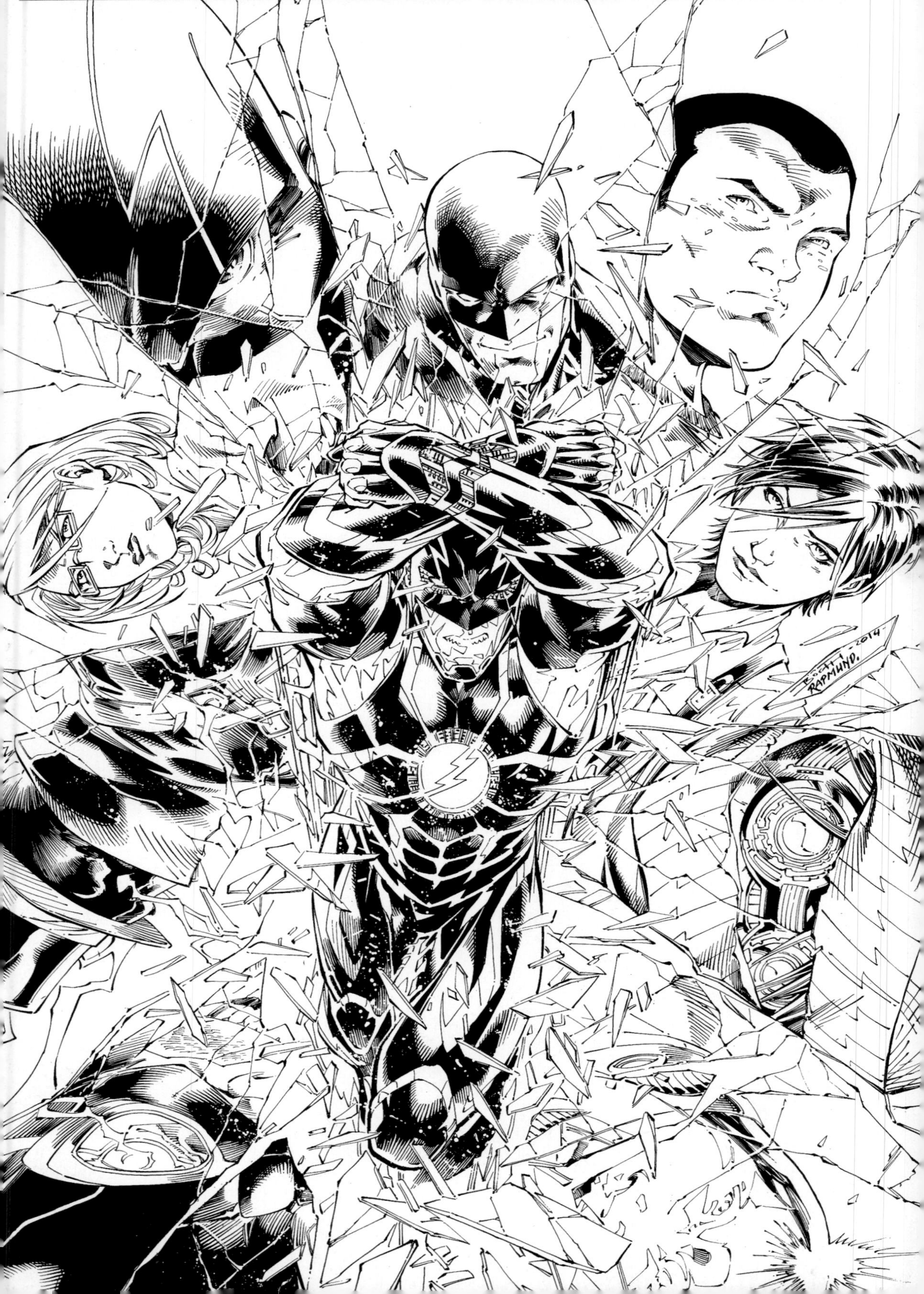

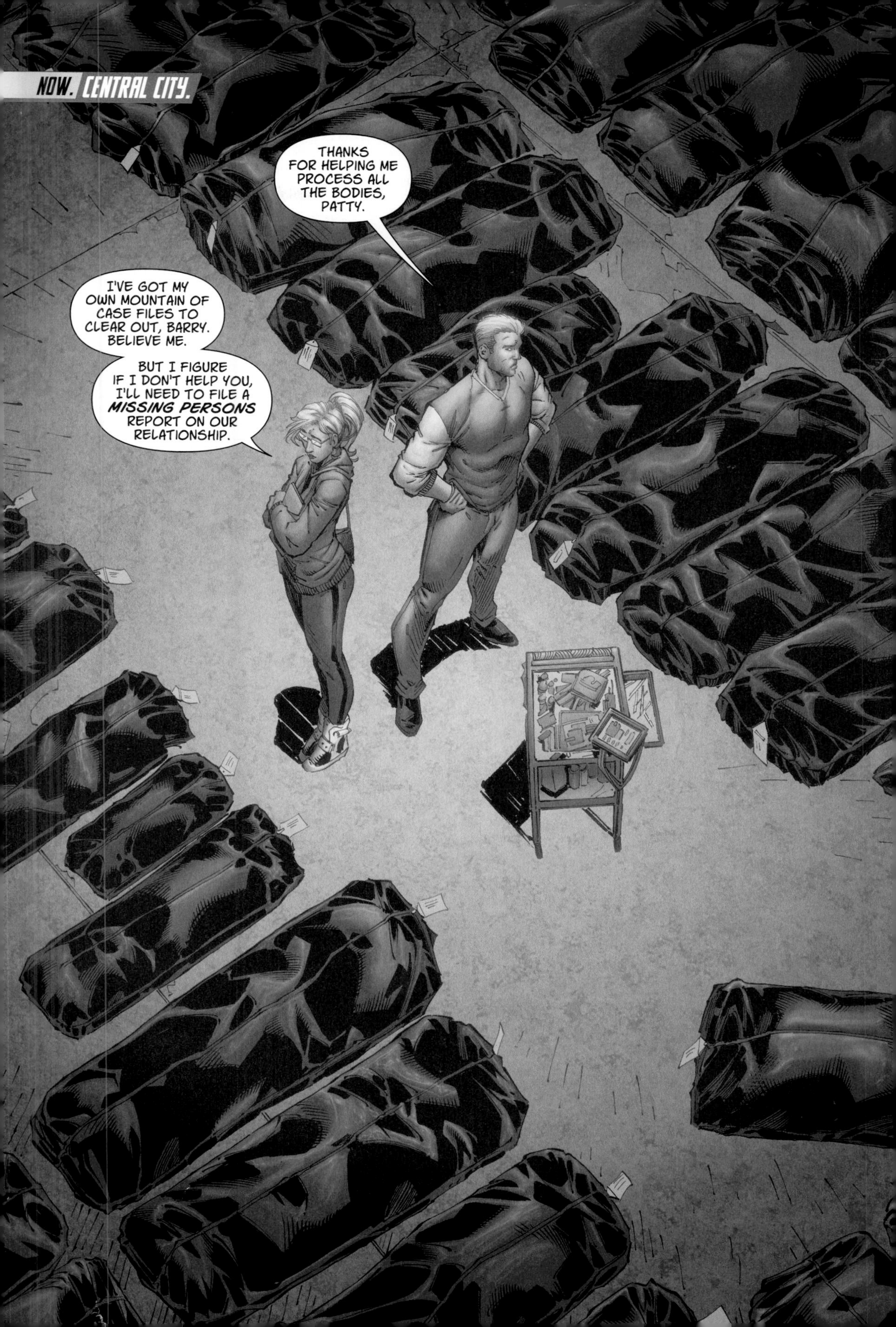
NOW. CENTRAL CITY.
THANKS FOR HELPING ME PROCESS ALL THE BODIES, PATTY.
I'VE GOT MY OWN MOUNTAIN OF CASE FILES TO CLEAR OUT, BARRY. BELIEVE ME.
BUT I FIGURE IF I DON'T HELP YOU, I'LL NEED TO FILE A *MISSING PERSONS* REPORT ON OUR RELATIONSHIP.

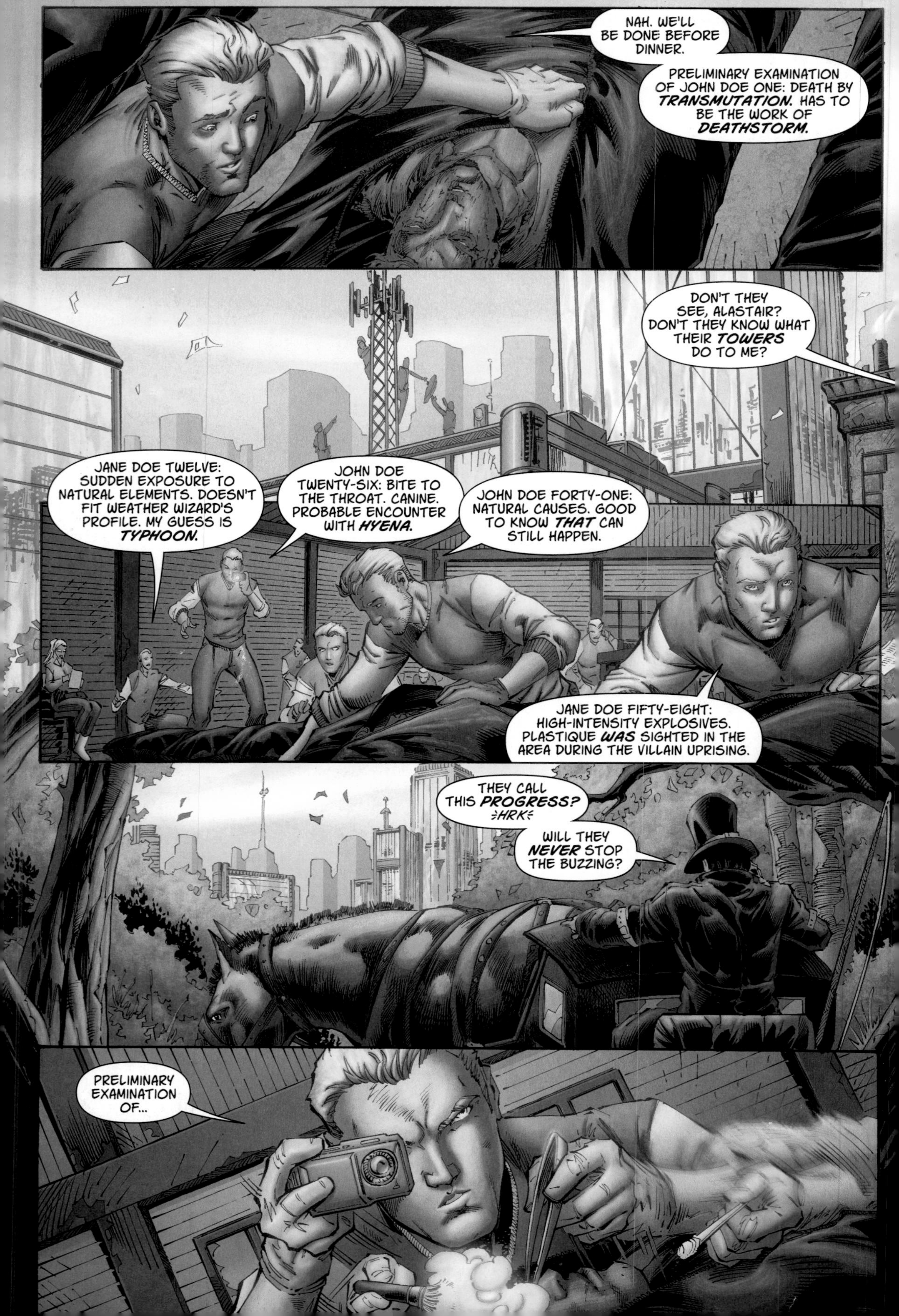
NAH. WE'LL BE DONE BEFORE DINNER.
PRELIMINARY EXAMINATION OF JOHN DOE ONE: DEATH BY TRANSMUTATION. HAS TO BE THE WORK OF DEATHSTORM.
DON'T THEY SEE, ALASTAIR? DON'T THEY KNOW WHAT THEIR TOWERS DO TO ME?
JANE DOE TWELVE: SUDDEN EXPOSURE TO NATURAL ELEMENTS. DOESN'T FIT WEATHER WIZARD'S PROFILE. MY GUESS IS TYPHOON.
JOHN DOE TWENTY-SIX: BITE TO THE THROAT. CANINE. PROBABLE ENCOUNTER WITH HYENA.
JOHN DOE FORTY-ONE: NATURAL CAUSES. GOOD TO KNOW THAT CAN STILL HAPPEN.
JANE DOE FIFTY-EIGHT: HIGH-INTENSITY EXPLOSIVES. PLASTIQUE WAS SIGHTED IN THE AREA DURING THE VILLAIN UPRISING.
THEY CALL THIS PROGRESS? HRK
WILL THEY NEVER STOP THE BUZZING?
PRELIMINARY EXAMINATION OF...

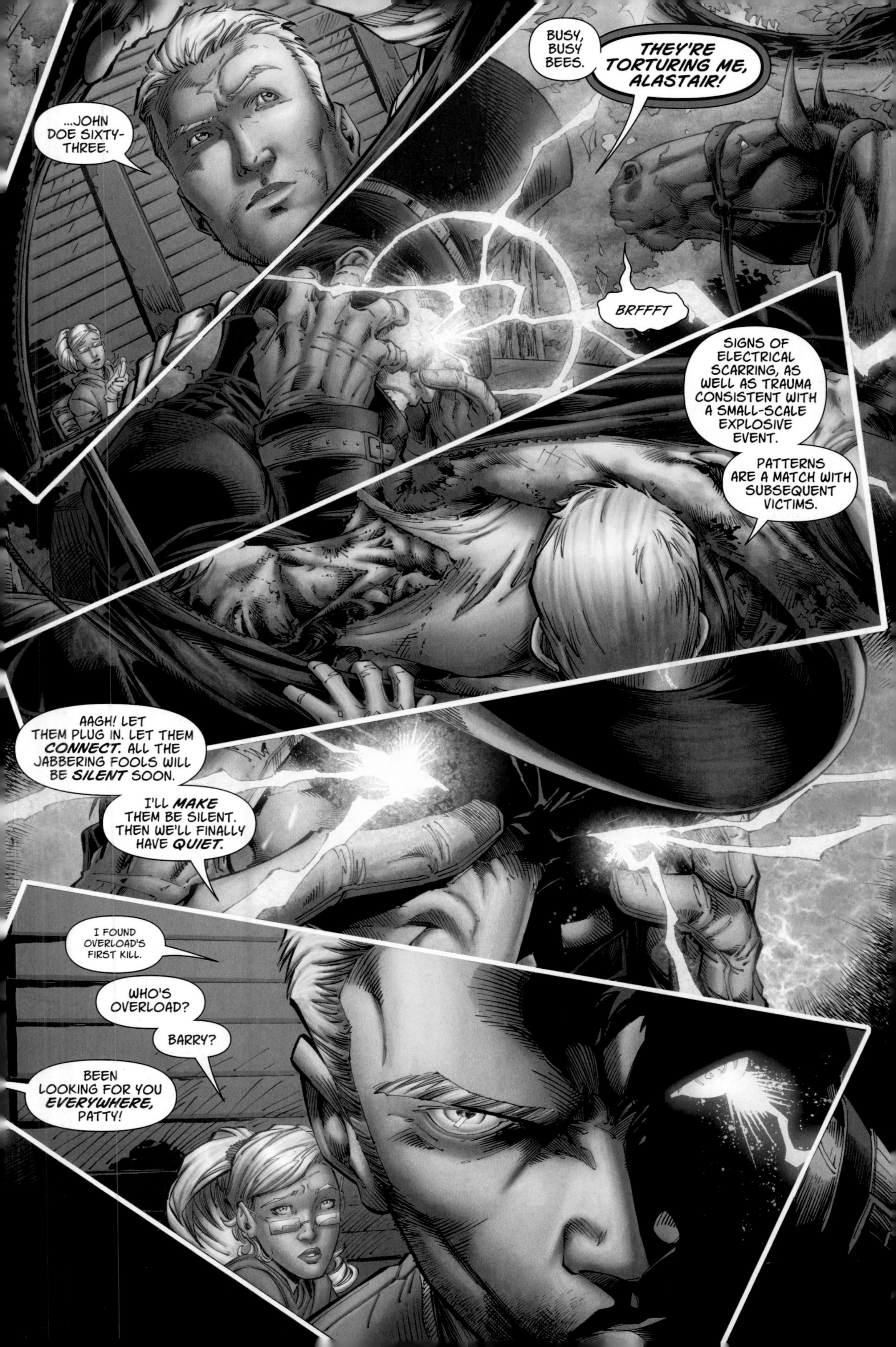

...JOHN DOE SIXTY-THREE.
BUSY, BUSY BEES.
THEY'RE TORTURING ME, ALASTAIR!
BRFFFT
SIGNS OF ELECTRICAL SCARRING, AS WELL AS TRAUMA CONSISTENT WITH A SMALL-SCALE EXPLOSIVE EVENT.
PATTERNS ARE A MATCH WITH SUBSEQUENT VICTIMS.
AAGH! LET THEM PLUG IN. LET THEM CONNECT. ALL THE JABBERING FOOLS WILL BE SILENT SOON.
I'LL MAKE THEM BE SILENT. THEN WE'LL FINALLY HAVE QUIET.
I FOUND OVERLOAD'S FIRST KILL.
WHO'S OVERLOAD?
BARRY?
BEEN LOOKING FOR YOU EVERYWHERE, PATTY!

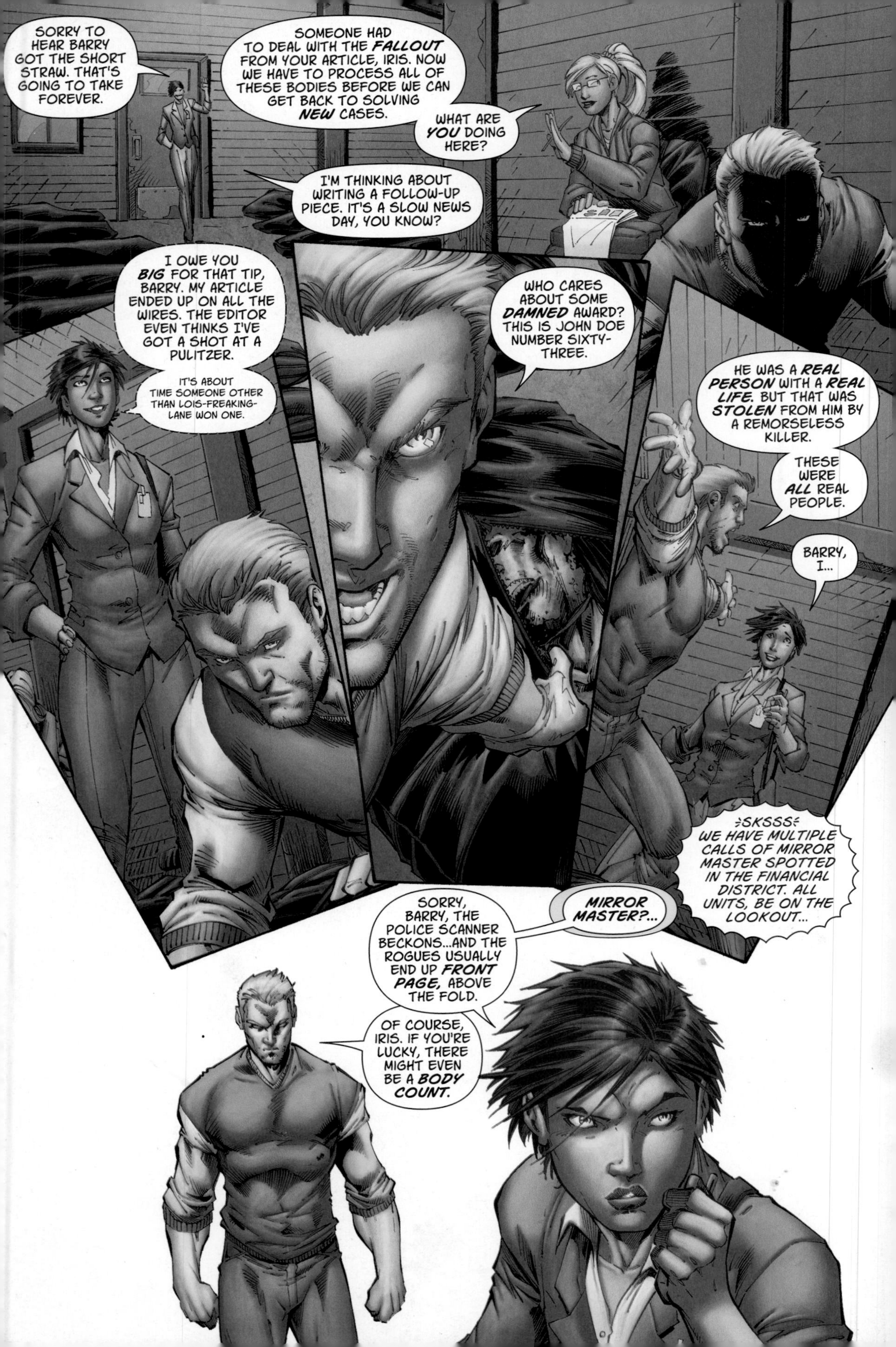
SORRY TO HEAR BARRY GOT THE SHORT STRAW. THAT'S GOING TO TAKE FOREVER.
SOMEONE HAD TO DEAL WITH THE FALLOUT FROM YOUR ARTICLE, IRIS. NOW WE HAVE TO PROCESS ALL OF THESE BODIES BEFORE WE CAN GET BACK TO SOLVING NEW CASES.
WHAT ARE YOU DOING HERE?
I'M THINKING ABOUT WRITING A FOLLOW-UP PIECE. IT'S A SLOW NEWS DAY, YOU KNOW?
I OWE YOU BIG FOR THAT TIP, BARRY. MY ARTICLE ENDED UP ON ALL THE WIRES. THE EDITOR EVEN THINKS I'VE GOT A SHOT AT A PULITZER.
IT'S ABOUT TIME SOMEONE OTHER THAN LOIS-FREAKING-LANE WON ONE.
WHO CARES ABOUT SOME DAMNED AWARD? THIS IS JOHN DOE NUMBER SIXTY-THREE.
HE WAS A REAL PERSON WITH A REAL LIFE. BUT THAT WAS STOLEN FROM HIM BY A REMORSELESS KILLER.
THESE WERE ALL REAL PEOPLE.
BARRY, I...
SKSSS WE HAVE MULTIPLE CALLS OF MIRROR MASTER SPOTTED IN THE FINANCIAL DISTRICT. ALL UNITS, BE ON THE LOOKOUT...
MIRROR MASTER?...
SORRY, BARRY, THE POLICE SCANNER BECKONS...AND THE ROGUES USUALLY END UP FRONT PAGE, ABOVE THE FOLD.
OF COURSE, IRIS. IF YOU'RE LUCKY, THERE MIGHT EVEN BE A BODY COUNT.

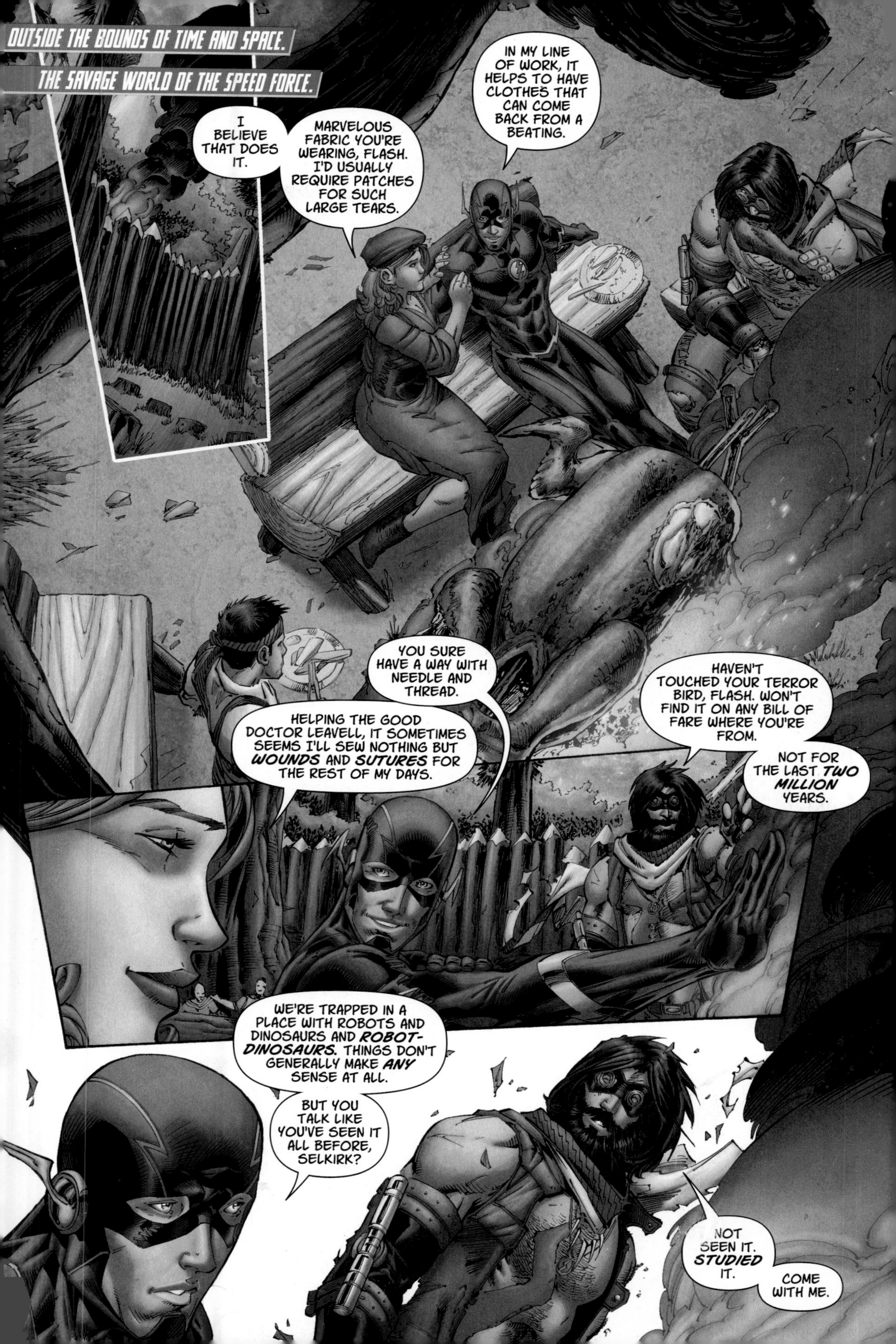

OUTSIDE THE BOUNDS OF TIME AND SPACE.
THE SAVAGE WORLD OF THE SPEED FORCE.
I BELIEVE THAT DOES IT.
MARVELOUS FABRIC YOU'RE WEARING, FLASH. I'D USUALLY REQUIRE PATCHES FOR SUCH LARGE TEARS.
IN MY LINE OF WORK, IT HELPS TO HAVE CLOTHES THAT CAN COME BACK FROM A BEATING.
YOU SURE HAVE A WAY WITH NEEDLE AND THREAD.
HELPING THE GOOD DOCTOR LEAVELL, IT SOMETIMES SEEMS I'LL SEW NOTHING BUT WOUNDS AND SUTURES FOR THE REST OF MY DAYS.
HAVEN'T TOUCHED YOUR TERROR BIRD, FLASH. WON'T FIND IT ON ANY BILL OF FARE WHERE YOU'RE FROM.
NOT FOR THE LAST TWO MILLION YEARS.
WE'RE TRAPPED IN A PLACE WITH ROBOTS AND DINOSAURS AND ROBOT-DINOSAURS. THINGS DON'T GENERALLY MAKE ANY SENSE AT ALL.
BUT YOU TALK LIKE YOU'VE SEEN IT ALL BEFORE, SELKIRK?
NOT SEEN IT. STUDIED IT.
COME WITH ME.

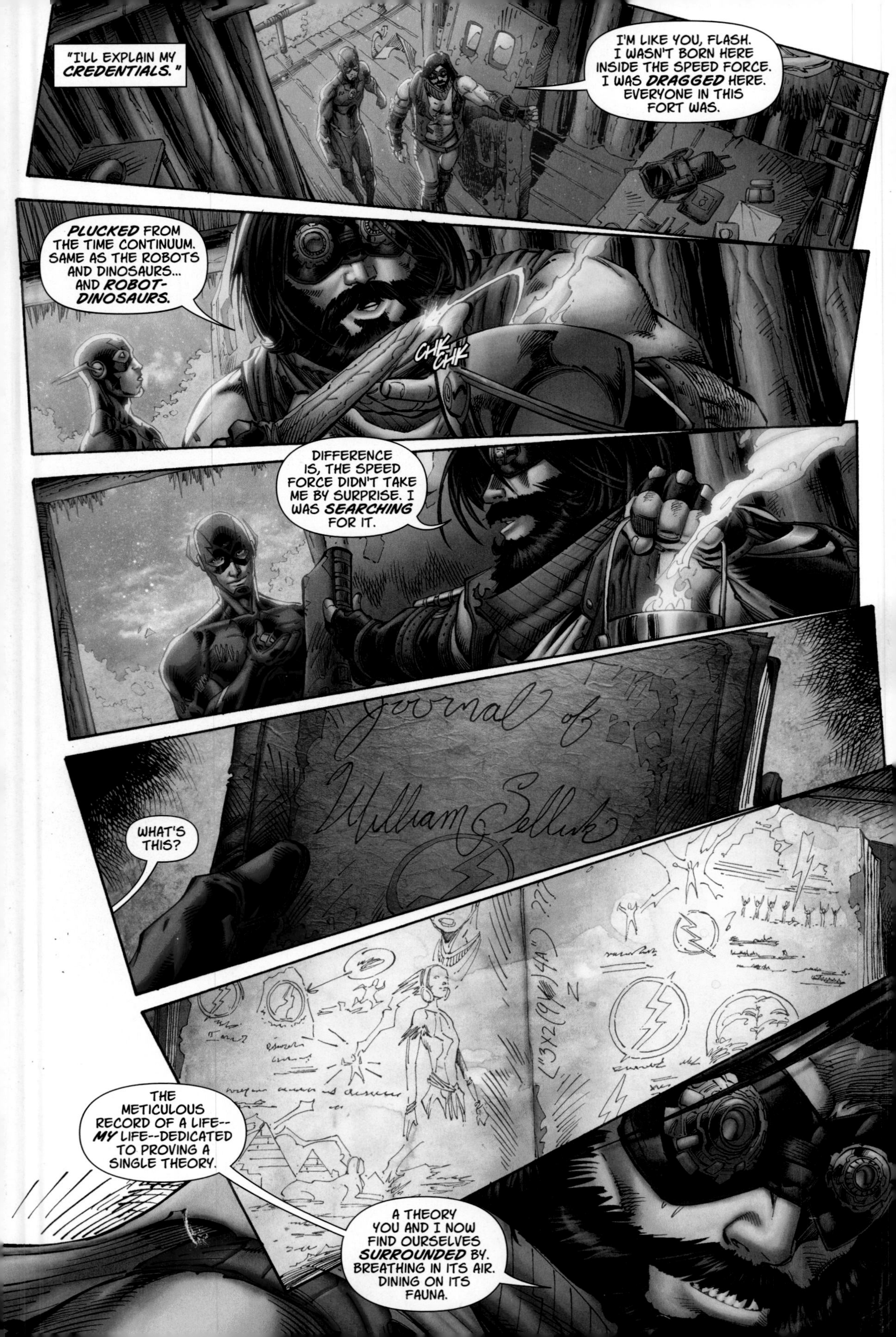
"I'LL EXPLAIN MY CREDENTIALS."
I'M LIKE YOU, FLASH. I WASN'T BORN HERE INSIDE THE SPEED FORCE. I WAS DRAGGED HERE. EVERYONE IN THIS FORT WAS.
PLUCKED FROM THE TIME CONTINUUM. SAME AS THE ROBOTS AND DINOSAURS... AND ROBOT-DINOSAURS.
CHK CHK
DIFFERENCE IS, THE SPEED FORCE DIDN'T TAKE ME BY SURPRISE. I WAS SEARCHING FOR IT.
Journal of William Sellick
WHAT'S THIS?
THE METICULOUS RECORD OF A LIFE--MY LIFE--DEDICATED TO PROVING A SINGLE THEORY.
A THEORY YOU AND I NOW FIND OURSELVES SURROUNDED BY. BREATHING IN ITS AIR. DINING ON ITS FAUNA.

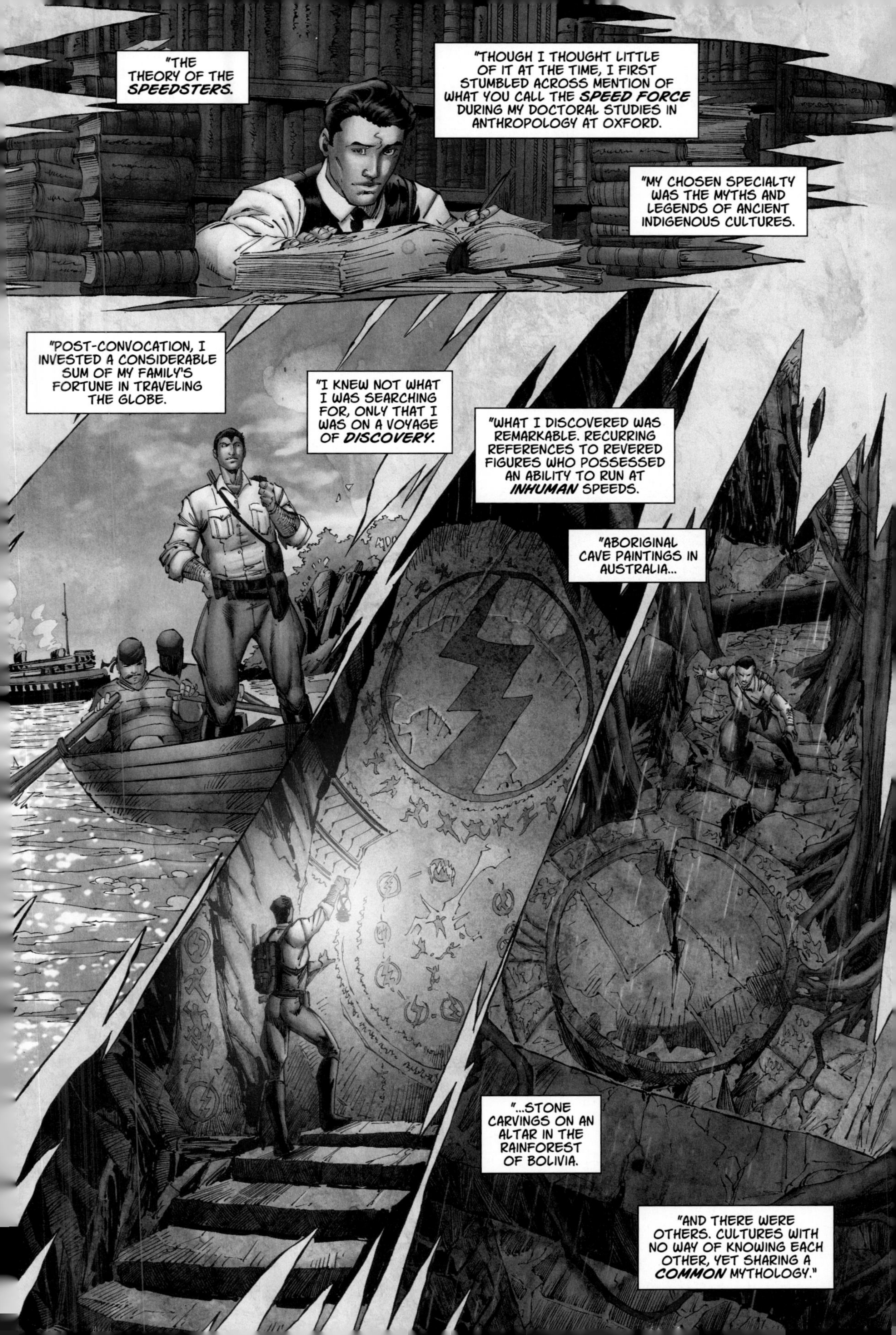
"THE THEORY OF THE SPEEDSTERS.
"THOUGH I THOUGHT LITTLE OF IT AT THE TIME, I FIRST STUMBLED ACROSS MENTION OF WHAT YOU CALL THE SPEED FORCE DURING MY DOCTORAL STUDIES IN ANTHROPOLOGY AT OXFORD.
"MY CHOSEN SPECIALTY WAS THE MYTHS AND LEGENDS OF ANCIENT INDIGENOUS CULTURES.
"POST-CONVOCATION, I INVESTED A CONSIDERABLE SUM OF MY FAMILY'S FORTUNE IN TRAVELING THE GLOBE.
"I KNEW NOT WHAT I WAS SEARCHING FOR, ONLY THAT I WAS ON A VOYAGE OF DISCOVERY.
"WHAT I DISCOVERED WAS REMARKABLE. RECURRING REFERENCES TO REVERED FIGURES WHO POSSESSED AN ABILITY TO RUN AT INHUMAN SPEEDS.
"ABORIGINAL CAVE PAINTINGS IN AUSTRALIA...
"...STONE CARVINGS ON AN ALTAR IN THE RAINFOREST OF BOLIVIA.
"AND THERE WERE OTHERS. CULTURES WITH NO WAY OF KNOWING EACH OTHER, YET SHARING A COMMON MYTHOLOGY."

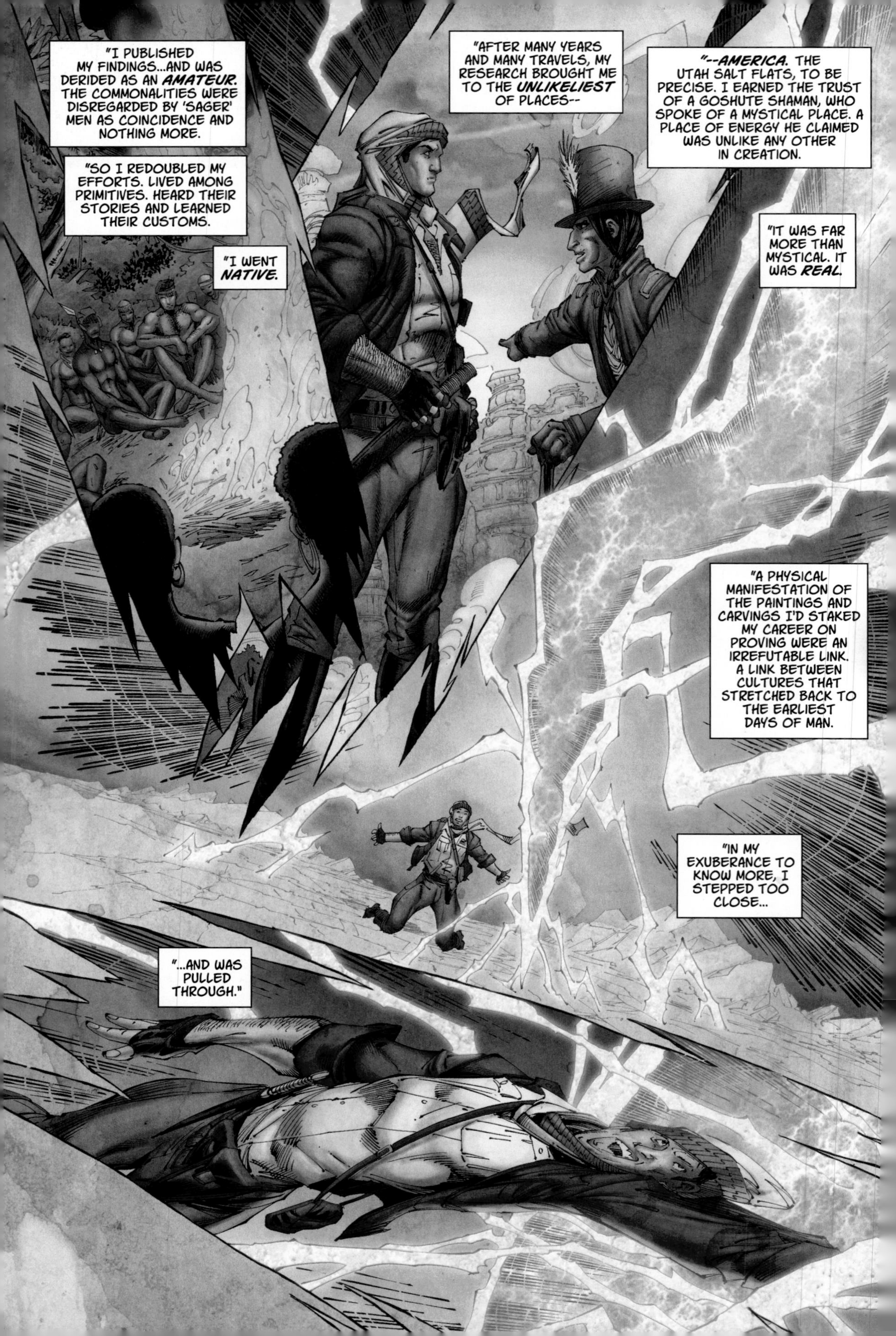
"I PUBLISHED MY FINDINGS...AND WAS DERIDED AS AN *AMATEUR*. THE COMMONALITIES WERE DISREGARDED BY 'SAGER' MEN AS COINCIDENCE AND NOTHING MORE.
"SO I REDOUBLED MY EFFORTS. LIVED AMONG PRIMITIVES. HEARD THEIR STORIES AND LEARNED THEIR CUSTOMS.
"I WENT *NATIVE*.
"AFTER MANY YEARS AND MANY TRAVELS, MY RESEARCH BROUGHT ME TO THE *UNLIKELIEST* OF PLACES--
"--*AMERICA*. THE UTAH SALT FLATS, TO BE PRECISE. I EARNED THE TRUST OF A GOSHUTE SHAMAN, WHO SPOKE OF A MYSTICAL PLACE. A PLACE OF ENERGY HE CLAIMED WAS UNLIKE ANY OTHER IN CREATION.
"IT WAS FAR MORE THAN MYSTICAL. IT WAS *REAL*.
"A PHYSICAL MANIFESTATION OF THE PAINTINGS AND CARVINGS I'D STAKED MY CAREER ON PROVING WERE AN IRREFUTABLE LINK. A LINK BETWEEN CULTURES THAT STRETCHED BACK TO THE EARLIEST DAYS OF MAN.
"IN MY EXUBERANCE TO KNOW MORE, I STEPPED TOO CLOSE...
"...AND WAS PULLED THROUGH."

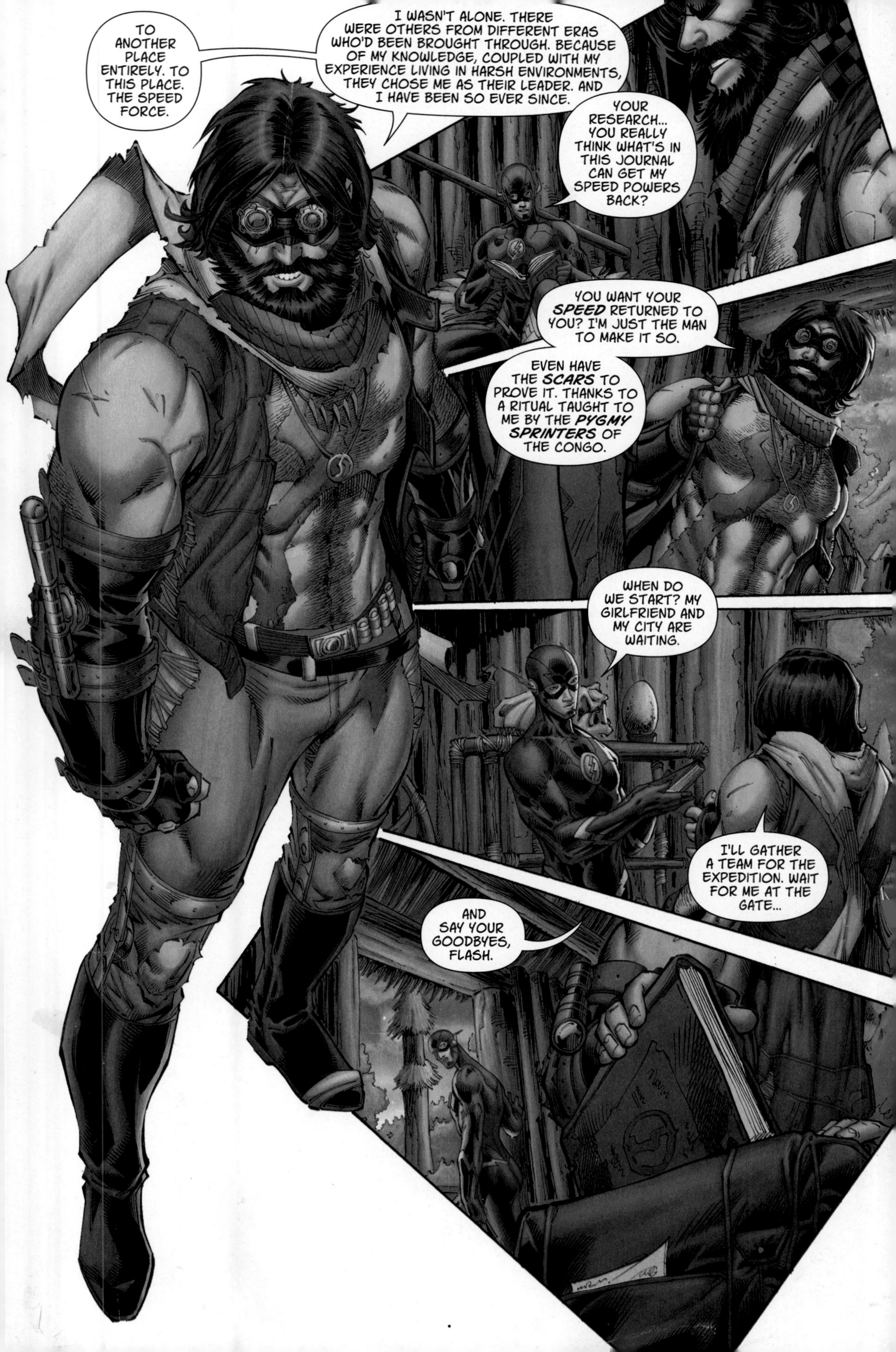
TO ANOTHER PLACE ENTIRELY. TO THIS PLACE. THE SPEED FORCE.
I WASN'T ALONE. THERE WERE OTHERS FROM DIFFERENT ERAS WHO'D BEEN BROUGHT THROUGH. BECAUSE OF MY KNOWLEDGE, COUPLED WITH MY EXPERIENCE LIVING IN HARSH ENVIRONMENTS, THEY CHOSE ME AS THEIR LEADER. AND I HAVE BEEN SO EVER SINCE.
YOUR RESEARCH... YOU REALLY THINK WHAT'S IN THIS JOURNAL CAN GET MY SPEED POWERS BACK?
YOU WANT YOUR SPEED RETURNED TO YOU? I'M JUST THE MAN TO MAKE IT SO.
EVEN HAVE THE SCARS TO PROVE IT. THANKS TO A RITUAL TAUGHT TO ME BY THE PYGMY SPRINTERS OF THE CONGO.
WHEN DO WE START? MY GIRLFRIEND AND MY CITY ARE WAITING.
I'LL GATHER A TEAM FOR THE EXPEDITION. WAIT FOR ME AT THE GATE...
AND SAY YOUR GOODBYES, FLASH.

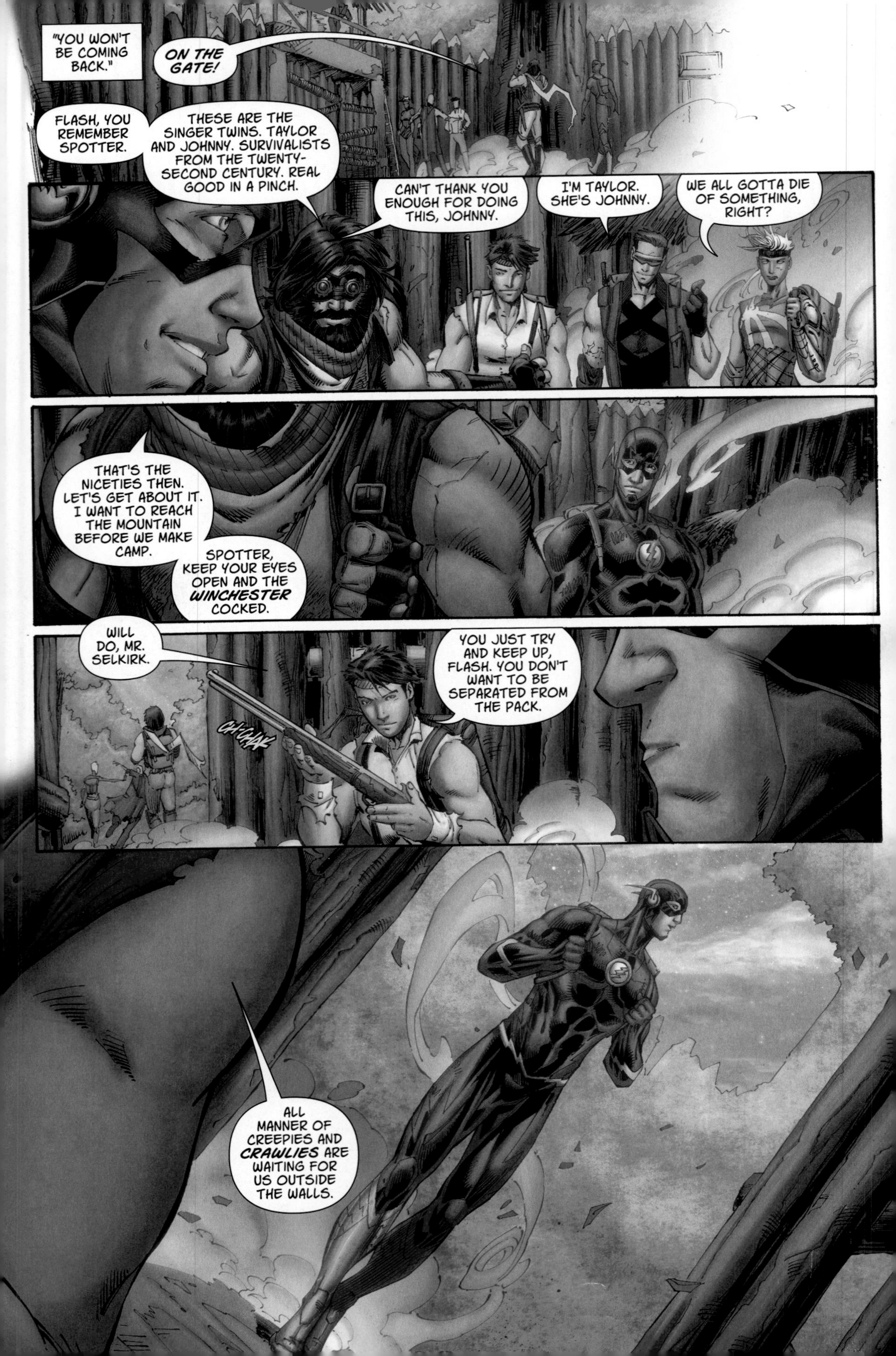
"YOU WON'T BE COMING BACK."
ON THE GATE!
FLASH, YOU REMEMBER SPOTTER.
THESE ARE THE SINGER TWINS. TAYLOR AND JOHNNY. SURVIVALISTS FROM THE TWENTY-SECOND CENTURY. REAL GOOD IN A PINCH.
CAN'T THANK YOU ENOUGH FOR DOING THIS, JOHNNY.
I'M TAYLOR. SHE'S JOHNNY.
WE ALL GOTTA DIE OF SOMETHING, RIGHT?
THAT'S THE NICETIES THEN. LET'S GET ABOUT IT. I WANT TO REACH THE MOUNTAIN BEFORE WE MAKE CAMP.
SPOTTER, KEEP YOUR EYES OPEN AND THE WINCHESTER COCKED.
WILL DO, MR. SELKIRK.
CH-CHAK
YOU JUST TRY AND KEEP UP, FLASH. YOU DON'T WANT TO BE SEPARATED FROM THE PACK.
ALL MANNER OF CREEPIES AND CRAWLIES ARE WAITING FOR US OUTSIDE THE WALLS.

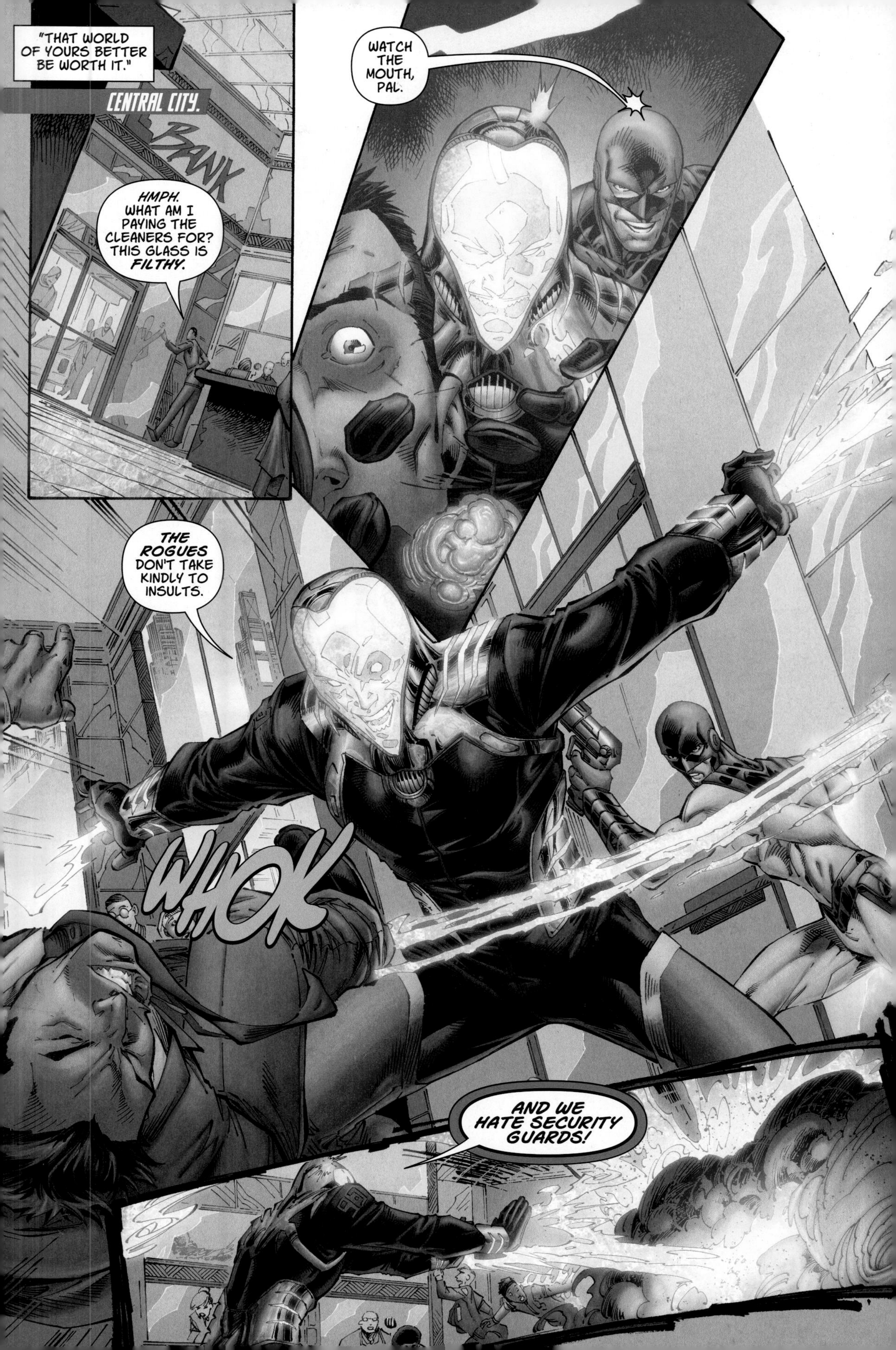
"THAT WORLD OF YOURS BETTER BE WORTH IT."
CENTRAL CITY.
BANK
HMPH. WHAT AM I PAYING THE CLEANERS FOR? THIS GLASS IS *FILTHY*.
WATCH THE MOUTH, PAL.
THE ROGUES DON'T TAKE KINDLY TO INSULTS.
WHOK
AND WE HATE SECURITY GUARDS!

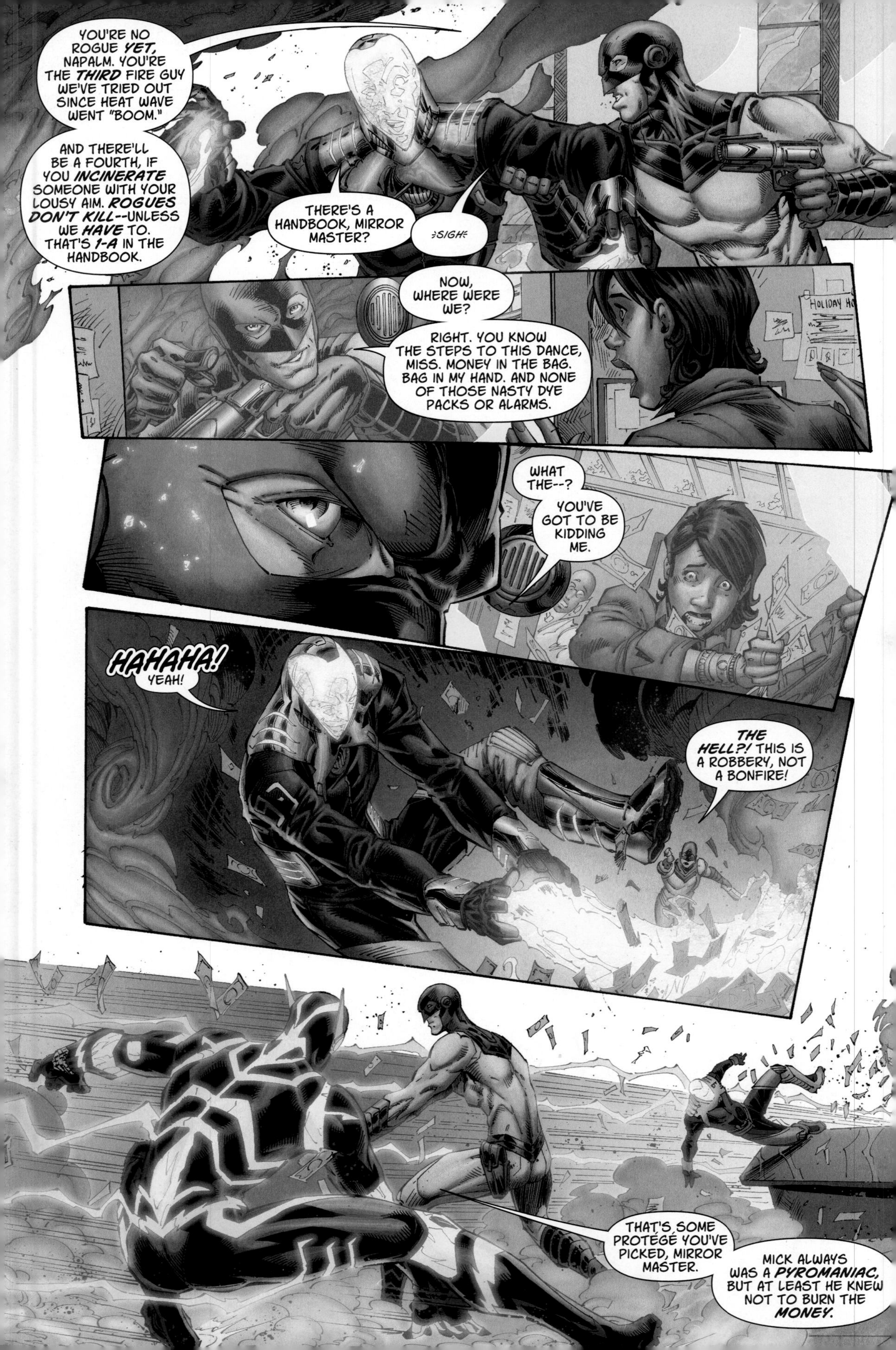
YOU'RE NO ROGUE YET, NAPALM. YOU'RE THE THIRD FIRE GUY WE'VE TRIED OUT SINCE HEAT WAVE WENT "BOOM."
AND THERE'LL BE A FOURTH, IF YOU INCINERATE SOMEONE WITH YOUR LOUSY AIM. ROGUES DON'T KILL--UNLESS WE HAVE TO. THAT'S 1-A IN THE HANDBOOK.
THERE'S A HANDBOOK, MIRROR MASTER?
SIGH
NOW, WHERE WERE WE?
RIGHT. YOU KNOW THE STEPS TO THIS DANCE, MISS. MONEY IN THE BAG. BAG IN MY HAND. AND NONE OF THOSE NASTY DYE PACKS OR ALARMS.
WHAT THE--?
YOU'VE GOT TO BE KIDDING ME.
HAHAHA! YEAH!
THE HELL?! THIS IS A ROBBERY, NOT A BONFIRE!
THAT'S SOME PROTEGÉ YOU'VE PICKED, MIRROR MASTER.
MICK ALWAYS WAS A PYROMANIAC, BUT AT LEAST HE KNEW NOT TO BURN THE MONEY.

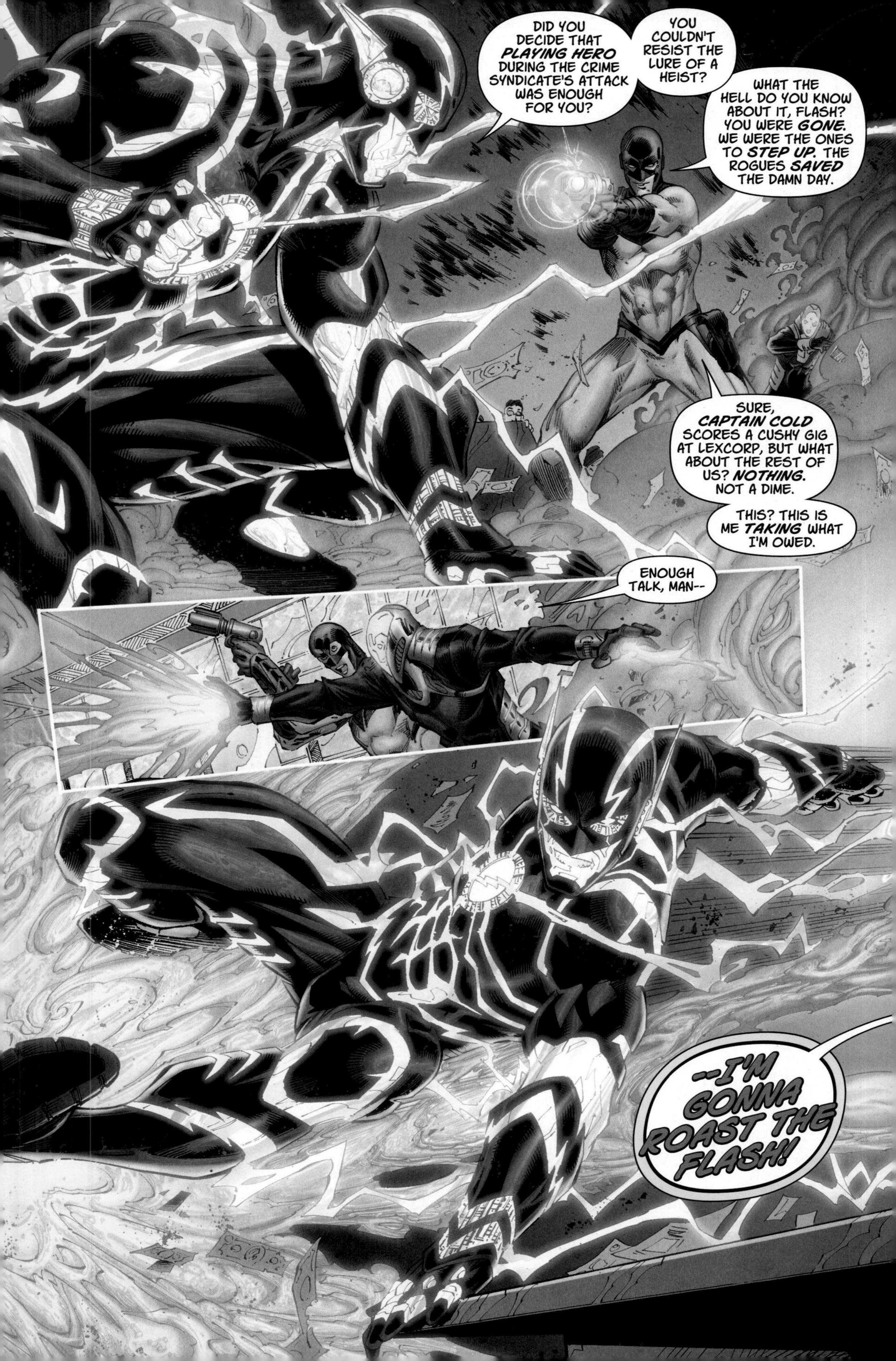
DID YOU DECIDE THAT PLAYING HERO DURING THE CRIME SYNDICATE'S ATTACK WAS ENOUGH FOR YOU?
YOU COULDN'T RESIST THE LURE OF A HEIST?
WHAT THE HELL DO YOU KNOW ABOUT IT, FLASH? YOU WERE GONE. WE WERE THE ONES TO STEP UP. THE ROGUES SAVED THE DAMN DAY.
SURE, CAPTAIN COLD SCORES A CUSHY GIG AT LEXCORP, BUT WHAT ABOUT THE REST OF US? NOTHING. NOT A DIME.
THIS? THIS IS ME TAKING WHAT I'M OWED.
ENOUGH TALK, MAN--
--I'M GONNA ROAST THE FLASH!

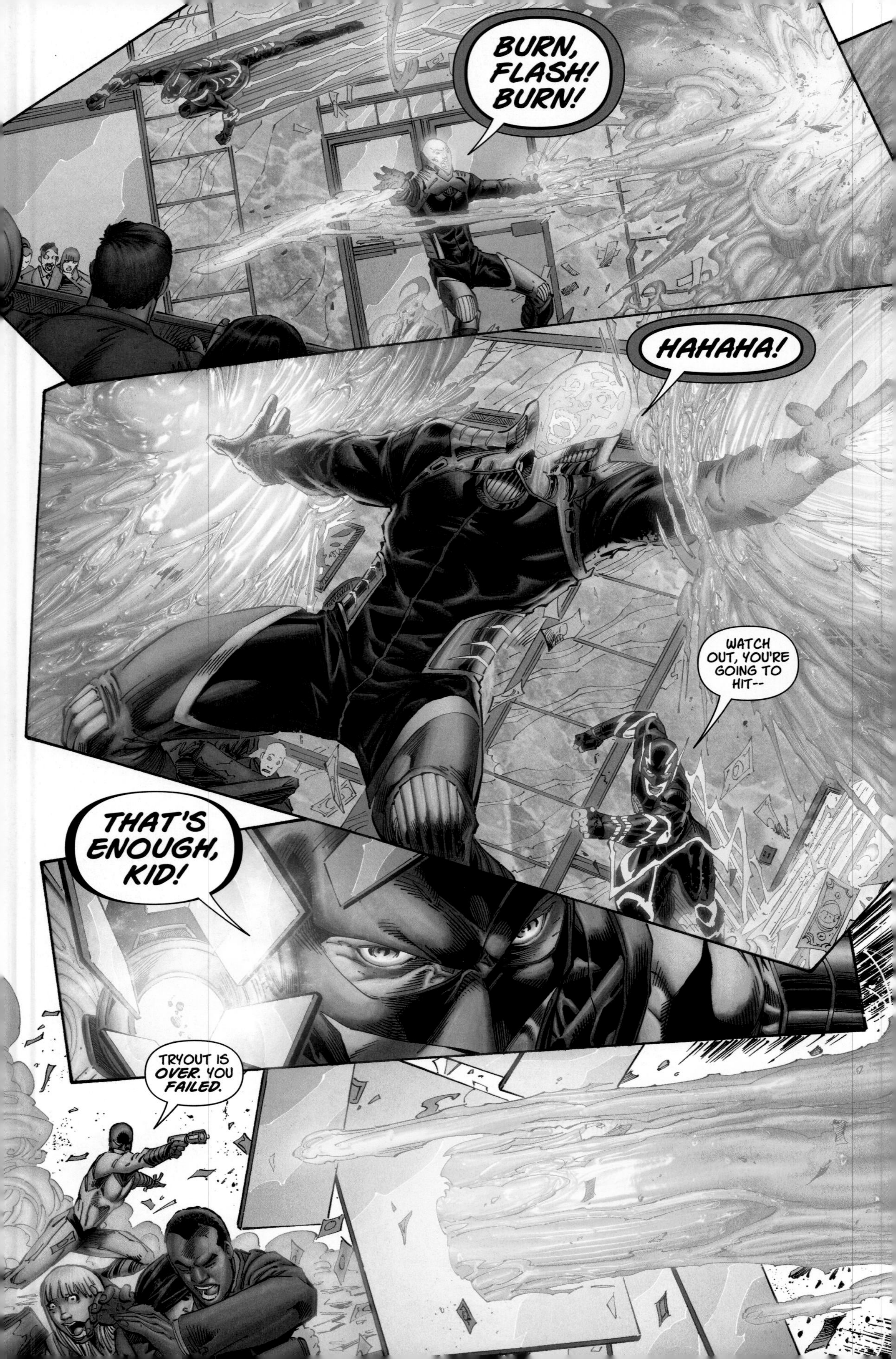
BURN, FLASH! BURN!
HAHAHA!
WATCH OUT, YOU'RE GOING TO HIT--
THAT'S ENOUGH, KID!
TRYOUT IS OVER. YOU FAILED.

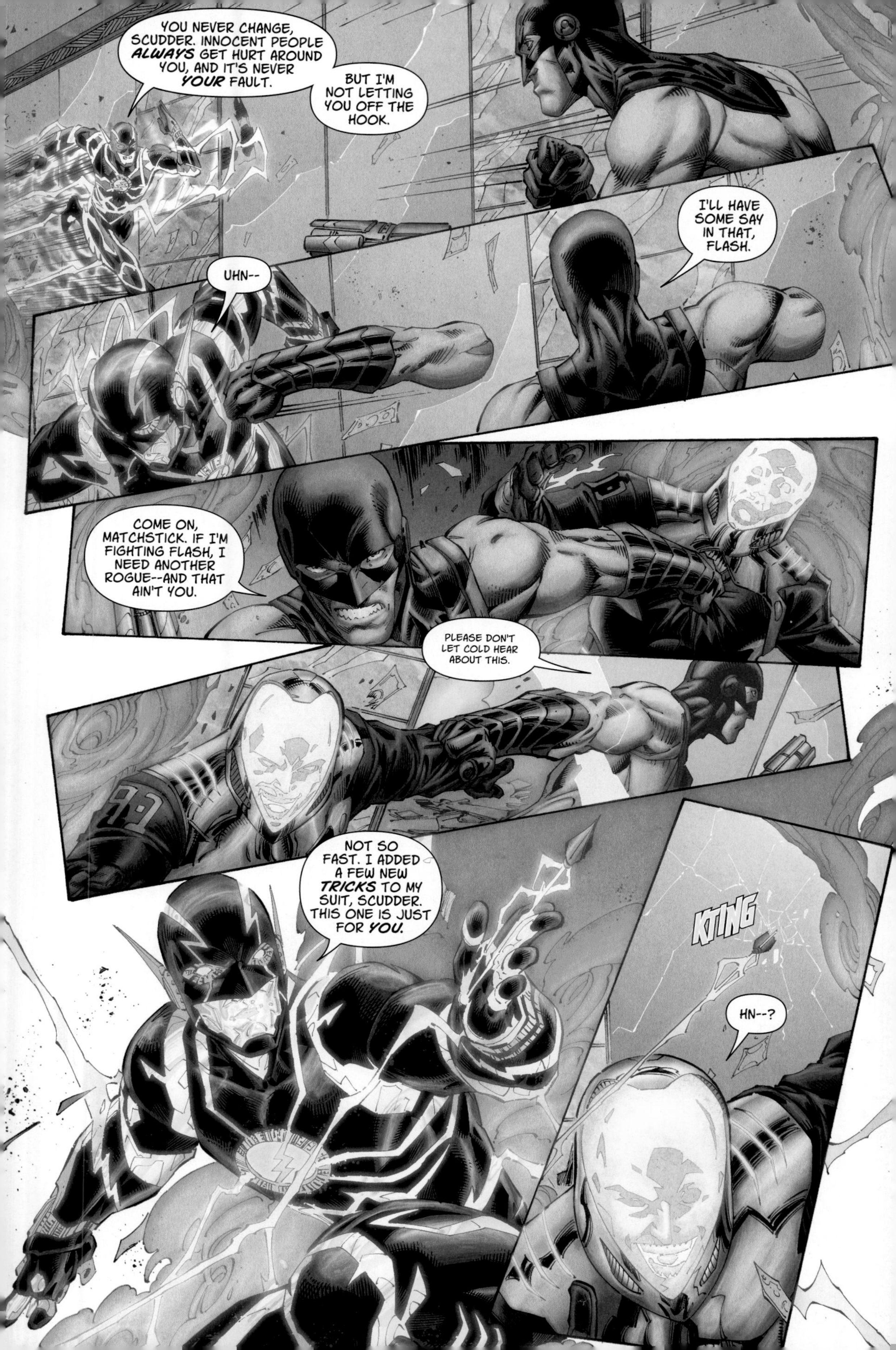
YOU NEVER CHANGE, SCUDDER. INNOCENT PEOPLE ALWAYS GET HURT AROUND YOU, AND IT'S NEVER YOUR FAULT.
BUT I'M NOT LETTING YOU OFF THE HOOK.
I'LL HAVE SOME SAY IN THAT, FLASH.
UHN--
COME ON, MATCHSTICK. IF I'M FIGHTING FLASH, I NEED ANOTHER ROGUE--AND THAT AIN'T YOU.
PLEASE DON'T LET COLD HEAR ABOUT THIS.
NOT SO FAST. I ADDED A FEW NEW TRICKS TO MY SUIT, SCUDDER. THIS ONE IS JUST FOR YOU.
KTING
HN--?

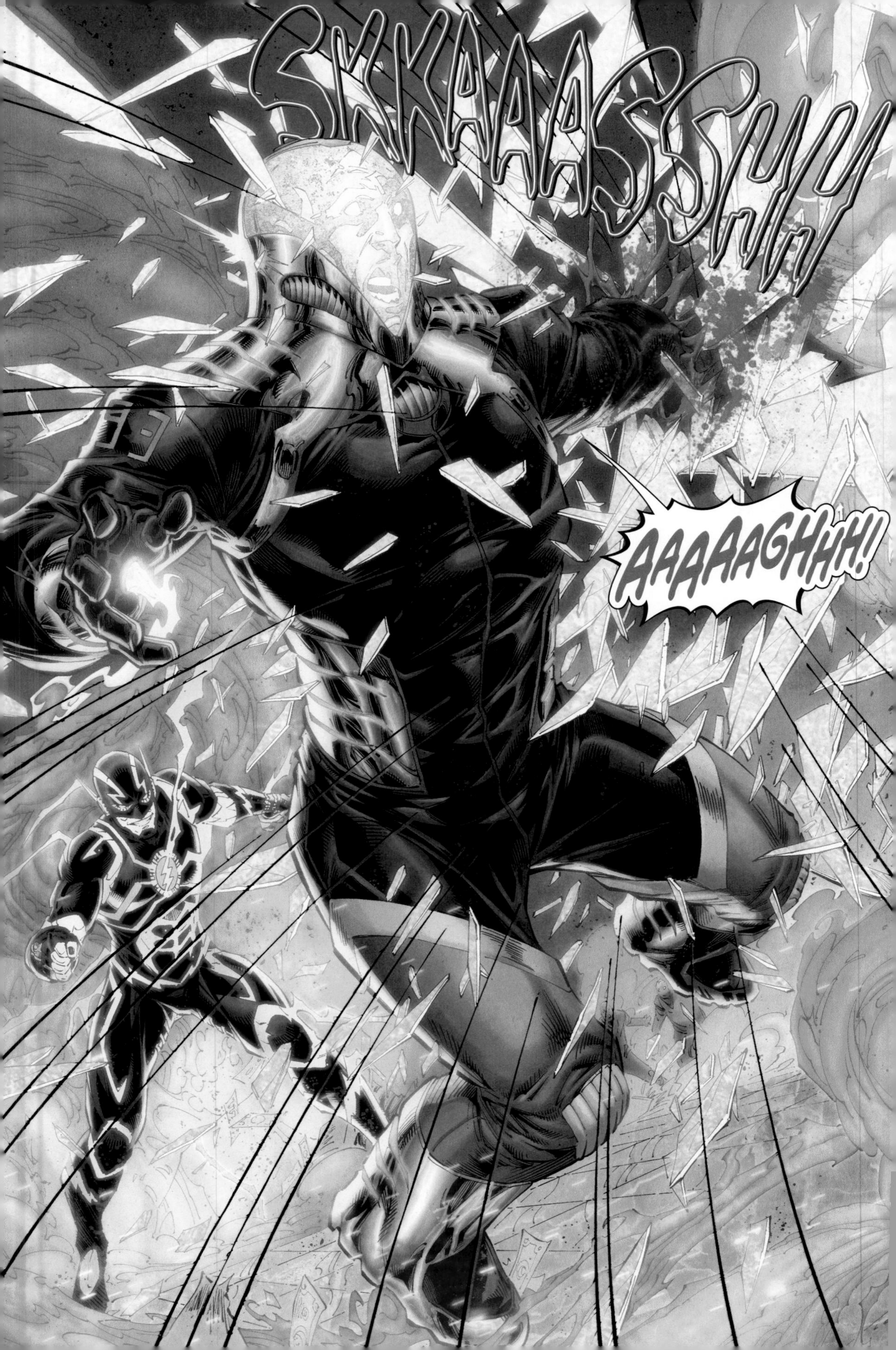
SKKAAASSHHH
AAAAAGHHH!

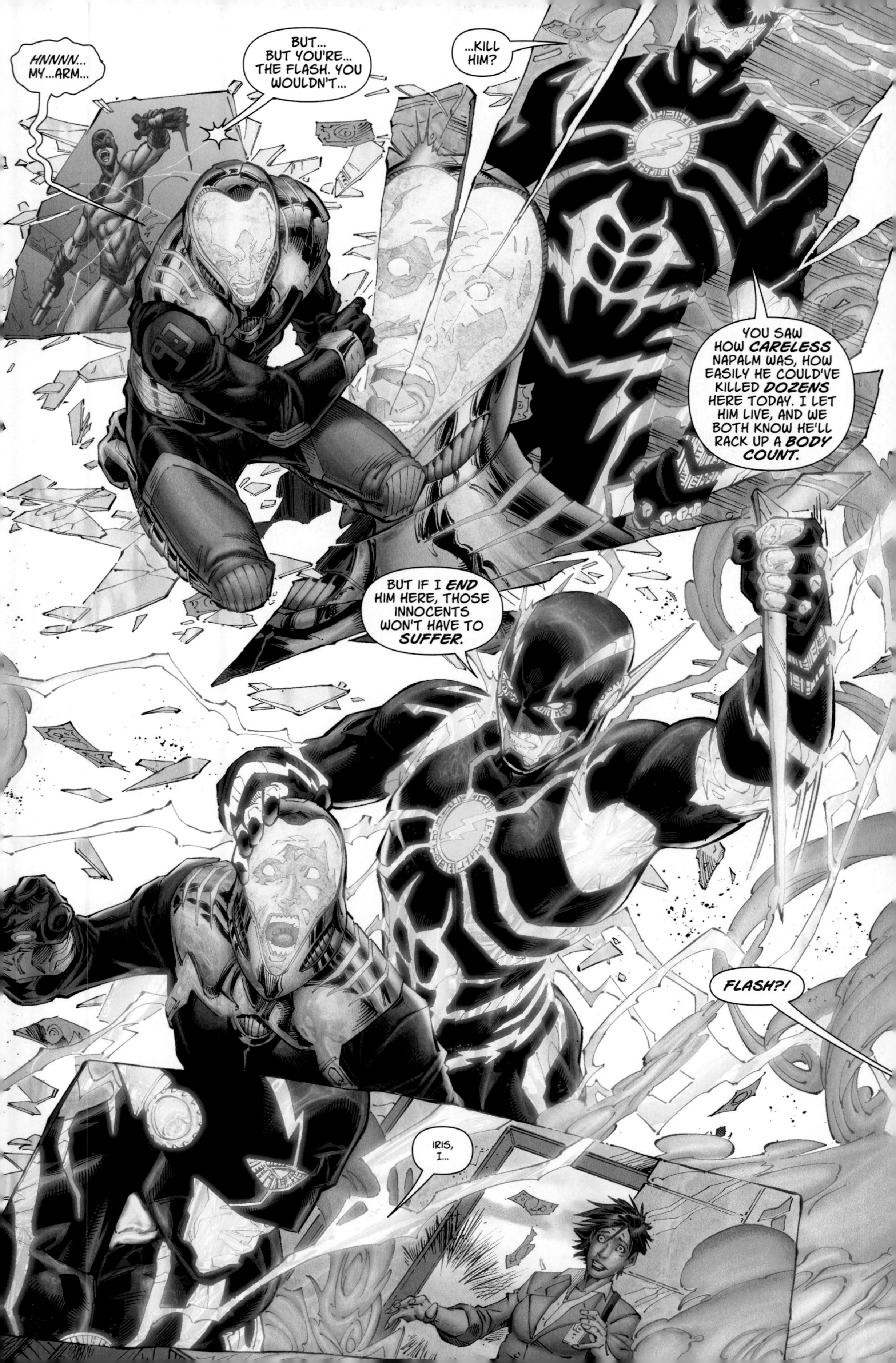
HNNNN... MY...ARM...
BUT... BUT YOU'RE... THE FLASH. YOU WOULDN'T...
...KILL HIM?
YOU SAW HOW CARELESS NAPALM WAS, HOW EASILY HE COULD'VE KILLED DOZENS HERE TODAY. I LET HIM LIVE, AND WE BOTH KNOW HE'LL RACK UP A BODY COUNT.
BUT IF I END HIM HERE, THOSE INNOCENTS WON'T HAVE TO SUFFER.
FLASH?!
IRIS, I...

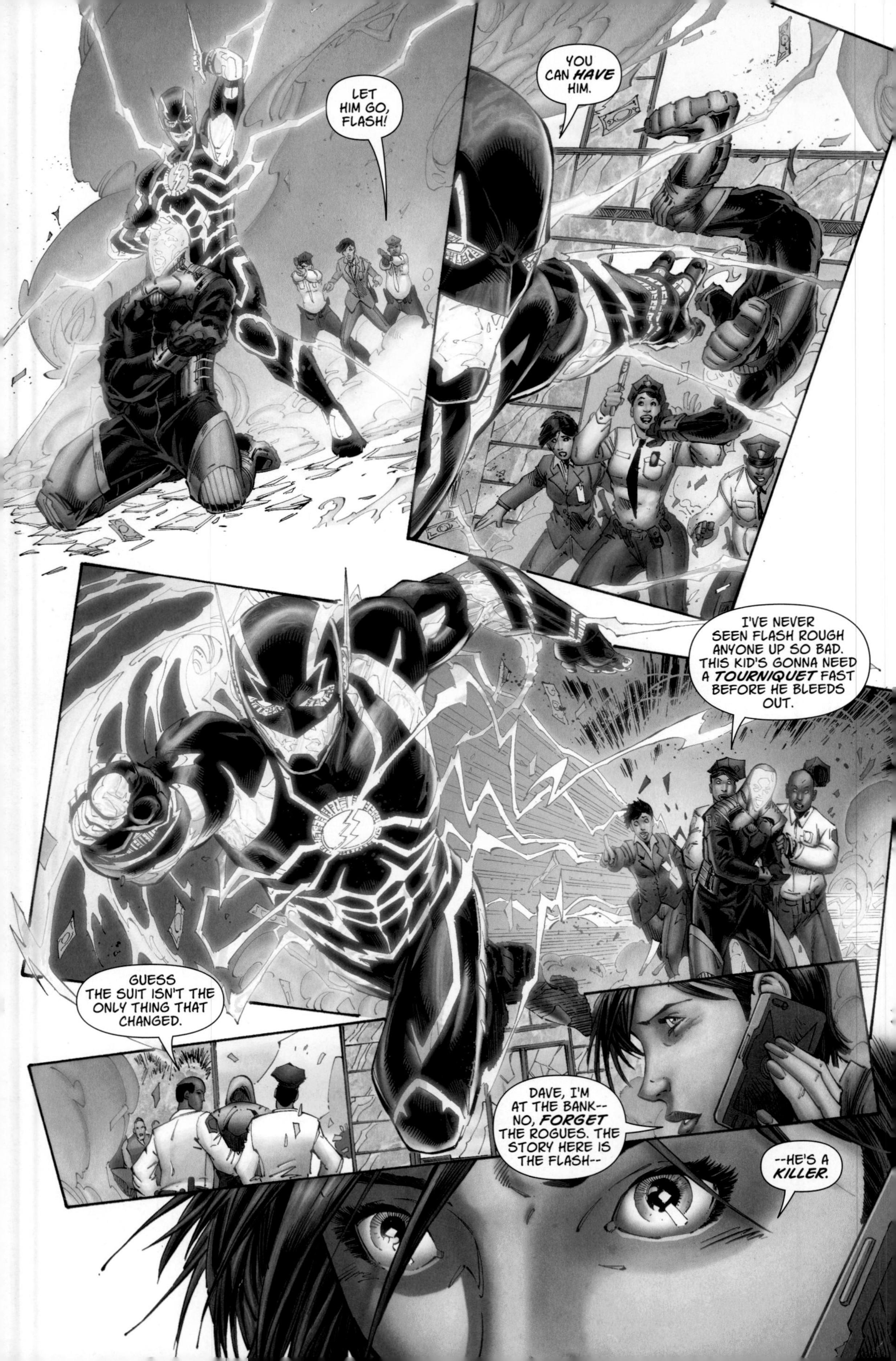
LET HIM GO, FLASH!
YOU CAN HAVE HIM.
I'VE NEVER SEEN FLASH ROUGH ANYONE UP SO BAD. THIS KID'S GONNA NEED A TOURNIQUET FAST BEFORE HE BLEEDS OUT.
GUESS THE SUIT ISN'T THE ONLY THING THAT CHANGED.
DAVE, I'M AT THE BANK-- NO, FORGET THE ROGUES. THE STORY HERE IS THE FLASH--
--HE'S A KILLER.

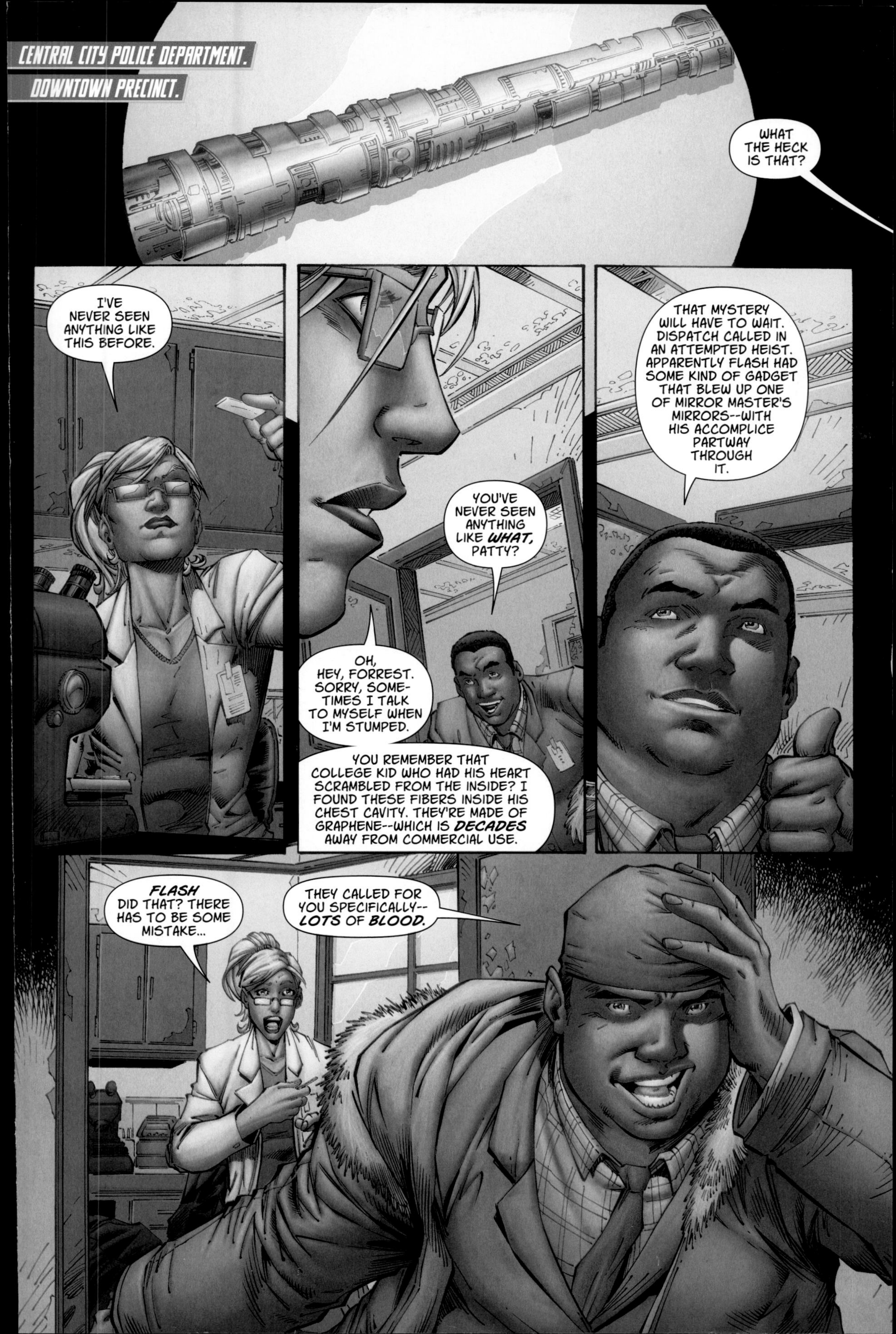
CENTRAL CITY POLICE DEPARTMENT.
DOWNTOWN PRECINCT.
WHAT THE HECK IS THAT?
I'VE NEVER SEEN ANYTHING LIKE THIS BEFORE.
YOU'VE NEVER SEEN ANYTHING LIKE WHAT, PATTY?
OH, HEY, FORREST. SORRY, SOMETIMES I TALK TO MYSELF WHEN I'M STUMPED.
YOU REMEMBER THAT COLLEGE KID WHO HAD HIS HEART SCRAMBLED FROM THE INSIDE? I FOUND THESE FIBERS INSIDE HIS CHEST CAVITY. THEY'RE MADE OF GRAPHENE--WHICH IS DECADES AWAY FROM COMMERCIAL USE.
THAT MYSTERY WILL HAVE TO WAIT. DISPATCH CALLED IN AN ATTEMPTED HEIST. APPARENTLY FLASH HAD SOME KIND OF GADGET THAT BLEW UP ONE OF MIRROR MASTER'S MIRRORS--WITH HIS ACCOMPLICE PARTWAY THROUGH IT.
FLASH DID THAT? THERE HAS TO BE SOME MISTAKE...
THEY CALLED FOR YOU SPECIFICALLY--LOTS OF BLOOD.

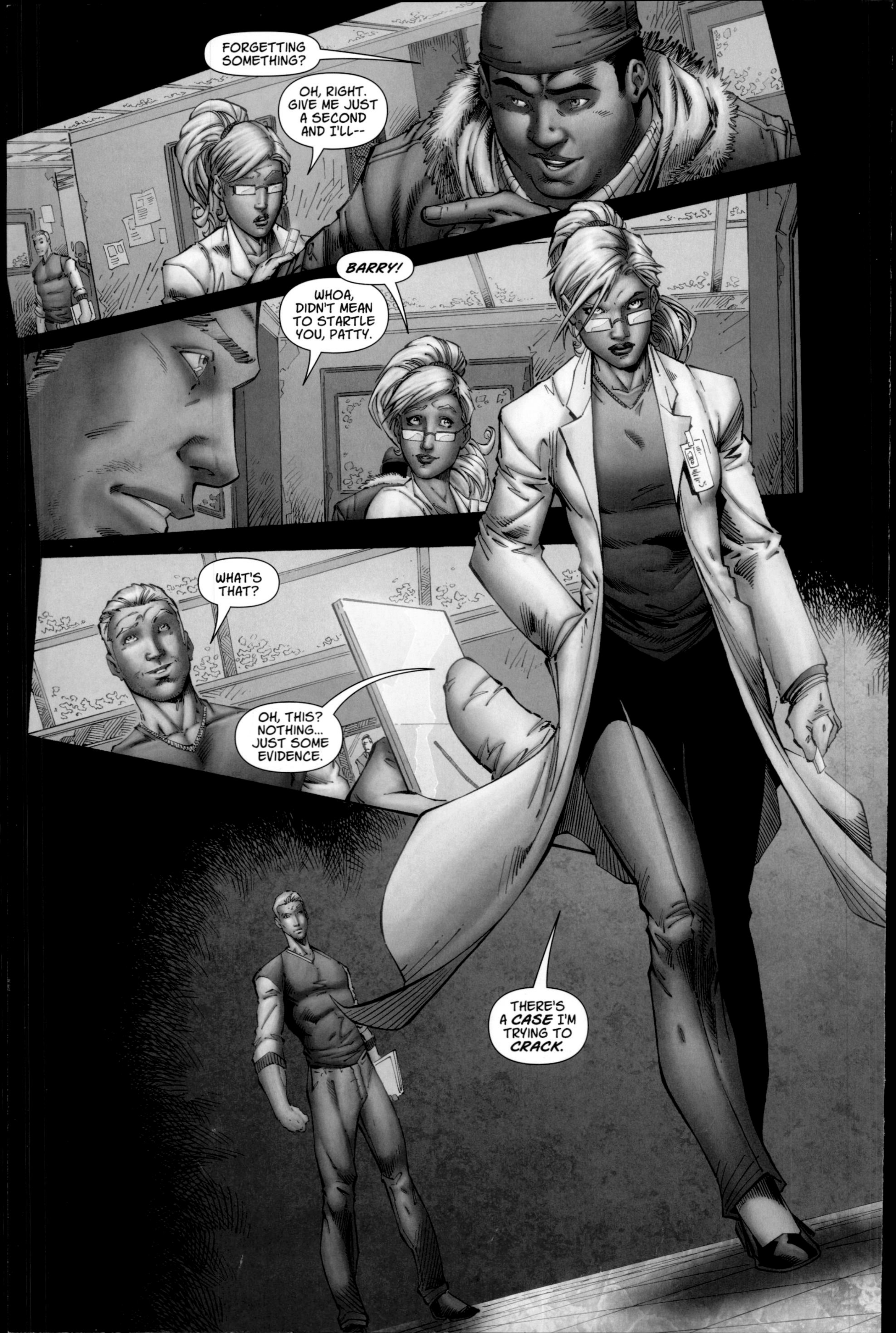
FORGETTING SOMETHING?
OH, RIGHT. GIVE ME JUST A SECOND AND I'LL--
BARRY!
WHOA, DIDN'T MEAN TO STARTLE YOU, PATTY.
WHAT'S THAT?
OH, THIS? NOTHING... JUST SOME EVIDENCE.
THERE'S A CASE I'M TRYING TO CRACK.

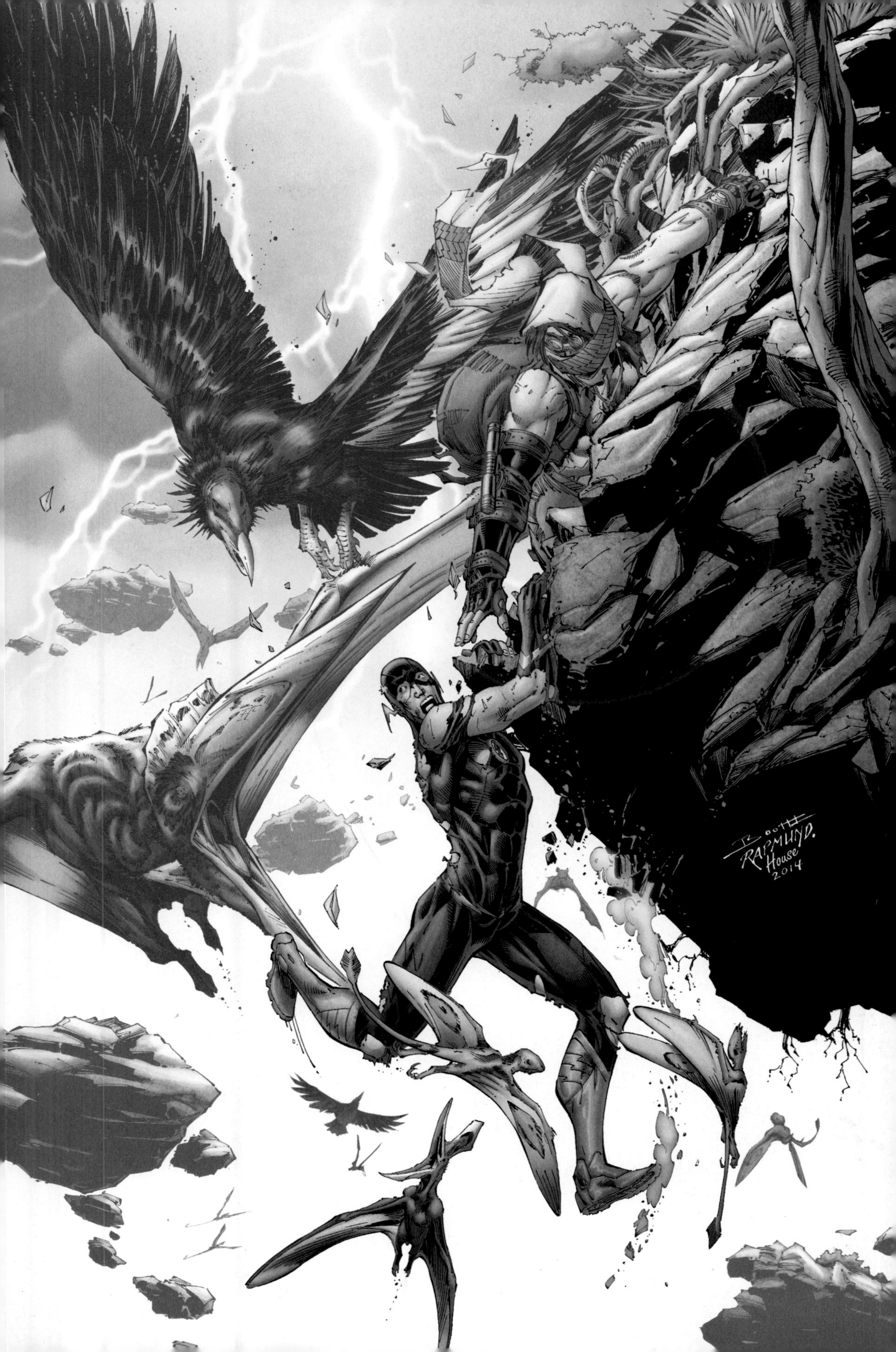
BOOTH
RAPMUND.
House
2014

POWER LOSS

ROBERT VENDITTI & VAN JENSEN writers BRETT BOOTH penciller NORM RAPMUND inker ANDREW DALHOUSE colorist PAT BROSSEAU letterer
cover by BRETT BOOTH, NORM RAPMUND & ANDREW DALHOUSE

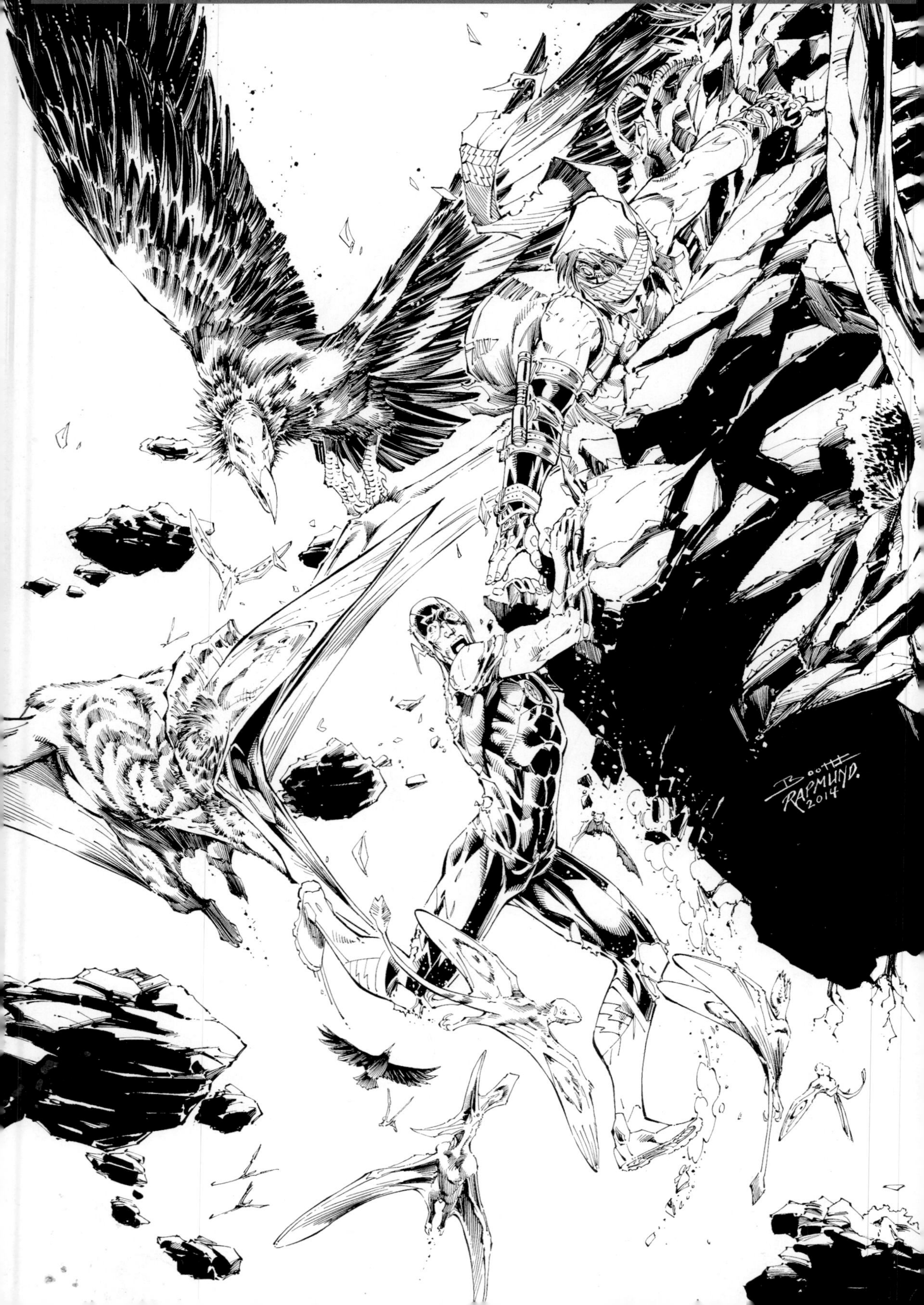

BOOTH
RAPMUND.
2014

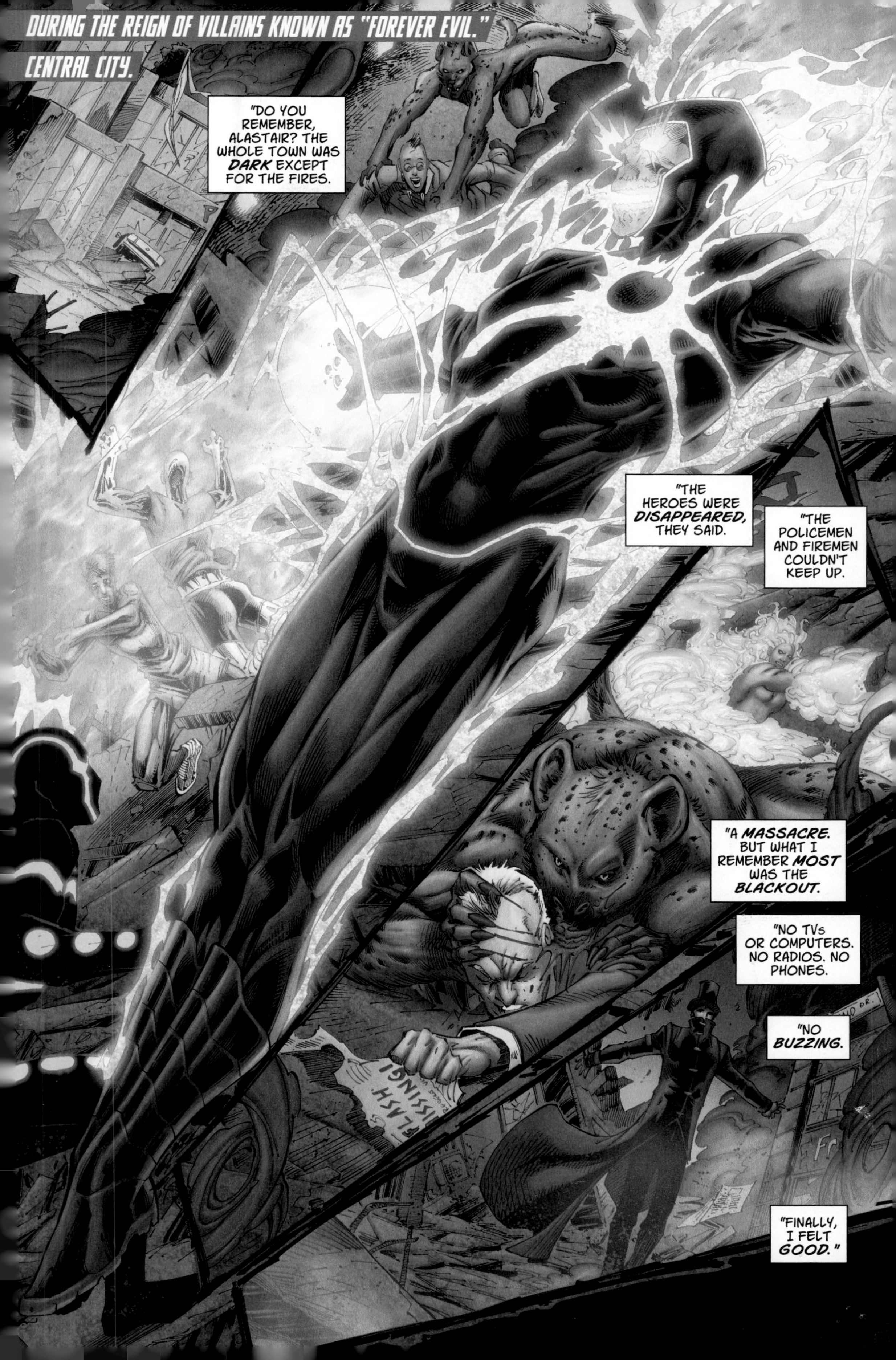
DURING THE REIGN OF VILLAINS KNOWN AS "FOREVER EVIL."
CENTRAL CITY.
"DO YOU REMEMBER, ALASTAIR? THE WHOLE TOWN WAS DARK EXCEPT FOR THE FIRES.
"THE HEROES WERE DISAPPEARED, THEY SAID.
"THE POLICEMEN AND FIREMEN COULDN'T KEEP UP.
"A MASSACRE. BUT WHAT I REMEMBER MOST WAS THE BLACKOUT.
"NO TVs OR COMPUTERS. NO RADIOS. NO PHONES.
"NO BUZZING.
"FINALLY, I FELT GOOD."

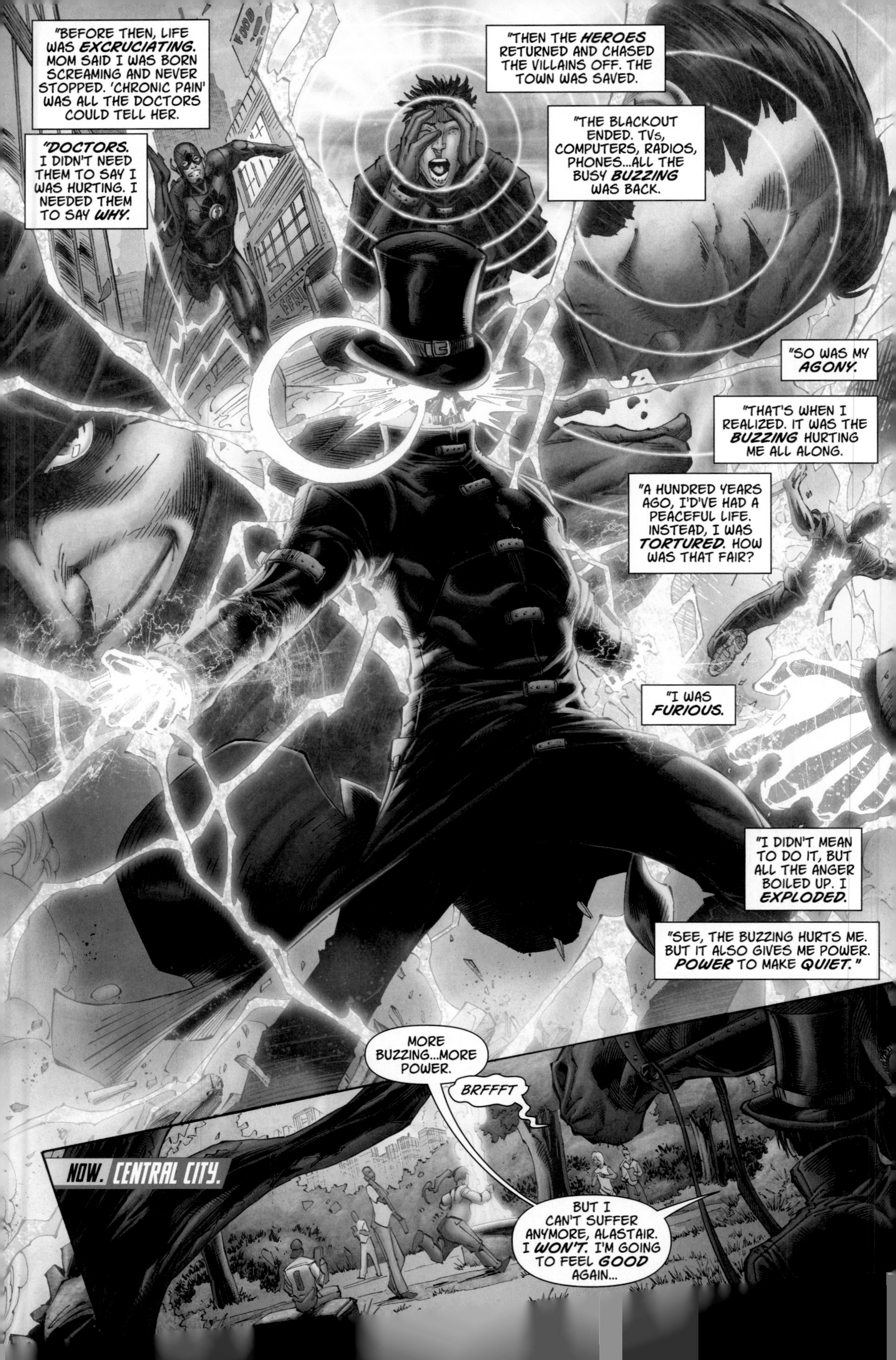
"BEFORE THEN, LIFE WAS EXCRUCIATING. MOM SAID I WAS BORN SCREAMING AND NEVER STOPPED. 'CHRONIC PAIN' WAS ALL THE DOCTORS COULD TELL HER.
"DOCTORS. I DIDN'T NEED THEM TO SAY I WAS HURTING. I NEEDED THEM TO SAY WHY.
"THEN THE HEROES RETURNED AND CHASED THE VILLAINS OFF. THE TOWN WAS SAVED.
"THE BLACKOUT ENDED. TVs, COMPUTERS, RADIOS, PHONES...ALL THE BUSY BUZZING WAS BACK.
"SO WAS MY AGONY.
"THAT'S WHEN I REALIZED. IT WAS THE BUZZING HURTING ME ALL ALONG.
"A HUNDRED YEARS AGO, I'D'VE HAD A PEACEFUL LIFE. INSTEAD, I WAS TORTURED. HOW WAS THAT FAIR?
"I WAS FURIOUS.
"I DIDN'T MEAN TO DO IT, BUT ALL THE ANGER BOILED UP. I EXPLODED.
"SEE, THE BUZZING HURTS ME. BUT IT ALSO GIVES ME POWER. POWER TO MAKE QUIET."
NOW. CENTRAL CITY.
MORE BUZZING...MORE POWER.
BRFFFT
BUT I CAN'T SUFFER ANYMORE, ALASTAIR. I WON'T. I'M GOING TO FEEL GOOD AGAIN...

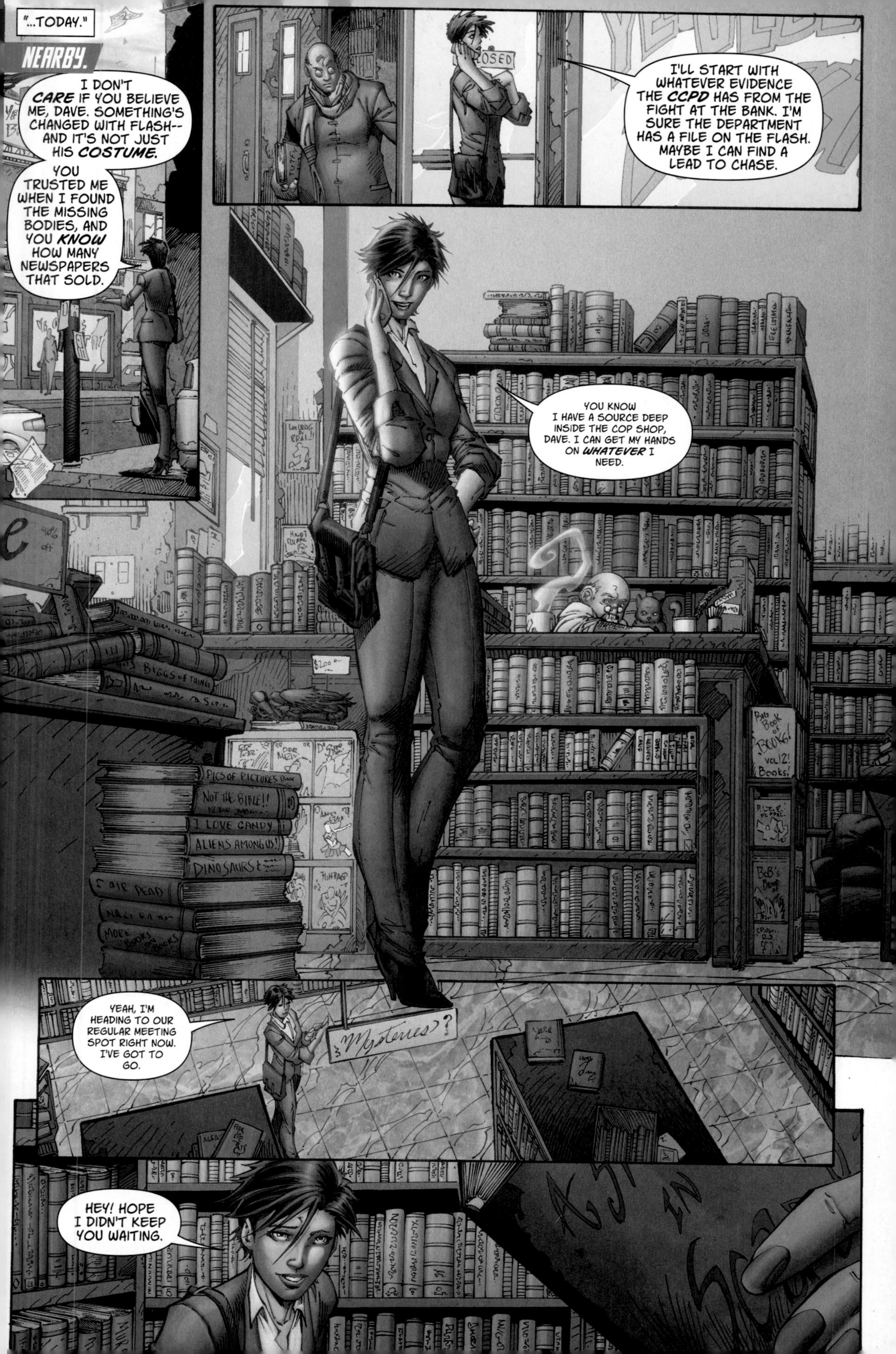
"...TODAY."
NEARBY.
I DON'T CARE IF YOU BELIEVE ME, DAVE. SOMETHING'S CHANGED WITH FLASH-- AND IT'S NOT JUST HIS COSTUME.
YOU TRUSTED ME WHEN I FOUND THE MISSING BODIES, AND YOU KNOW HOW MANY NEWSPAPERS THAT SOLD.
I'LL START WITH WHATEVER EVIDENCE THE CCPD HAS FROM THE FIGHT AT THE BANK. I'M SURE THE DEPARTMENT HAS A FILE ON THE FLASH. MAYBE I CAN FIND A LEAD TO CHASE.
YOU KNOW I HAVE A SOURCE DEEP INSIDE THE COP SHOP, DAVE. I CAN GET MY HANDS ON WHATEVER I NEED.
YEAH, I'M HEADING TO OUR REGULAR MEETING SPOT RIGHT NOW. I'VE GOT TO GO.
HEY! HOPE I DIDN'T KEEP YOU WAITING.

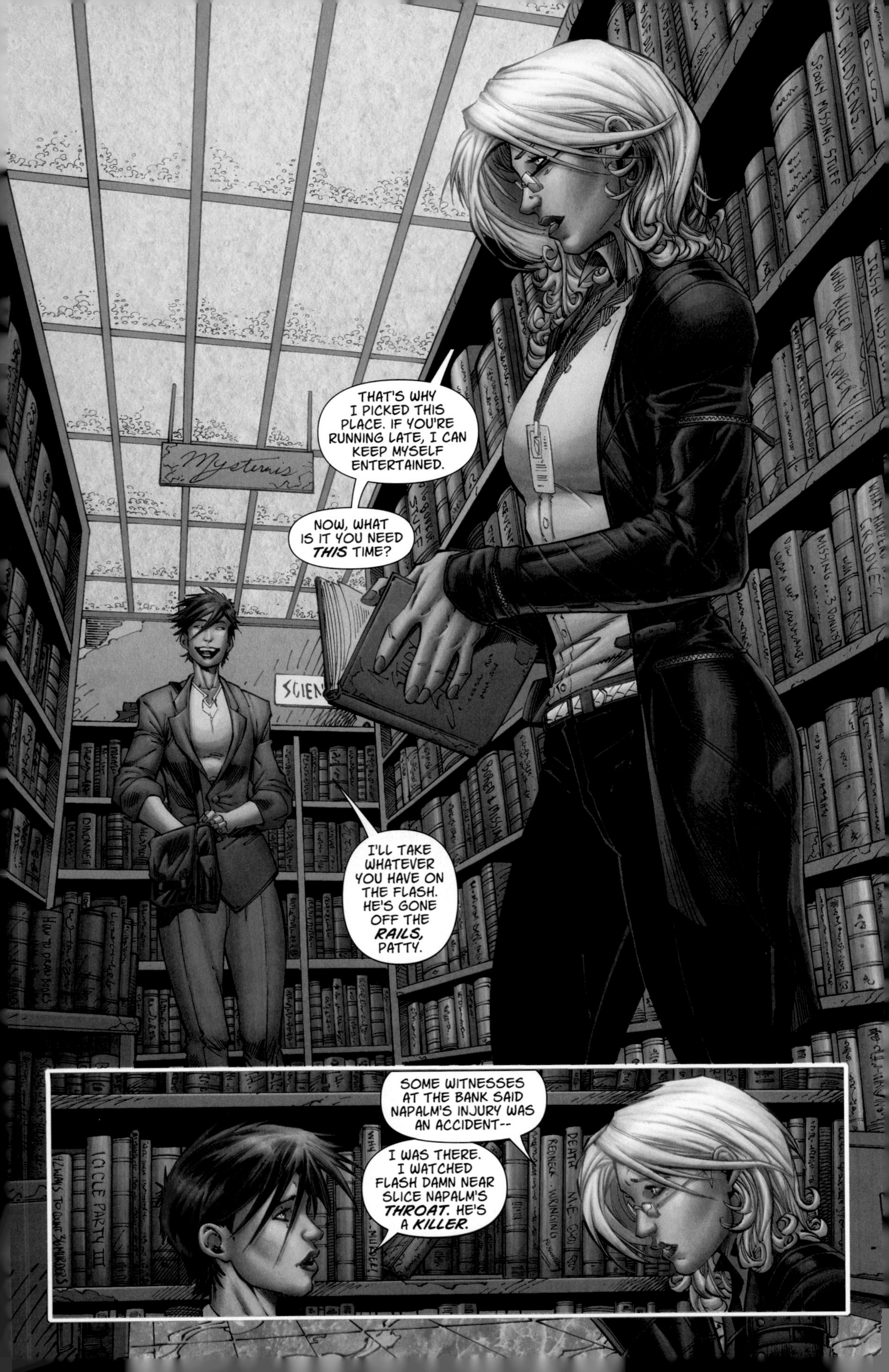

Mysteries
SCIEN
THAT'S WHY I PICKED THIS PLACE. IF YOU'RE RUNNING LATE, I CAN KEEP MYSELF ENTERTAINED.
NOW, WHAT IS IT YOU NEED *THIS* TIME?
I'LL TAKE WHATEVER YOU HAVE ON THE FLASH. HE'S GONE OFF THE *RAILS,* PATTY.
SOME WITNESSES AT THE BANK SAID NAPALM'S INJURY WAS AN ACCIDENT--
I WAS THERE. I WATCHED FLASH DAMN NEAR SLICE NAPALM'S *THROAT.* HE'S A *KILLER.*

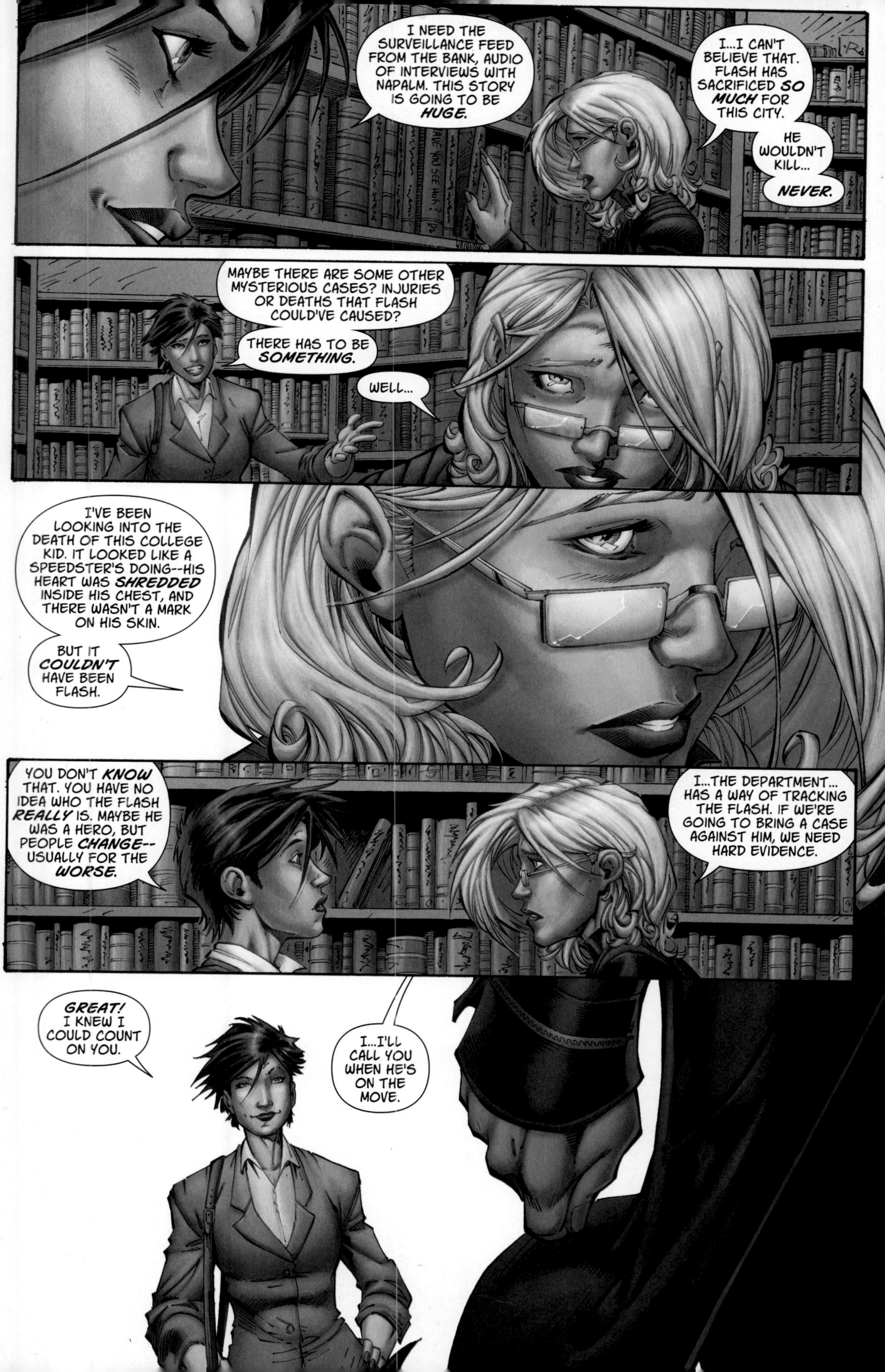
I NEED THE SURVEILLANCE FEED FROM THE BANK, AUDIO OF INTERVIEWS WITH NAPALM. THIS STORY IS GOING TO BE *HUGE*.
I...I CAN'T BELIEVE THAT. FLASH HAS SACRIFICED *SO MUCH* FOR THIS CITY.
HE WOULDN'T KILL...
NEVER.
MAYBE THERE ARE SOME OTHER MYSTERIOUS CASES? INJURIES OR DEATHS THAT FLASH COULD'VE CAUSED?
THERE HAS TO BE *SOMETHING*.
WELL...
I'VE BEEN LOOKING INTO THE DEATH OF THIS COLLEGE KID. IT LOOKED LIKE A SPEEDSTER'S DOING--HIS HEART WAS *SHREDDED* INSIDE HIS CHEST, AND THERE WASN'T A MARK ON HIS SKIN.
BUT IT *COULDN'T* HAVE BEEN FLASH.
YOU DON'T *KNOW* THAT. YOU HAVE NO IDEA WHO THE FLASH *REALLY* IS. MAYBE HE WAS A HERO, BUT PEOPLE *CHANGE*--USUALLY FOR THE *WORSE*.
I...THE DEPARTMENT...HAS A WAY OF TRACKING THE FLASH. IF WE'RE GOING TO BRING A CASE AGAINST HIM, WE NEED HARD EVIDENCE.
GREAT! I KNEW I COULD COUNT ON YOU.
I...I'LL CALL YOU WHEN HE'S ON THE MOVE.

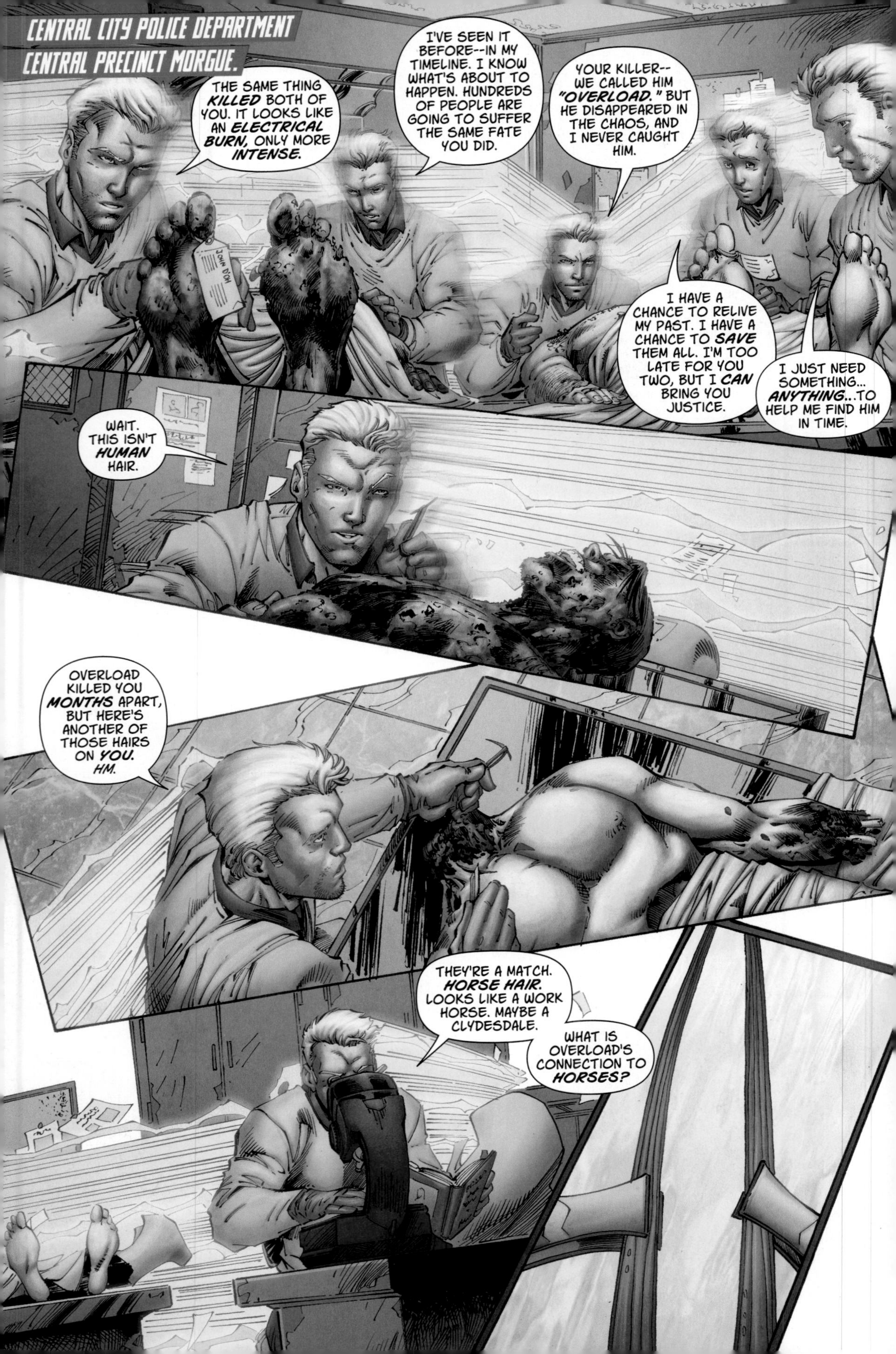
CENTRAL CITY POLICE DEPARTMENT
CENTRAL PRECINCT MORGUE.
THE SAME THING KILLED BOTH OF YOU. IT LOOKS LIKE AN ELECTRICAL BURN, ONLY MORE INTENSE.
I'VE SEEN IT BEFORE--IN MY TIMELINE. I KNOW WHAT'S ABOUT TO HAPPEN. HUNDREDS OF PEOPLE ARE GOING TO SUFFER THE SAME FATE YOU DID.
YOUR KILLER--WE CALLED HIM "OVERLOAD." BUT HE DISAPPEARED IN THE CHAOS, AND I NEVER CAUGHT HIM.
I HAVE A CHANCE TO RELIVE MY PAST. I HAVE A CHANCE TO SAVE THEM ALL. I'M TOO LATE FOR YOU TWO, BUT I CAN BRING YOU JUSTICE.
I JUST NEED SOMETHING... ANYTHING...TO HELP ME FIND HIM IN TIME.
WAIT. THIS ISN'T HUMAN HAIR.
OVERLOAD KILLED YOU MONTHS APART, BUT HERE'S ANOTHER OF THOSE HAIRS ON YOU. HM.
THEY'RE A MATCH. HORSE HAIR. LOOKS LIKE A WORK HORSE. MAYBE A CLYDESDALE.
WHAT IS OVERLOAD'S CONNECTION TO HORSES?

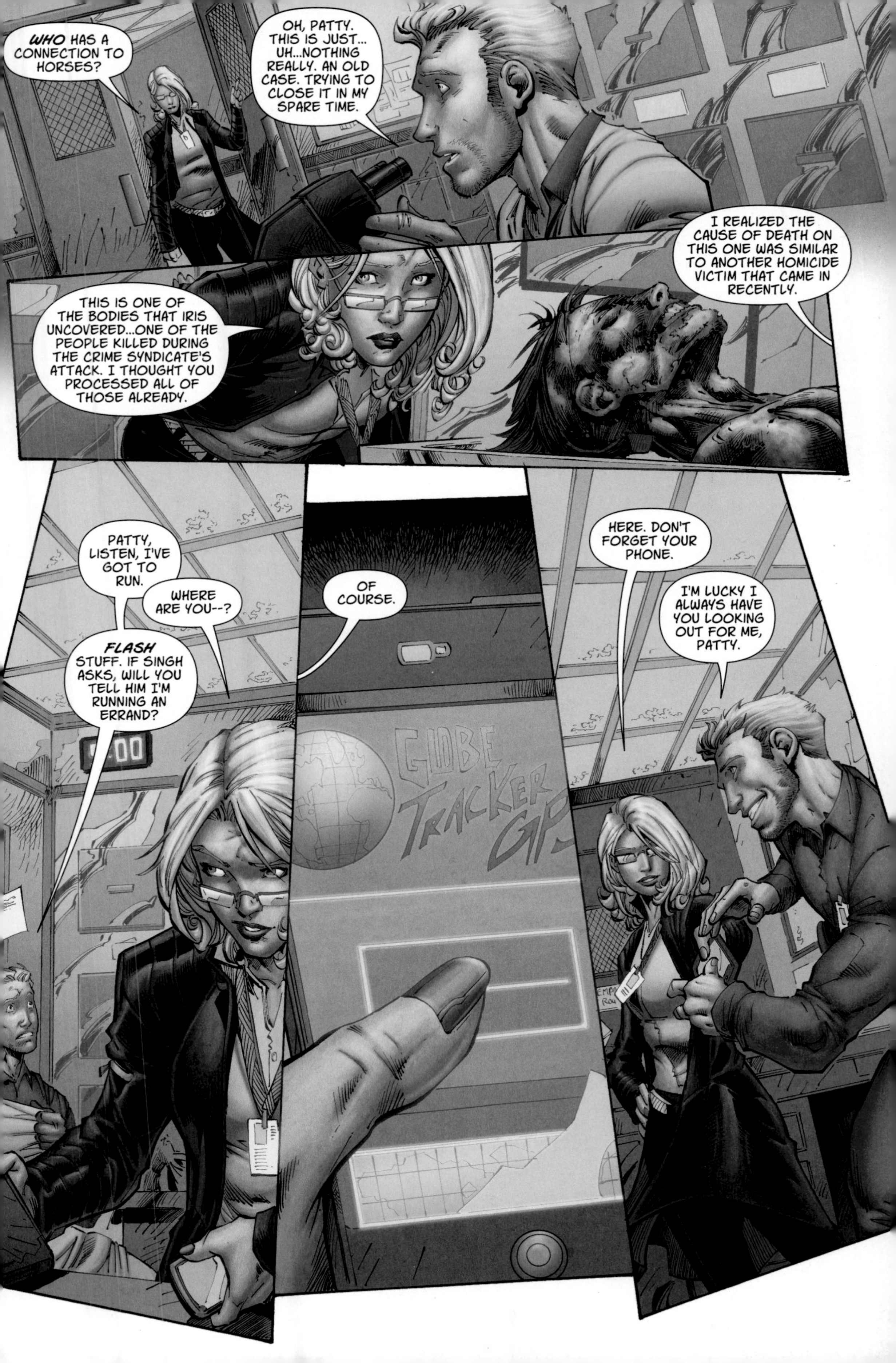
WHO HAS A CONNECTION TO HORSES?
OH, PATTY. THIS IS JUST... UH...NOTHING REALLY. AN OLD CASE. TRYING TO CLOSE IT IN MY SPARE TIME.
THIS IS ONE OF THE BODIES THAT IRIS UNCOVERED...ONE OF THE PEOPLE KILLED DURING THE CRIME SYNDICATE'S ATTACK. I THOUGHT YOU PROCESSED ALL OF THOSE ALREADY.
I REALIZED THE CAUSE OF DEATH ON THIS ONE WAS SIMILAR TO ANOTHER HOMICIDE VICTIM THAT CAME IN RECENTLY.
PATTY, LISTEN, I'VE GOT TO RUN.
WHERE ARE YOU--?
FLASH STUFF. IF SINGH ASKS, WILL YOU TELL HIM I'M RUNNING AN ERRAND?
OF COURSE.
GLOBE TRACKER GPS
HERE. DON'T FORGET YOUR PHONE.
I'M LUCKY I ALWAYS HAVE YOU LOOKING OUT FOR ME, PATTY.

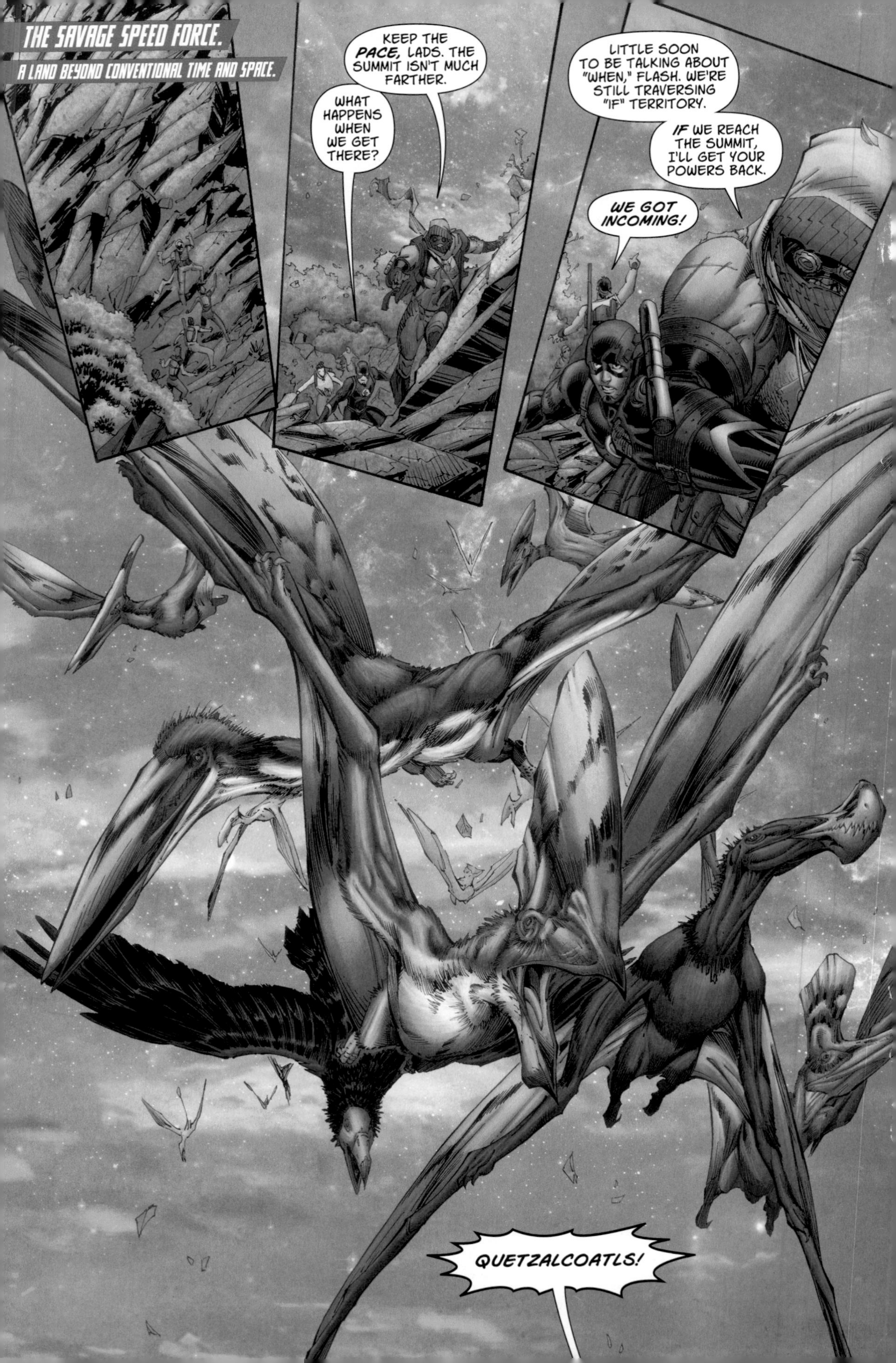
THE SAVAGE SPEED FORCE.
A LAND BEYOND CONVENTIONAL TIME AND SPACE.
KEEP THE PACE, LADS. THE SUMMIT ISN'T MUCH FARTHER.
WHAT HAPPENS WHEN WE GET THERE?
LITTLE SOON TO BE TALKING ABOUT "WHEN," FLASH. WE'RE STILL TRAVERSING "IF" TERRITORY.
IF WE REACH THE SUMMIT, I'LL GET YOUR POWERS BACK.
WE GOT INCOMING!
QUETZALCOATLS!

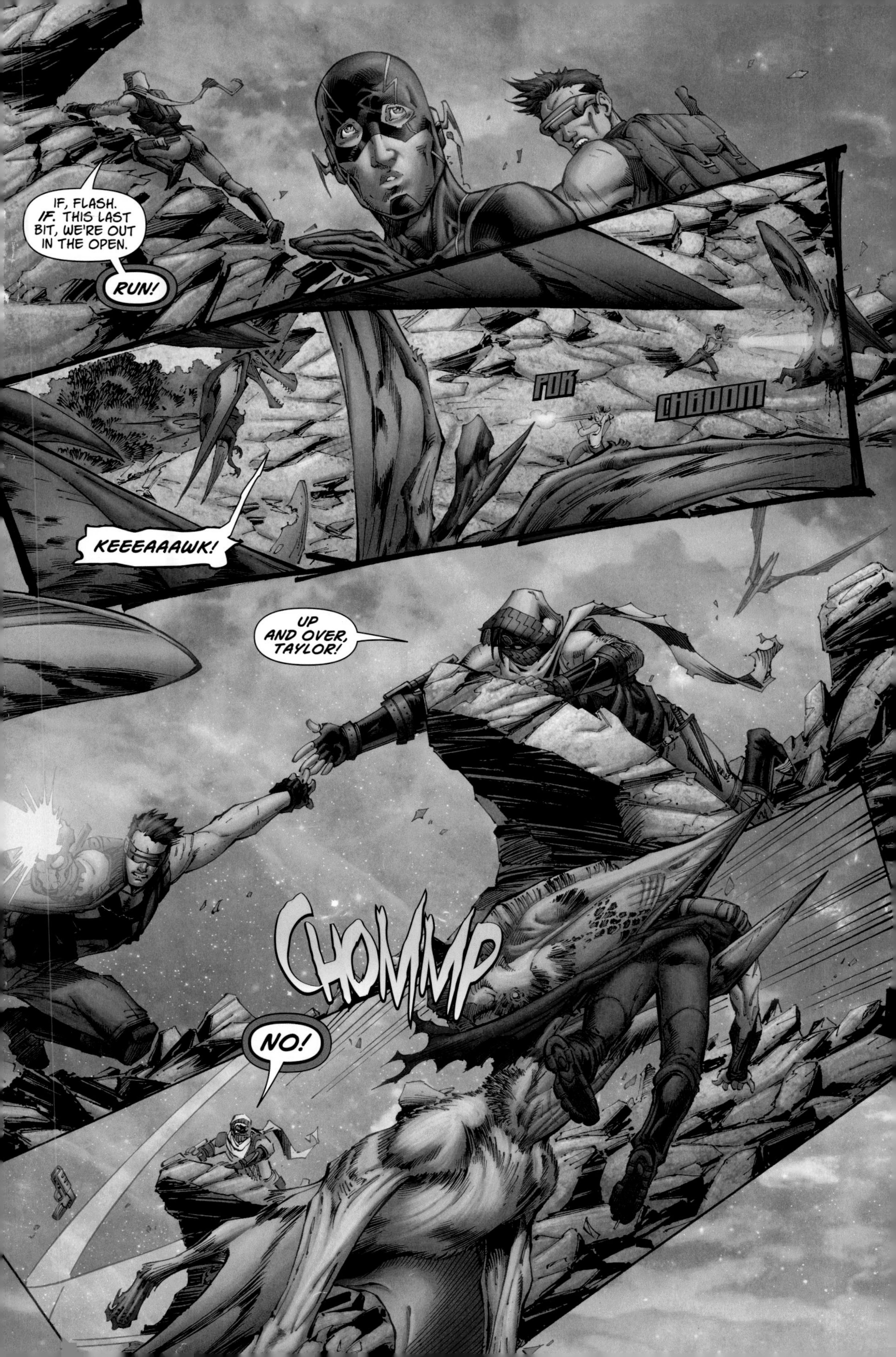

IF, FLASH. *IF.* THIS LAST BIT, WE'RE OUT IN THE OPEN.
RUN!
POK
CHBOOM
KEEEAAAWK!
UP AND OVER, TAYLOR!
CHOMMP
NO!

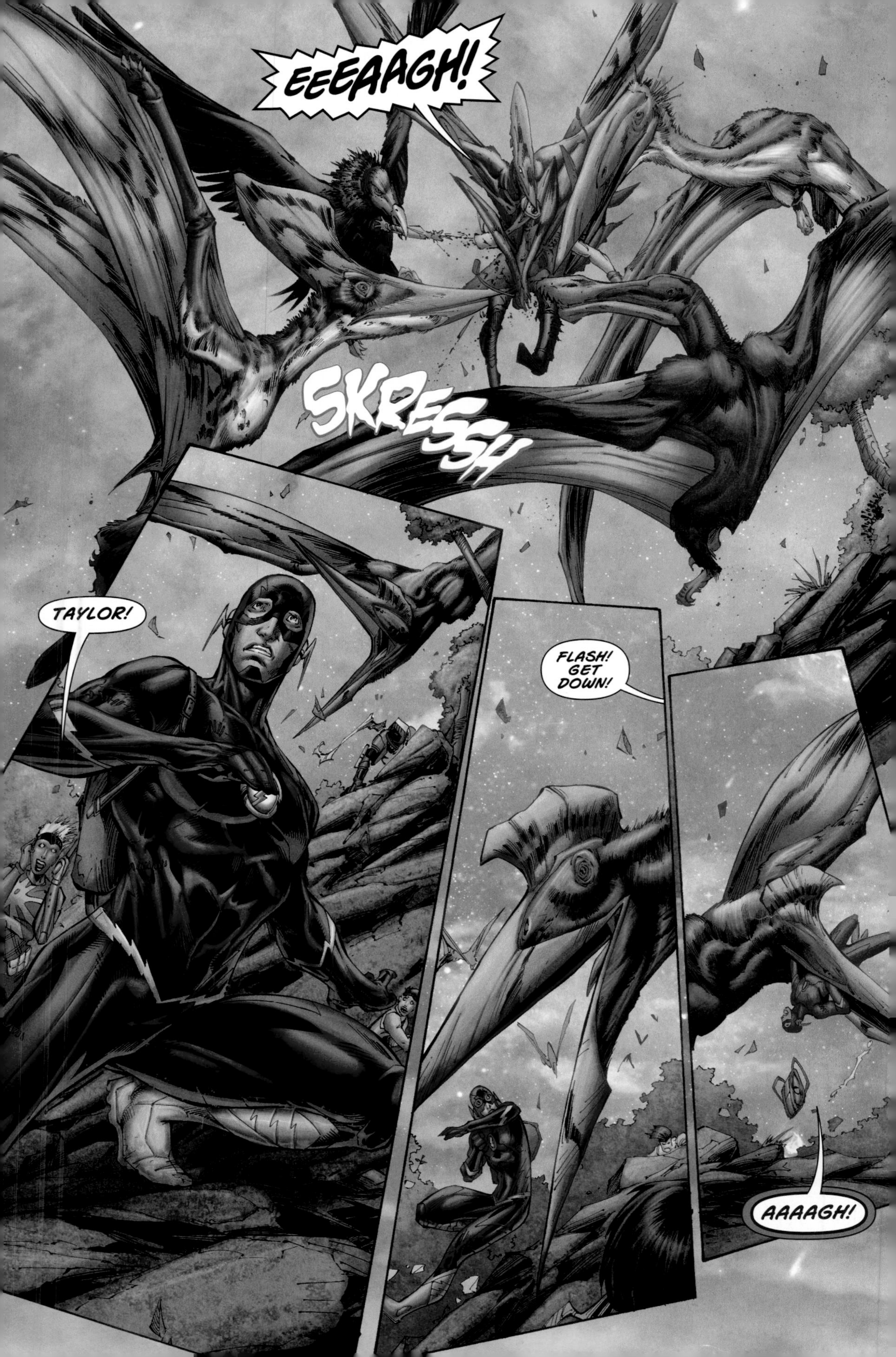
EEEAAGH!
SKRESSH
TAYLOR!
FLASH! GET DOWN!
AAAAGH!

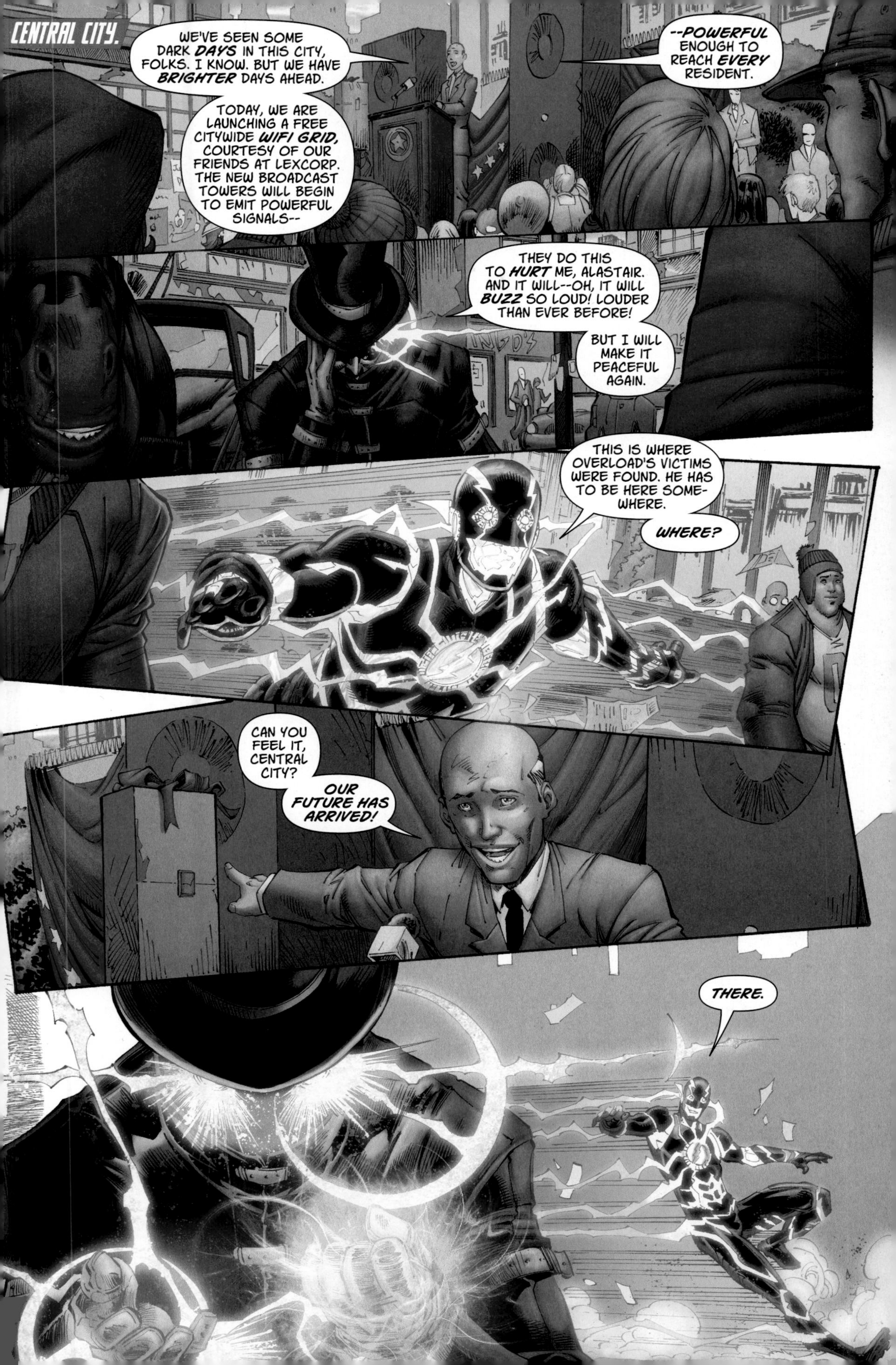
CENTRAL CITY.
WE'VE SEEN SOME DARK DAYS IN THIS CITY, FOLKS. I KNOW. BUT WE HAVE BRIGHTER DAYS AHEAD.
TODAY, WE ARE LAUNCHING A FREE CITYWIDE WIFI GRID, COURTESY OF OUR FRIENDS AT LEXCORP. THE NEW BROADCAST TOWERS WILL BEGIN TO EMIT POWERFUL SIGNALS--
--POWERFUL ENOUGH TO REACH EVERY RESIDENT.
THEY DO THIS TO HURT ME, ALASTAIR. AND IT WILL--OH, IT WILL BUZZ SO LOUD! LOUDER THAN EVER BEFORE!
BUT I WILL MAKE IT PEACEFUL AGAIN.
THIS IS WHERE OVERLOAD'S VICTIMS WERE FOUND. HE HAS TO BE HERE SOME-WHERE.
WHERE?
CAN YOU FEEL IT, CENTRAL CITY?
OUR FUTURE HAS ARRIVED!
THERE.

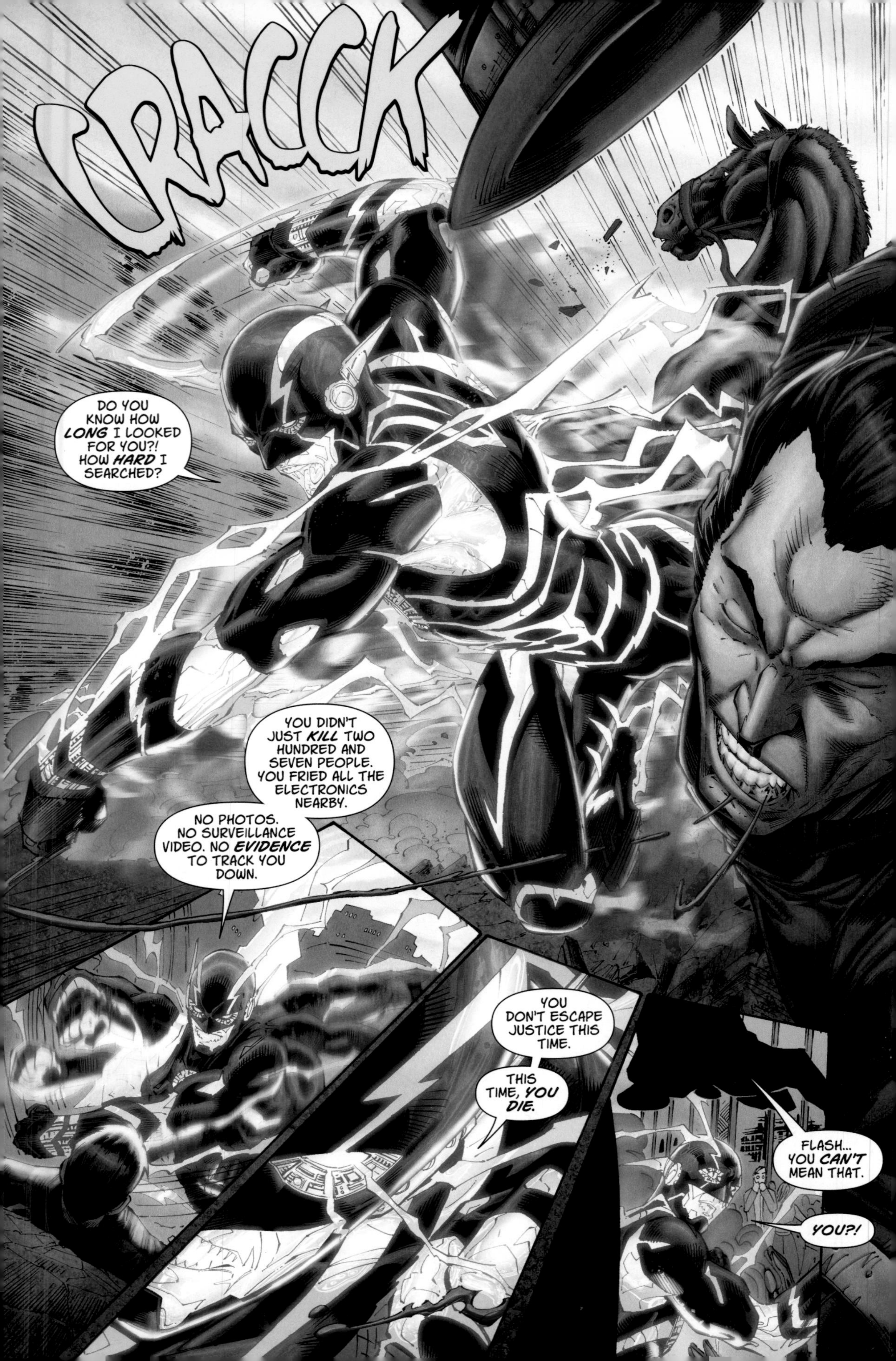
CRACCK
DO YOU KNOW HOW LONG I LOOKED FOR YOU?! HOW HARD I SEARCHED?
YOU DIDN'T JUST KILL TWO HUNDRED AND SEVEN PEOPLE. YOU FRIED ALL THE ELECTRONICS NEARBY.
NO PHOTOS. NO SURVEILLANCE VIDEO. NO EVIDENCE TO TRACK YOU DOWN.
YOU DON'T ESCAPE JUSTICE THIS TIME.
THIS TIME, YOU DIE.
FLASH... YOU CAN'T MEAN THAT.
YOU?!

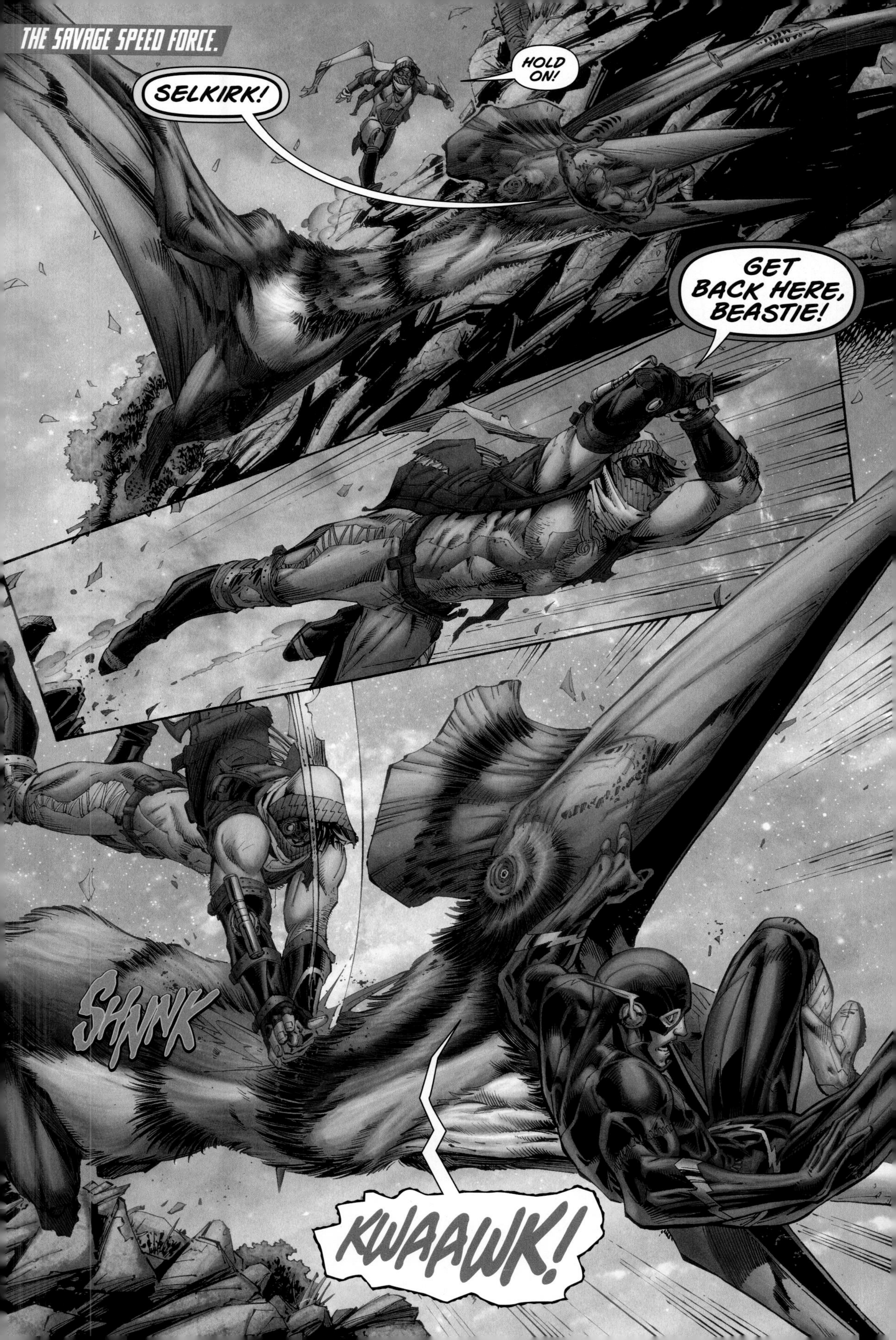
THE SAVAGE SPEED FORCE.
SELKIRK!
HOLD ON!
GET BACK HERE, BEASTIE!
SHNK
KWAAWK!

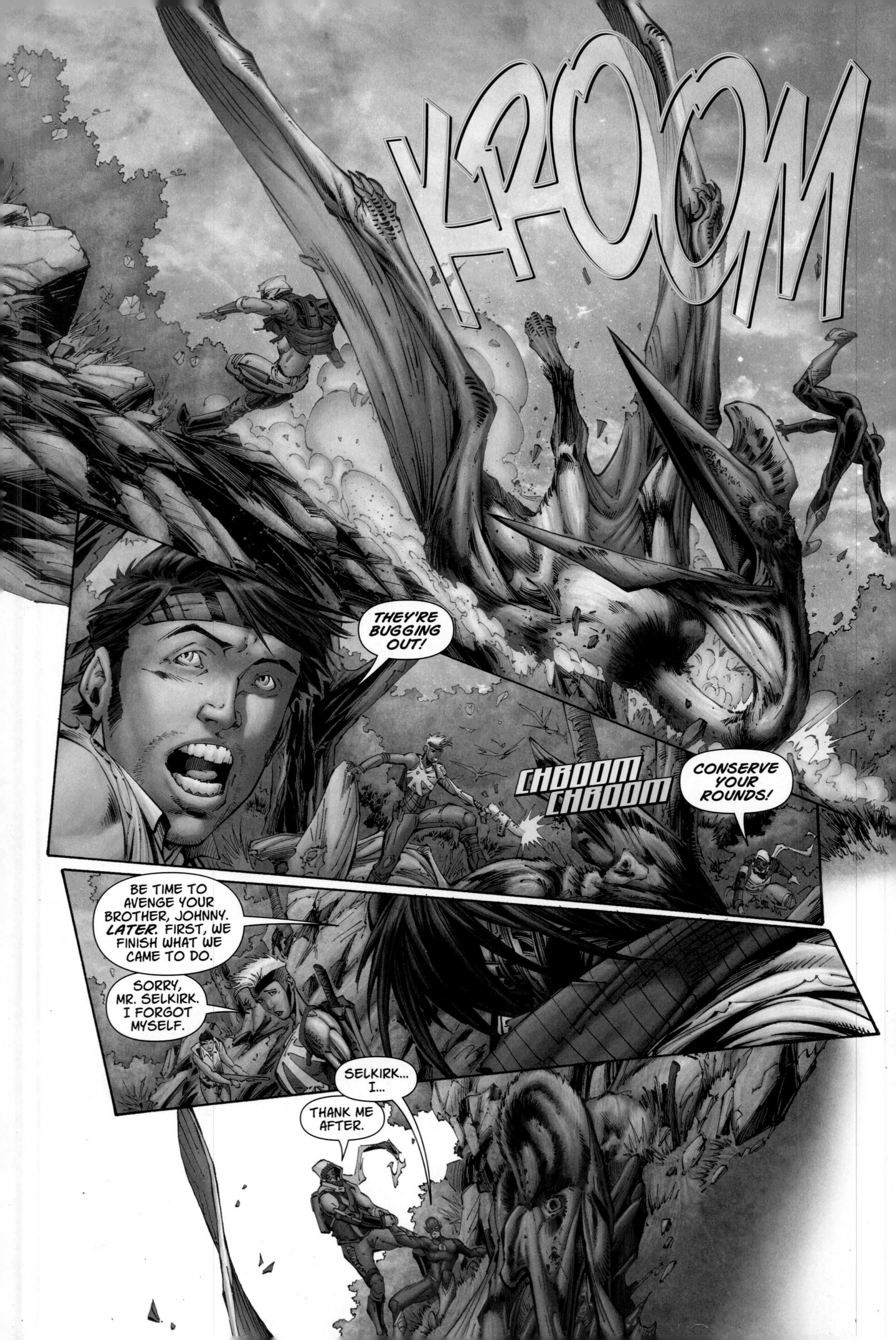
KROOM
THEY'RE BUGGING OUT!
CHROOM CHROOM
CONSERVE YOUR ROUNDS!
BE TIME TO AVENGE YOUR BROTHER, JOHNNY. LATER. FIRST, WE FINISH WHAT WE CAME TO DO.
SORRY, MR. SELKIRK. I FORGOT MYSELF.
SELKIRK... I...
THANK ME AFTER.

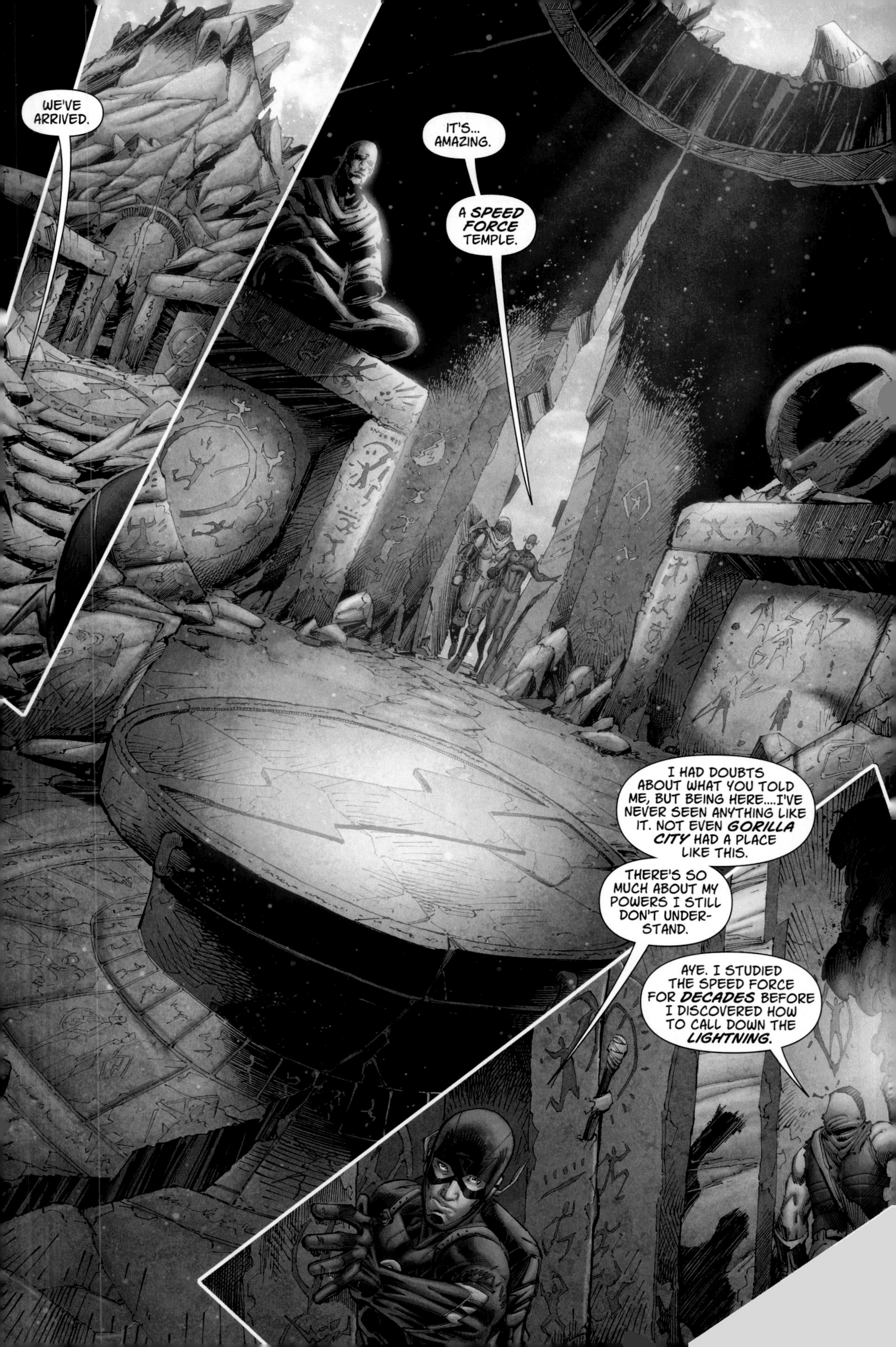
WE'VE ARRIVED.
IT'S... AMAZING.
A SPEED FORCE TEMPLE.
I HAD DOUBTS ABOUT WHAT YOU TOLD ME, BUT BEING HERE....I'VE NEVER SEEN ANYTHING LIKE IT. NOT EVEN GORILLA CITY HAD A PLACE LIKE THIS.
THERE'S SO MUCH ABOUT MY POWERS I STILL DON'T UNDER-STAND.
AYE. I STUDIED THE SPEED FORCE FOR DECADES BEFORE I DISCOVERED HOW TO CALL DOWN THE LIGHTNING.

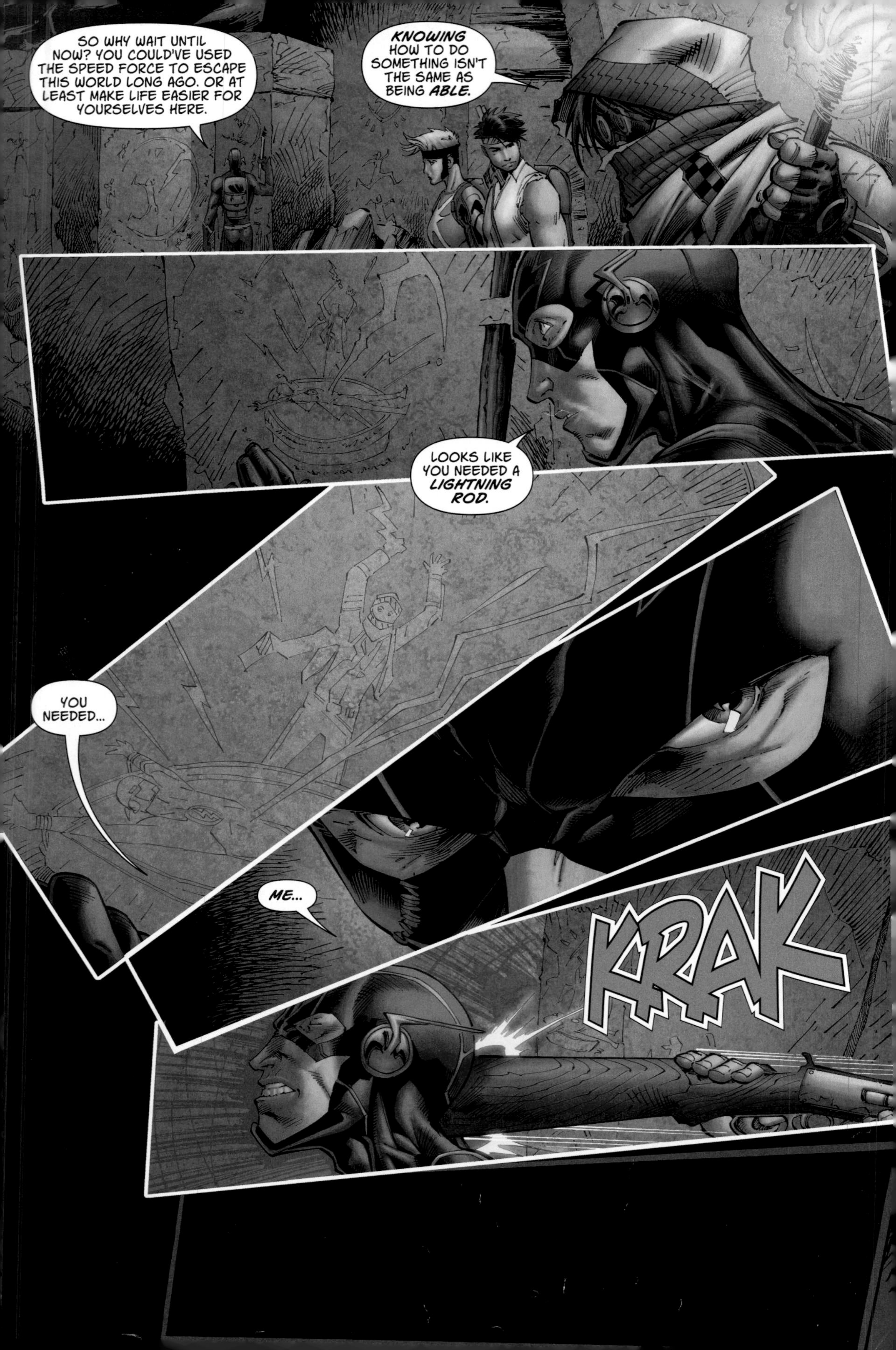
SO WHY WAIT UNTIL NOW? YOU COULD'VE USED THE SPEED FORCE TO ESCAPE THIS WORLD LONG AGO. OR AT LEAST MAKE LIFE EASIER FOR YOURSELVES HERE.
KNOWING HOW TO DO SOMETHING ISN'T THE SAME AS BEING *ABLE*.
LOOKS LIKE YOU NEEDED A *LIGHTNING ROD*.
YOU NEEDED...
ME...
KRAK

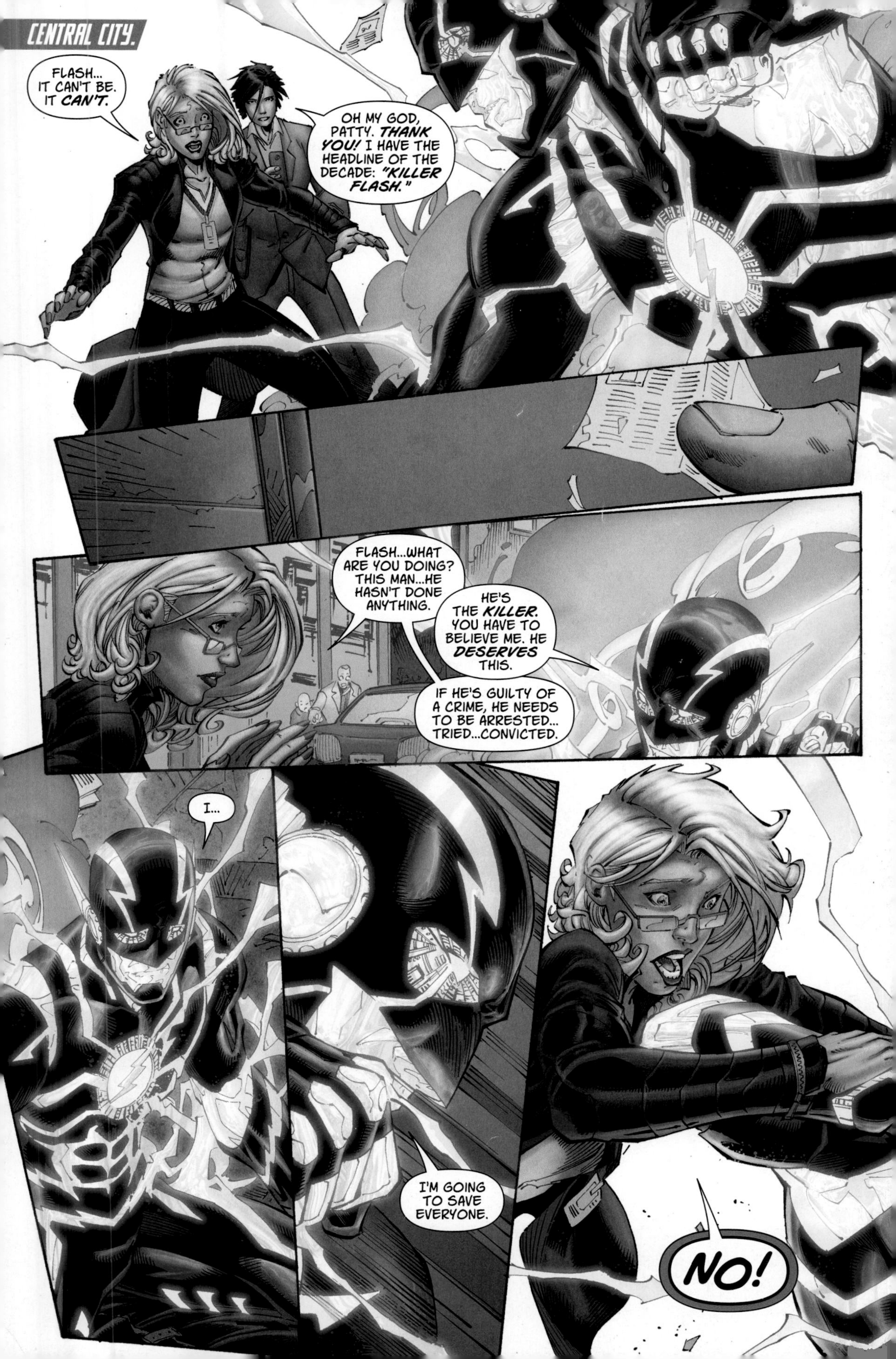
CENTRAL CITY.
FLASH... IT CAN'T BE. IT CAN'T.
OH MY GOD, PATTY. THANK YOU! I HAVE THE HEADLINE OF THE DECADE: "KILLER FLASH."
FLASH...WHAT ARE YOU DOING? THIS MAN...HE HASN'T DONE ANYTHING.
HE'S THE KILLER. YOU HAVE TO BELIEVE ME. HE DESERVES THIS.
IF HE'S GUILTY OF A CRIME, HE NEEDS TO BE ARRESTED... TRIED...CONVICTED.
I...
I'M GOING TO SAVE EVERYONE.
NO!

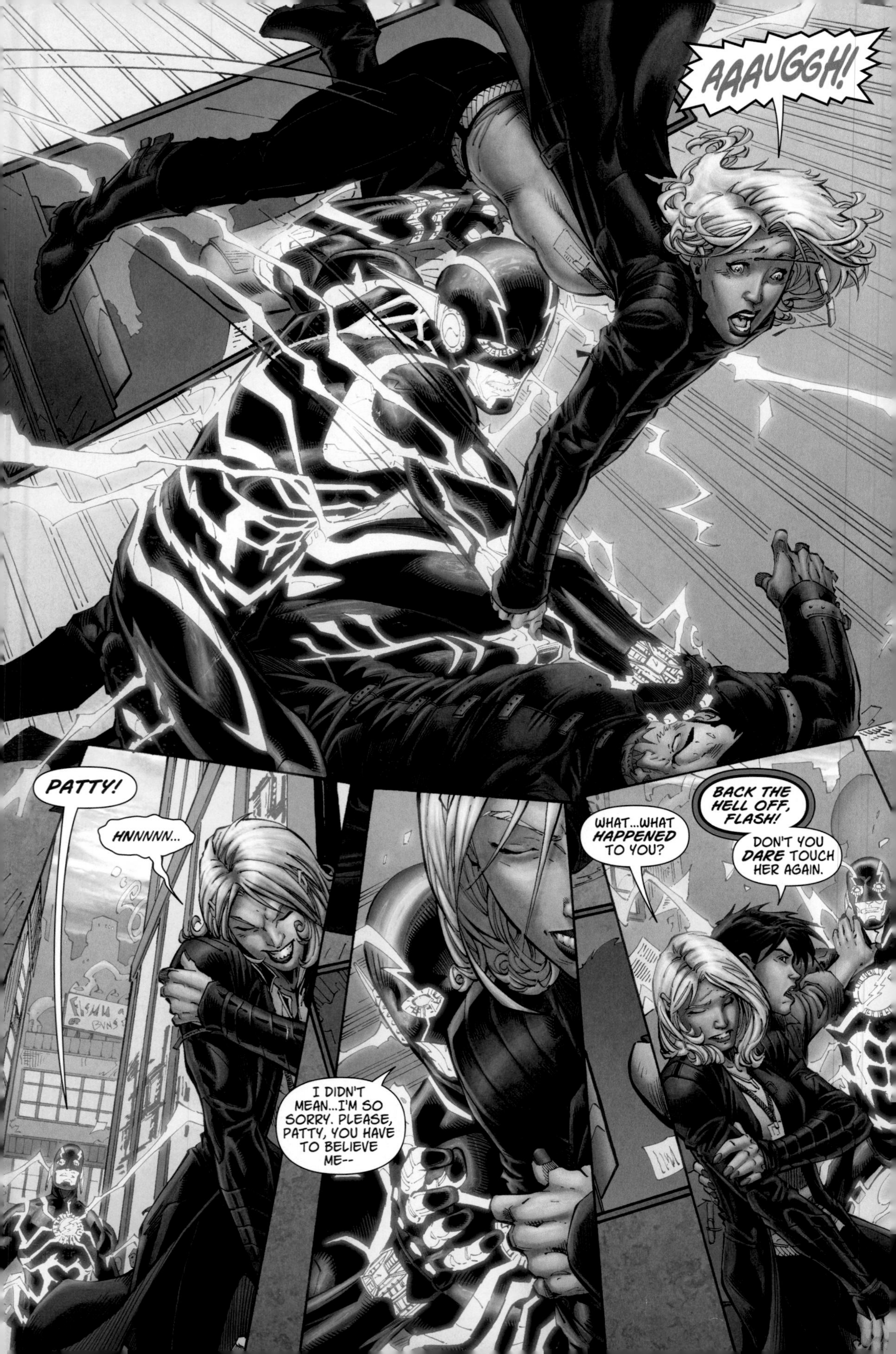
AAAUGGH!
PATTY!
HNNNNN...
I DIDN'T MEAN...I'M SO SORRY. PLEASE, PATTY, YOU HAVE TO BELIEVE ME--
WHAT...WHAT HAPPENED TO YOU?
BACK THE HELL OFF, FLASH!
DON'T YOU DARE TOUCH HER AGAIN.

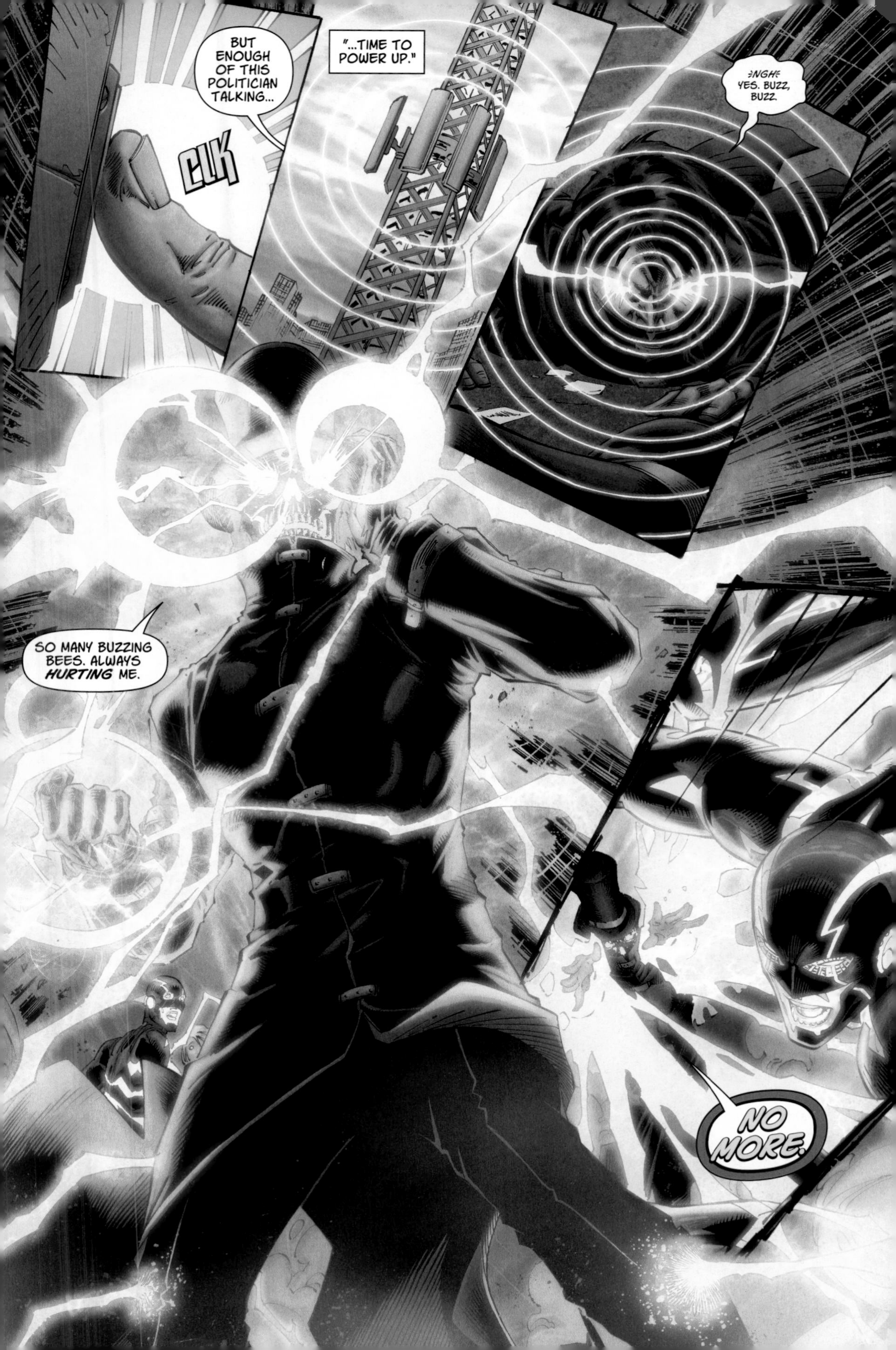
BUT ENOUGH OF THIS POLITICIAN TALKING...
CLK
"...TIME TO POWER UP."
NGH YES. BUZZ, BUZZ.
SO MANY BUZZING BEES. ALWAYS HURTING ME.
NO MORE.

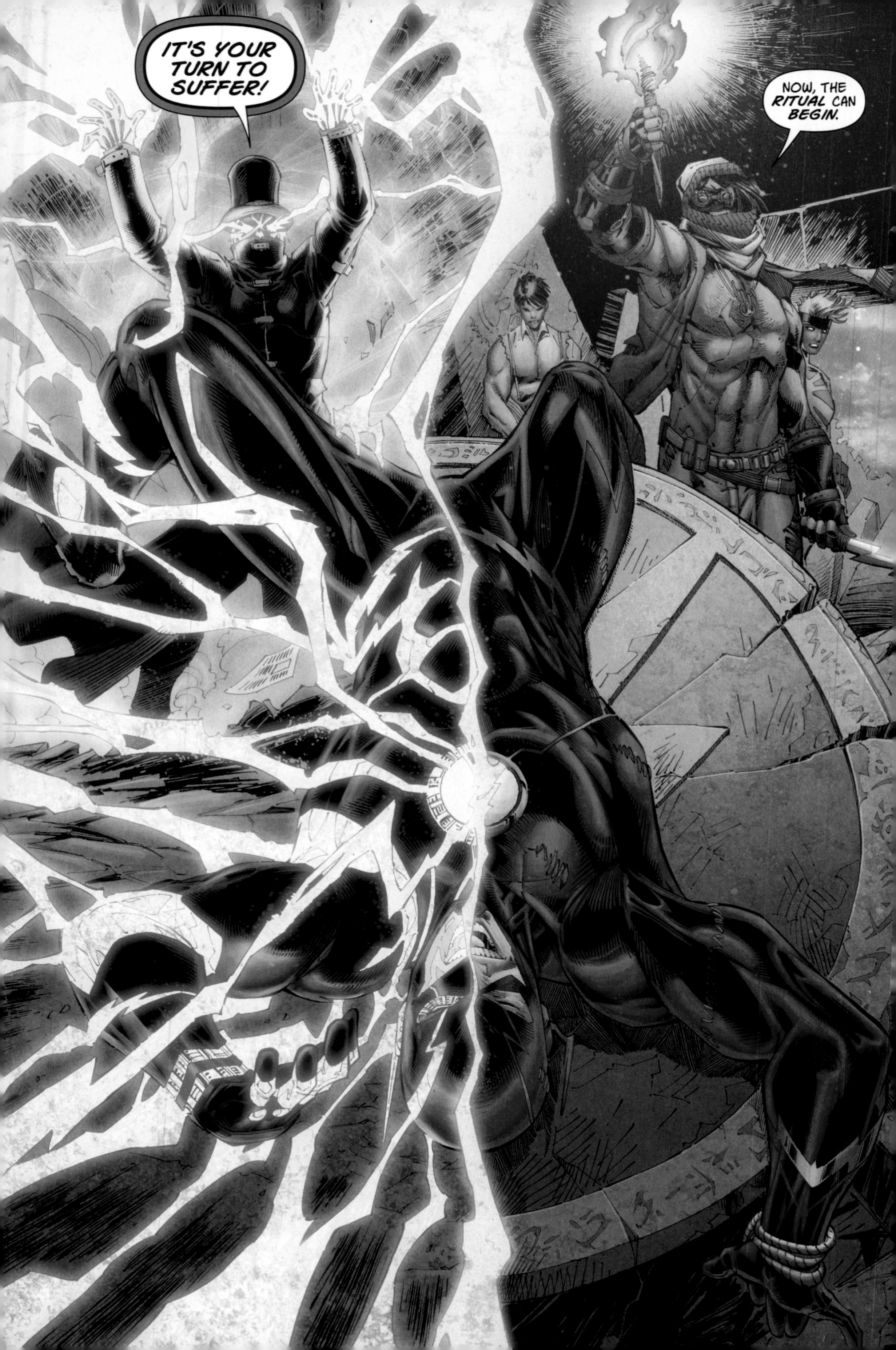
IT'S YOUR TURN TO SUFFER!
NOW, THE RITUAL CAN BEGIN.

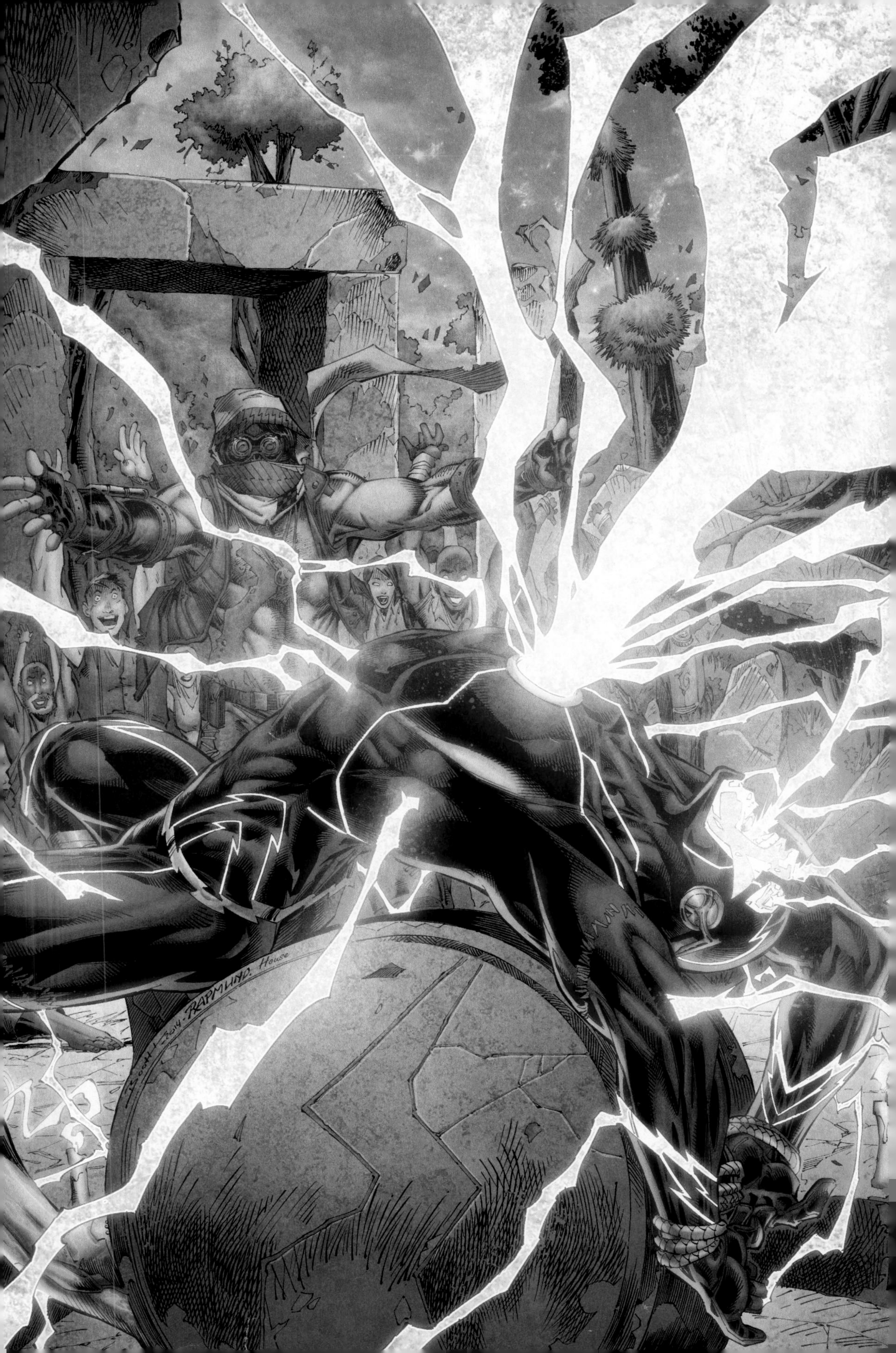

END OF THE ROAD

ROBERT VENDITTI & VAN JENSEN writers BRETT BOOTH penciller NORM RAPMUND inker ANDREW DALHOUSE colorist PAT BROSSEAU letterer
cover by BRETT BOOTH, NORM RAPMUND & ANDREW DALHOUSE

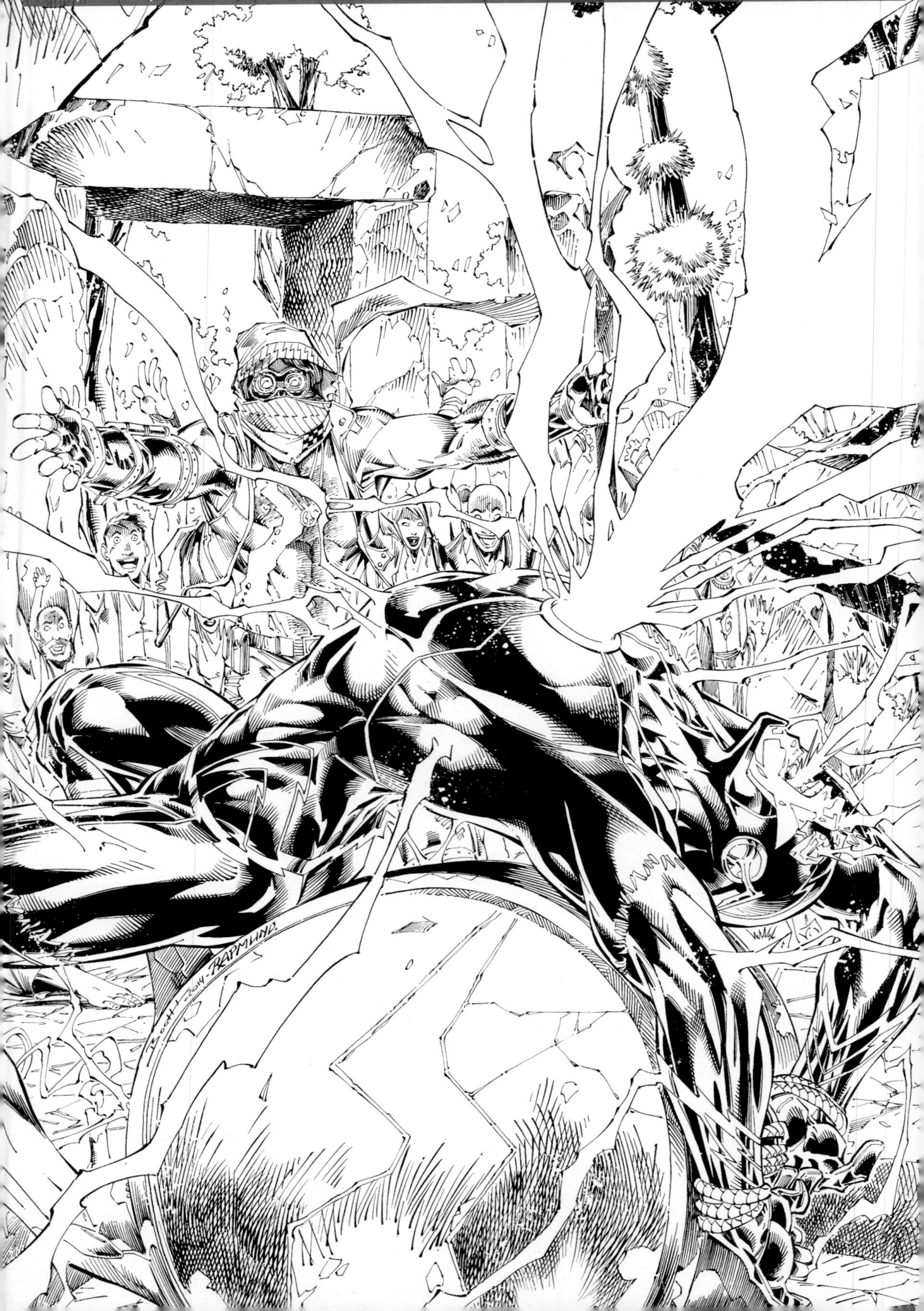

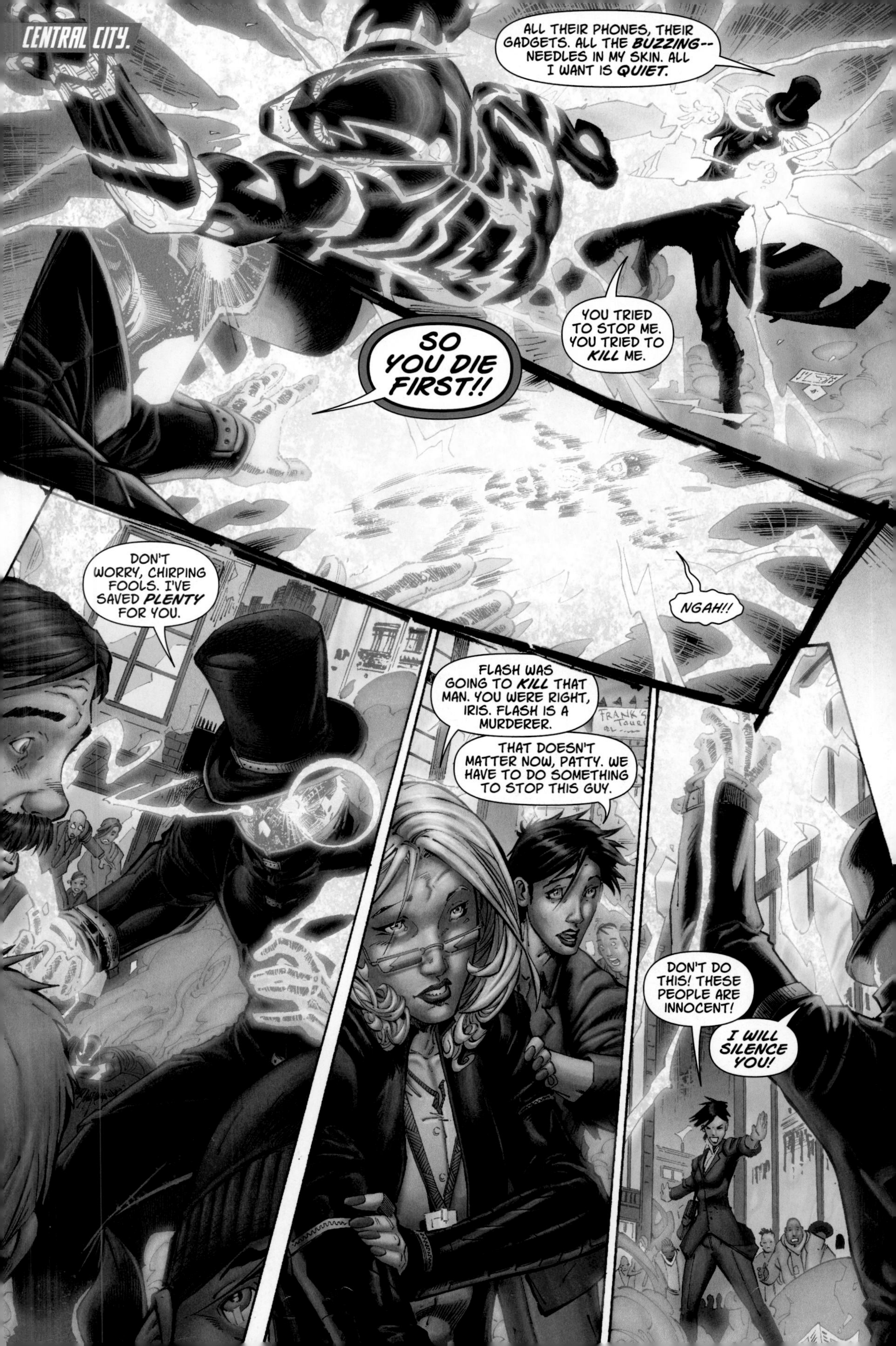
CENTRAL CITY.
ALL THEIR PHONES, THEIR GADGETS. ALL THE BUZZING-- NEEDLES IN MY SKIN. ALL I WANT IS QUIET.
YOU TRIED TO STOP ME. YOU TRIED TO KILL ME.
SO YOU DIE FIRST!!
NGAH!!
DON'T WORRY, CHIRPING FOOLS. I'VE SAVED PLENTY FOR YOU.
FLASH WAS GOING TO KILL THAT MAN. YOU WERE RIGHT, IRIS. FLASH IS A MURDERER.
THAT DOESN'T MATTER NOW, PATTY. WE HAVE TO DO SOMETHING TO STOP THIS GUY.
DON'T DO THIS! THESE PEOPLE ARE INNOCENT!
I WILL SILENCE YOU!

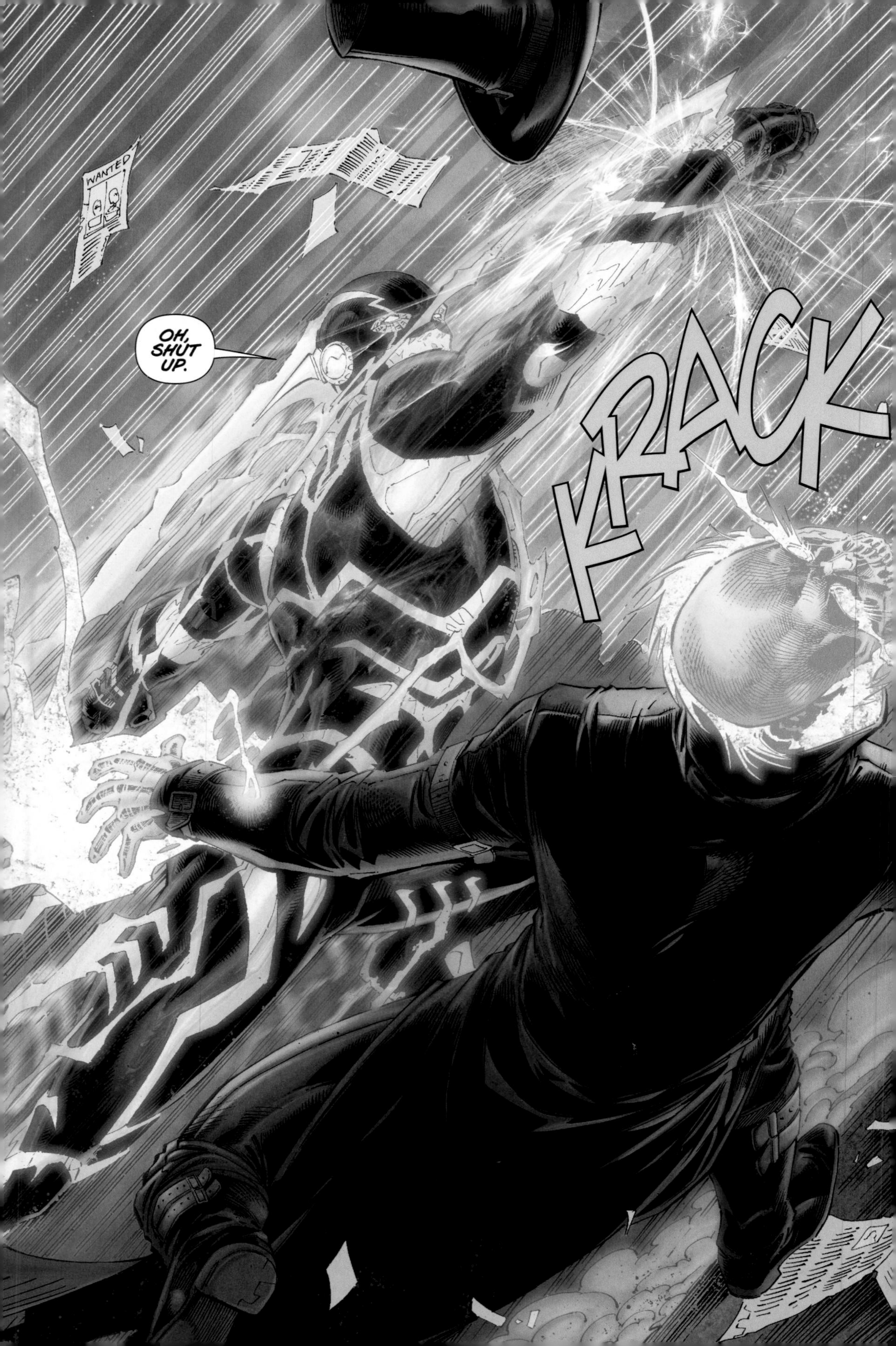
WANTED
OH, SHUT UP.
KRACK

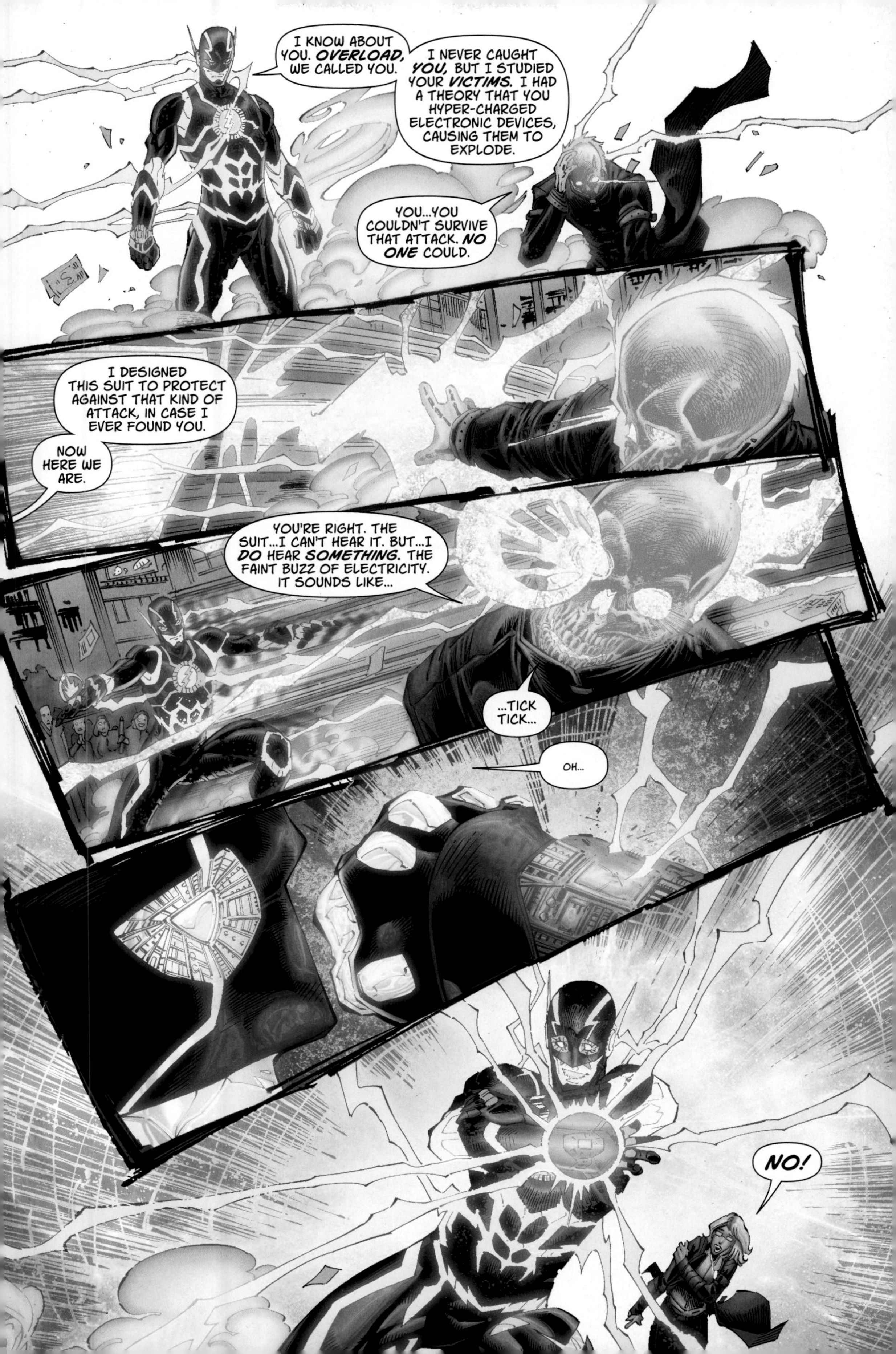
I KNOW ABOUT YOU. OVERLOAD, WE CALLED YOU.
I NEVER CAUGHT YOU, BUT I STUDIED YOUR VICTIMS. I HAD A THEORY THAT YOU HYPER-CHARGED ELECTRONIC DEVICES, CAUSING THEM TO EXPLODE.
YOU...YOU COULDN'T SURVIVE THAT ATTACK. NO ONE COULD.
I DESIGNED THIS SUIT TO PROTECT AGAINST THAT KIND OF ATTACK, IN CASE I EVER FOUND YOU.
NOW HERE WE ARE.
YOU'RE RIGHT. THE SUIT...I CAN'T HEAR IT. BUT...I DO HEAR SOMETHING. THE FAINT BUZZ OF ELECTRICITY. IT SOUNDS LIKE...
...TICK TICK...
OH...
NO!

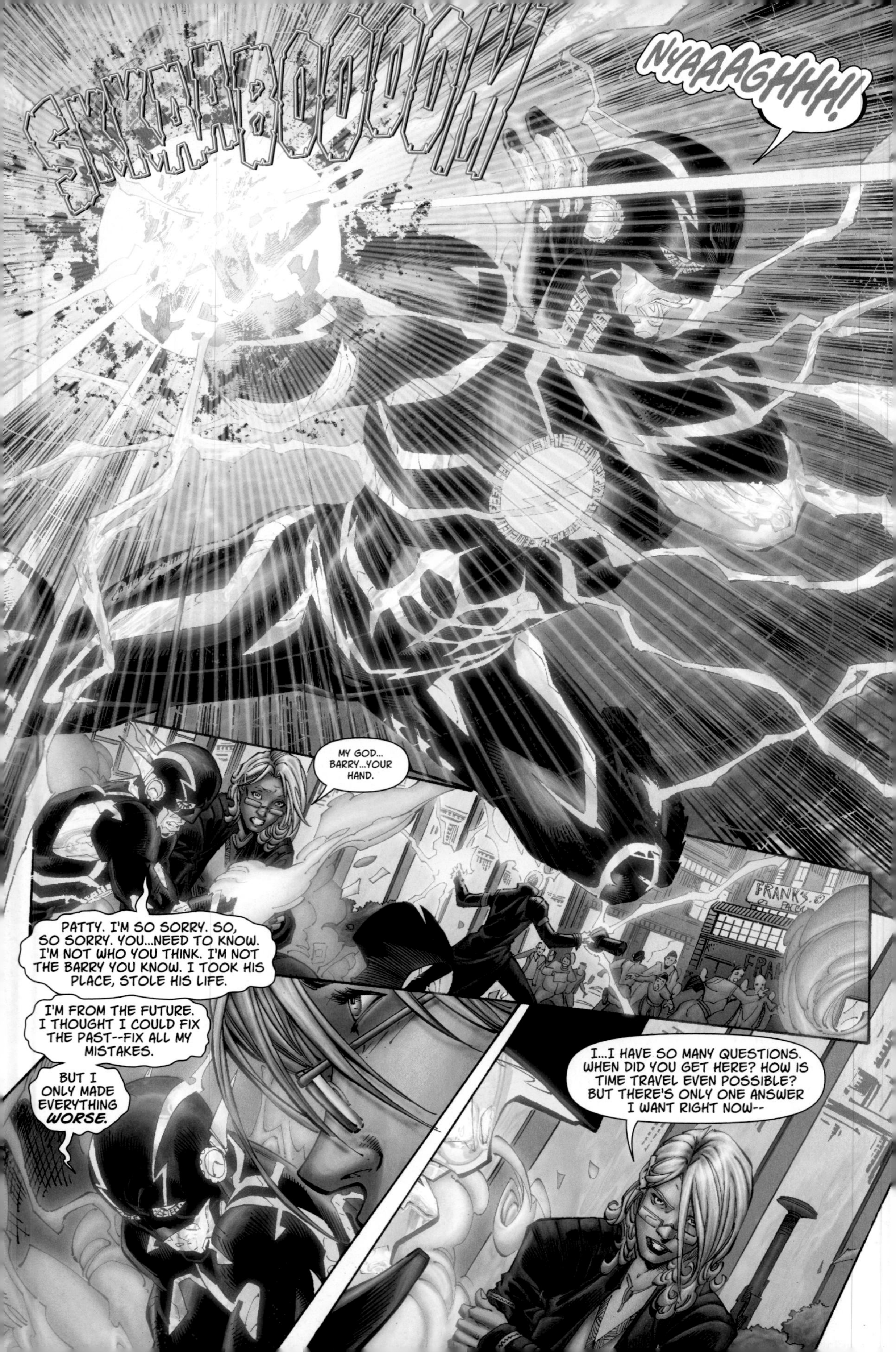
SKKRRBOOOOM
NYAAAGHHH!
MY GOD... BARRY...YOUR HAND.
PATTY. I'M SO SORRY. SO, SO SORRY. YOU...NEED TO KNOW. I'M NOT WHO YOU THINK. I'M NOT THE BARRY YOU KNOW. I TOOK HIS PLACE, STOLE HIS LIFE.
I'M FROM THE FUTURE. I THOUGHT I COULD FIX THE PAST--FIX ALL MY MISTAKES.
BUT I ONLY MADE EVERYTHING WORSE.
I...I HAVE SO MANY QUESTIONS. WHEN DID YOU GET HERE? HOW IS TIME TRAVEL EVEN POSSIBLE? BUT THERE'S ONLY ONE ANSWER I WANT RIGHT NOW--

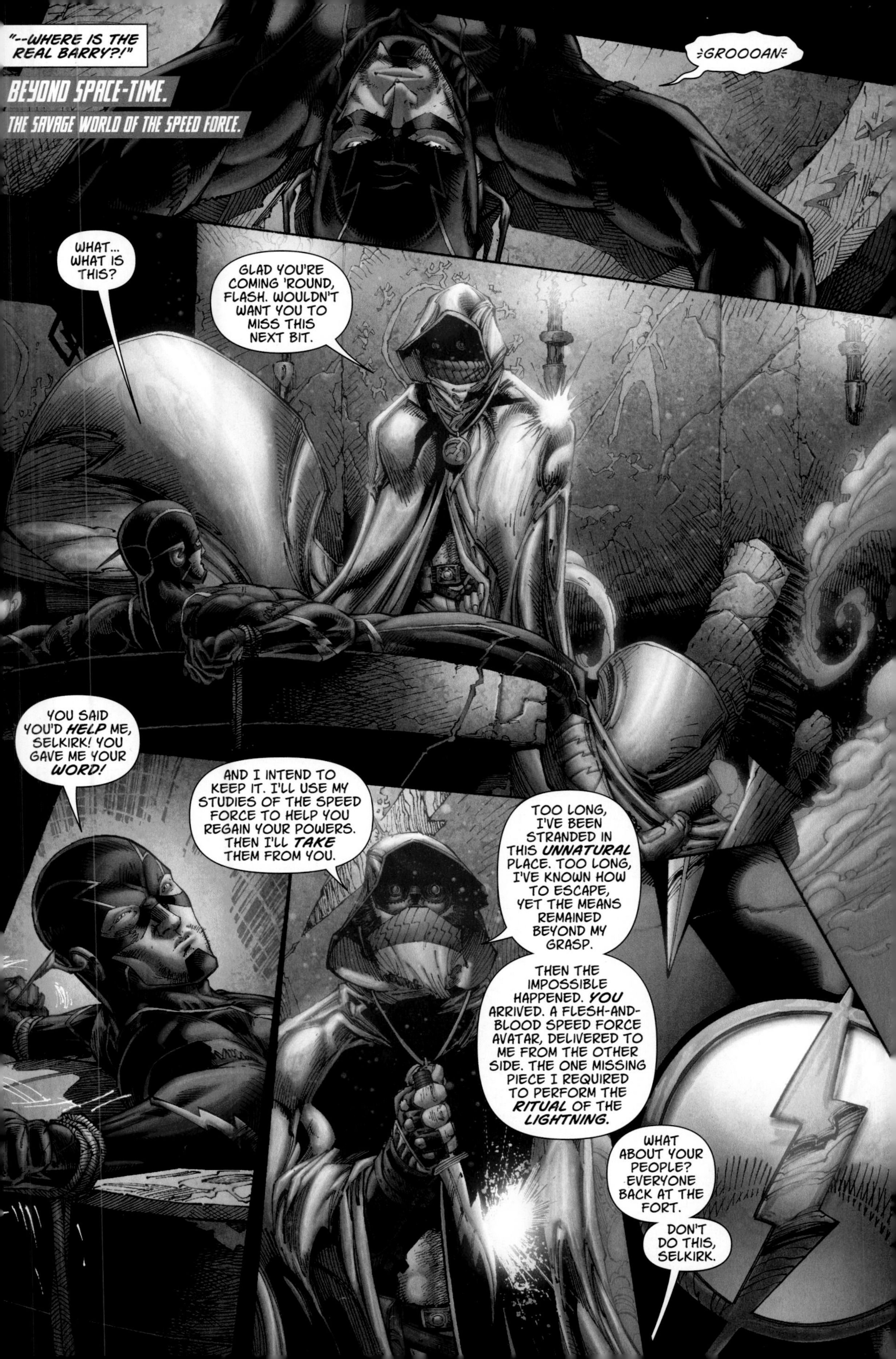
"--WHERE IS THE REAL BARRY?!"
BEYOND SPACE-TIME.
THE SAVAGE WORLD OF THE SPEED FORCE.
GROOOAN
WHAT... WHAT IS THIS?
GLAD YOU'RE COMING 'ROUND, FLASH. WOULDN'T WANT YOU TO MISS THIS NEXT BIT.
YOU SAID YOU'D HELP ME, SELKIRK! YOU GAVE ME YOUR WORD!
AND I INTEND TO KEEP IT. I'LL USE MY STUDIES OF THE SPEED FORCE TO HELP YOU REGAIN YOUR POWERS. THEN I'LL TAKE THEM FROM YOU.
TOO LONG, I'VE BEEN STRANDED IN THIS UNNATURAL PLACE. TOO LONG, I'VE KNOWN HOW TO ESCAPE, YET THE MEANS REMAINED BEYOND MY GRASP.
THEN THE IMPOSSIBLE HAPPENED. YOU ARRIVED. A FLESH-AND-BLOOD SPEED FORCE AVATAR, DELIVERED TO ME FROM THE OTHER SIDE. THE ONE MISSING PIECE I REQUIRED TO PERFORM THE RITUAL OF THE LIGHTNING.
WHAT ABOUT YOUR PEOPLE? EVERYONE BACK AT THE FORT.
DON'T DO THIS, SELKIRK.

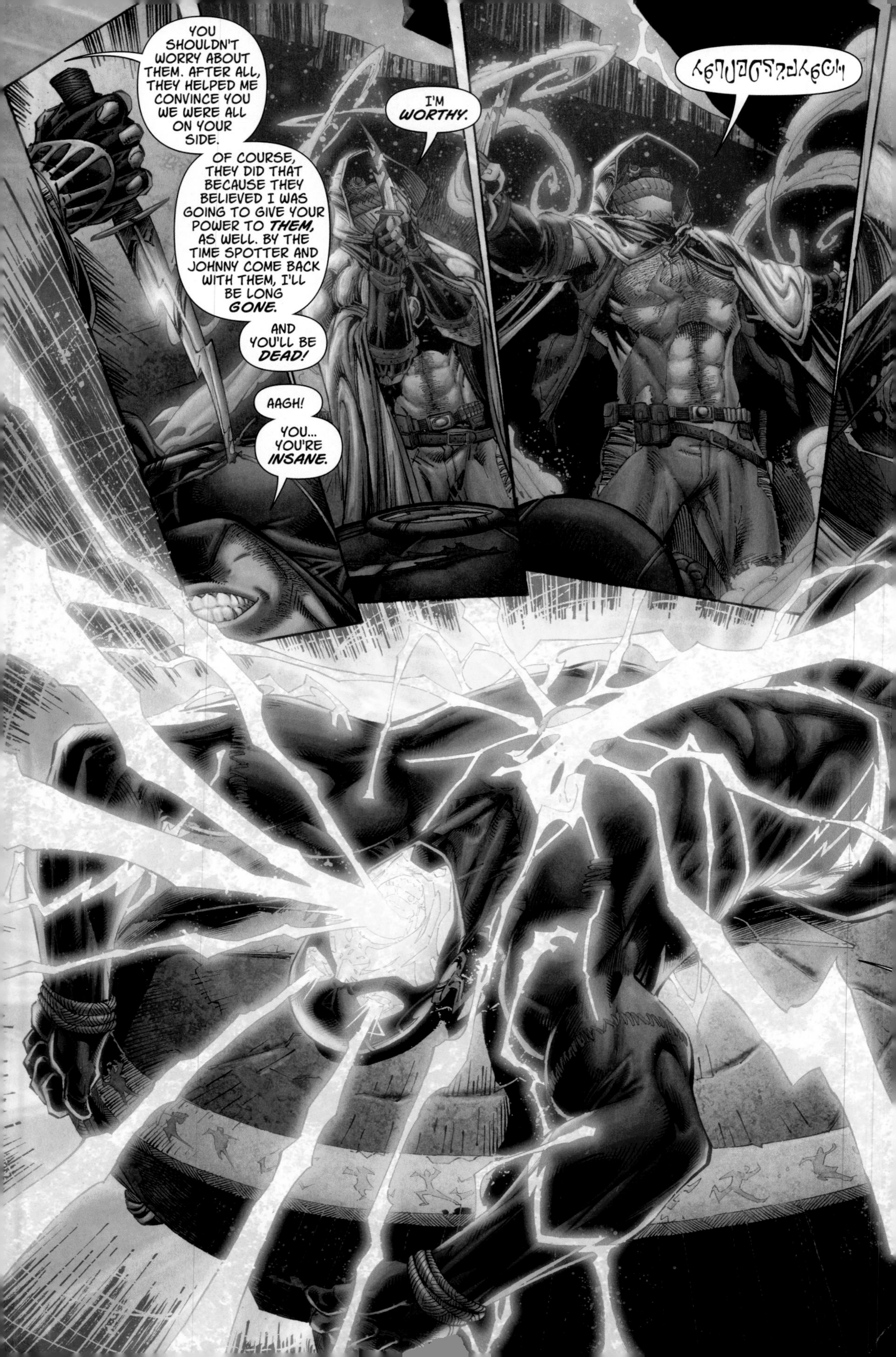
YOU SHOULDN'T WORRY ABOUT THEM. AFTER ALL, THEY HELPED ME CONVINCE YOU WE WERE ALL ON YOUR SIDE.
OF COURSE, THEY DID THAT BECAUSE THEY BELIEVED I WAS GOING TO GIVE YOUR POWER TO THEM, AS WELL. BY THE TIME SPOTTER AND JOHNNY COME BACK WITH THEM, I'LL BE LONG GONE.
AND YOU'LL BE DEAD!
AAGH!
YOU... YOU'RE INSANE.
I'M WORTHY.

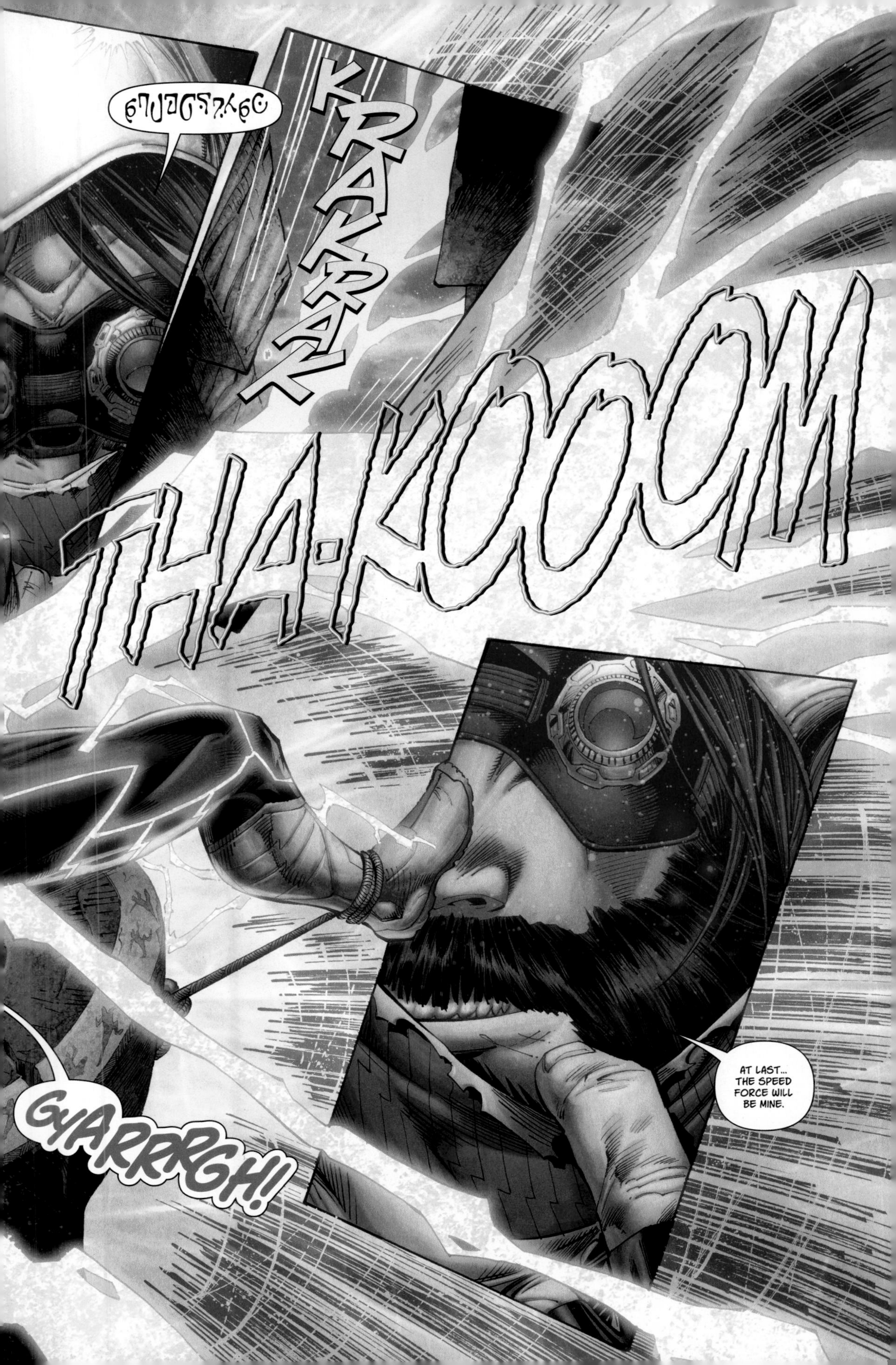
KRAKRAK
THA-KOOOM
GYARRRGH!
AT LAST... THE SPEED FORCE WILL BE MINE.

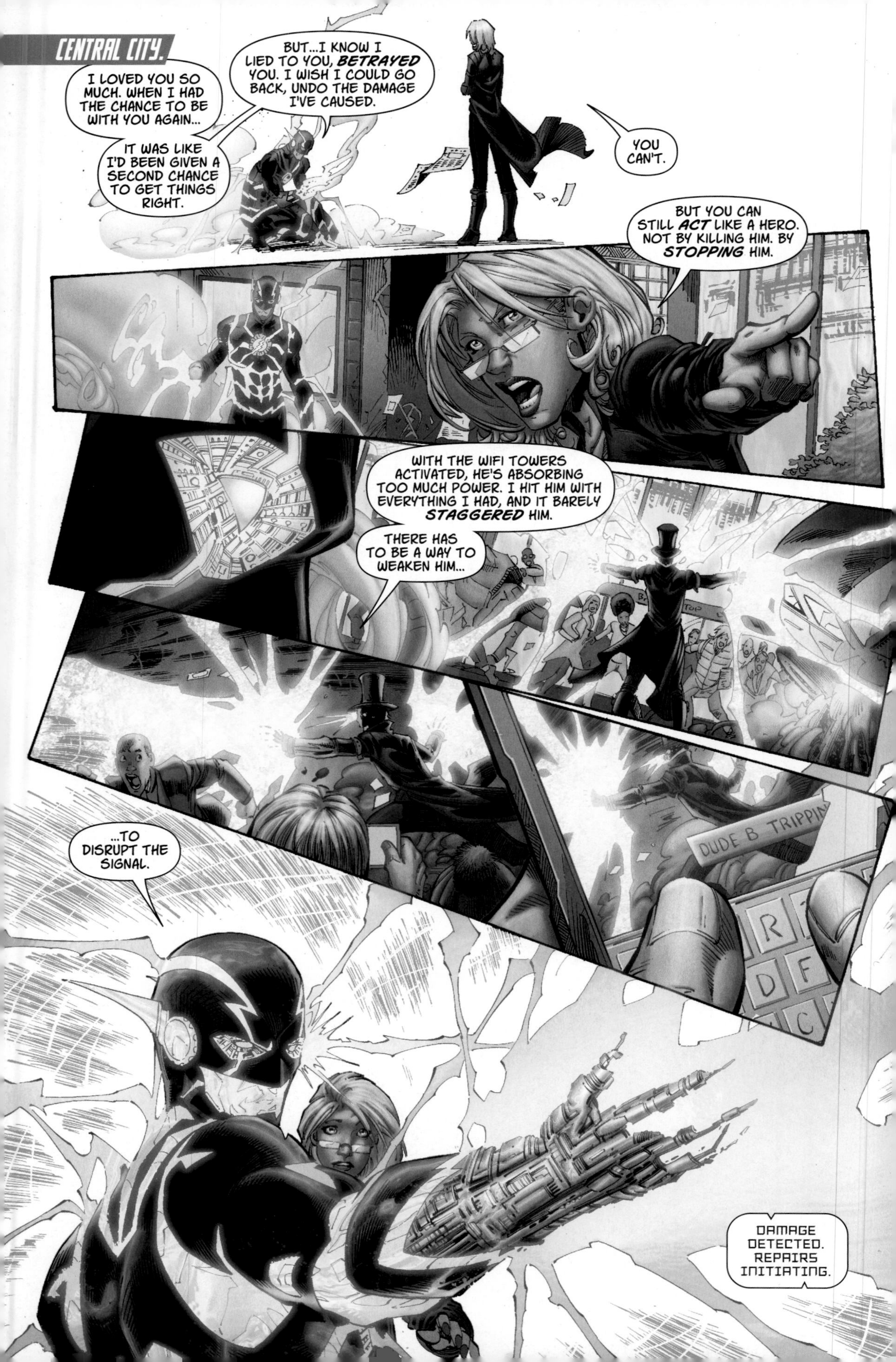
CENTRAL CITY.
I LOVED YOU SO MUCH. WHEN I HAD THE CHANCE TO BE WITH YOU AGAIN...
IT WAS LIKE I'D BEEN GIVEN A SECOND CHANCE TO GET THINGS RIGHT.
BUT...I KNOW I LIED TO YOU, BETRAYED YOU. I WISH I COULD GO BACK, UNDO THE DAMAGE I'VE CAUSED.
YOU CAN'T.
BUT YOU CAN STILL ACT LIKE A HERO. NOT BY KILLING HIM. BY STOPPING HIM.
WITH THE WIFI TOWERS ACTIVATED, HE'S ABSORBING TOO MUCH POWER. I HIT HIM WITH EVERYTHING I HAD, AND IT BARELY STAGGERED HIM.
THERE HAS TO BE A WAY TO WEAKEN HIM...
DUDE B TRIPPIN
...TO DISRUPT THE SIGNAL.
DAMAGE DETECTED. REPAIRS INITIATING.

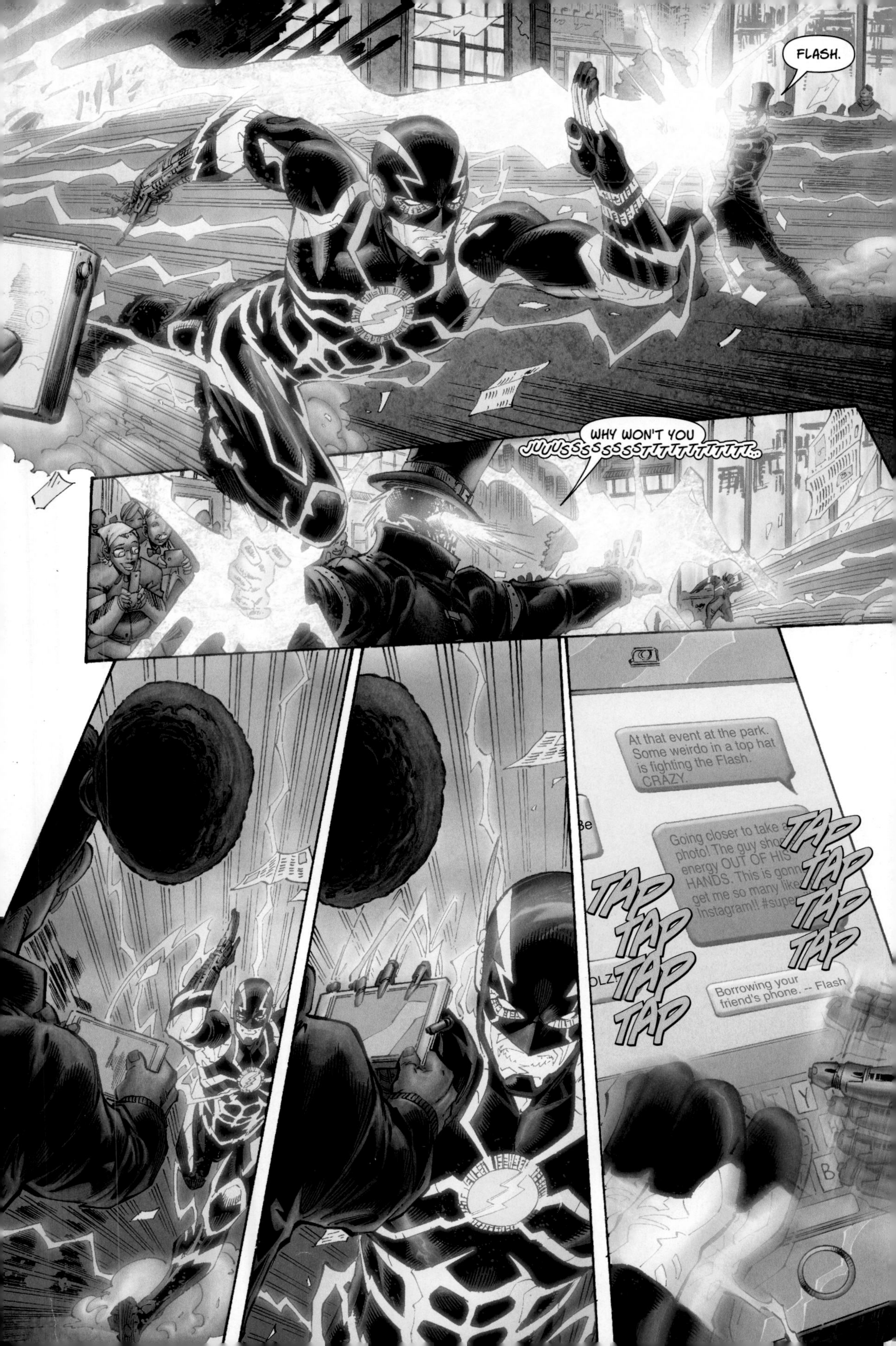
FLASH.
WHY WON'T YOU JUUUSSSSSSSSSTTTTTTTTTTTT...
At that event at the park. Some weirdo in a top hat is fighting the Flash. CRAZY.
Going closer to take a photo! The guy sho energy OUT OF HIS HANDS. This is gonn get me so many like Instagram!! #supe
TAP TAP TAP TAP
TAP TAP TAP TAP
Borrowing your friend's phone. -- Flash

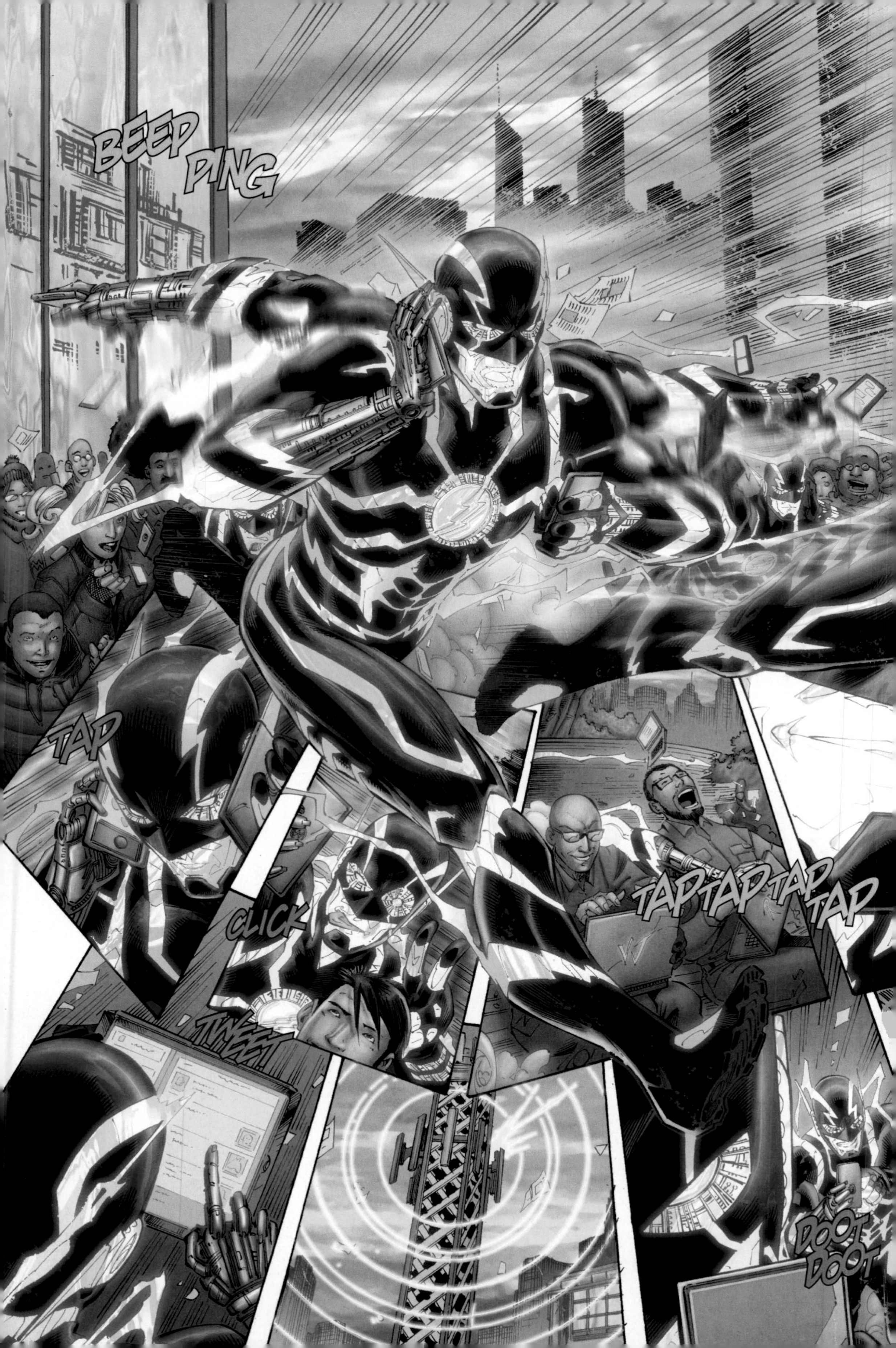
BEEP
PING
TAP
CLICK
TAP TAP TAP TAP
TWEET
DOOT DOOT

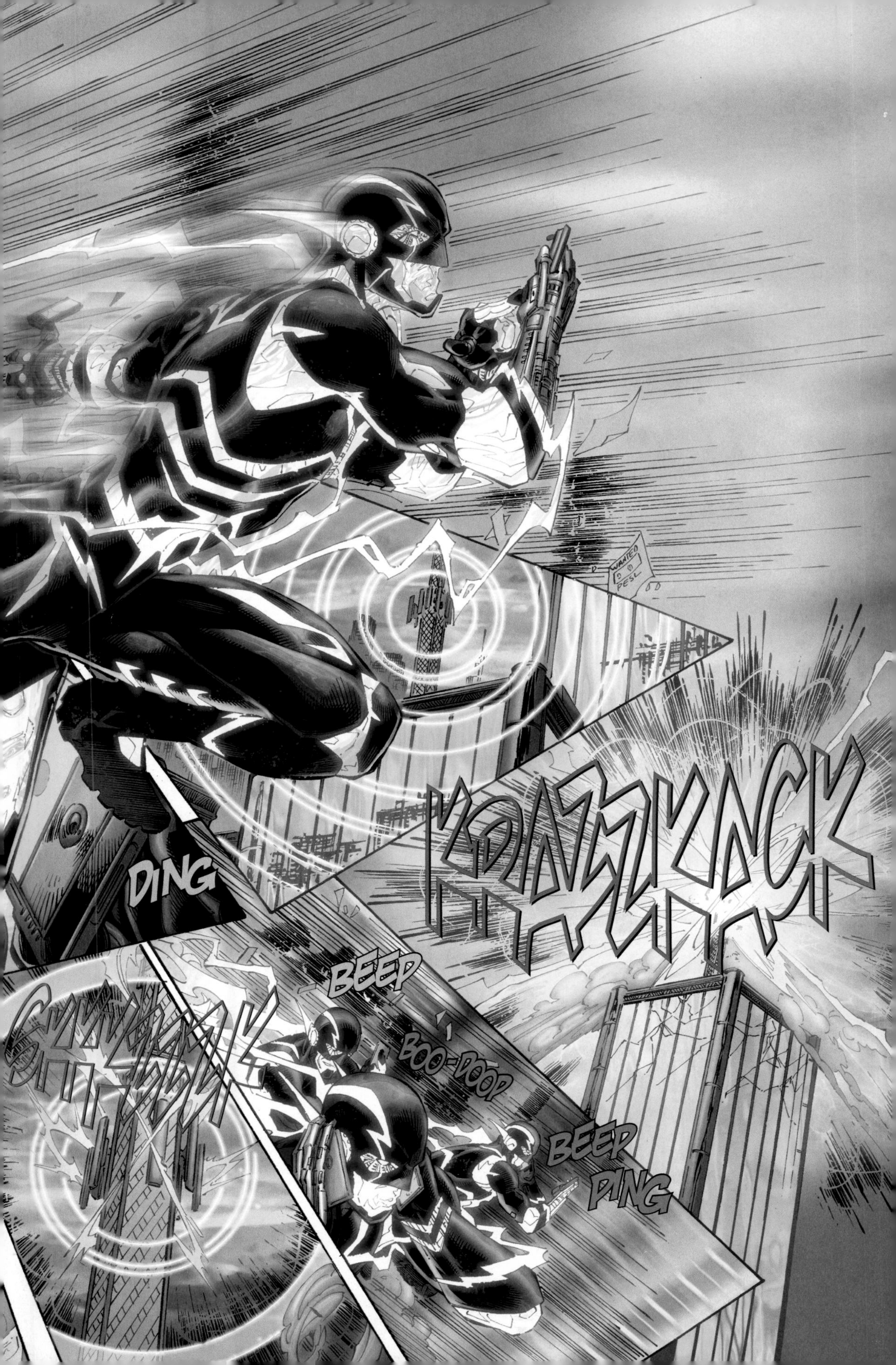
WANTED
PESL
DING
BEEP
BOO-DOOP
BEEP
DING

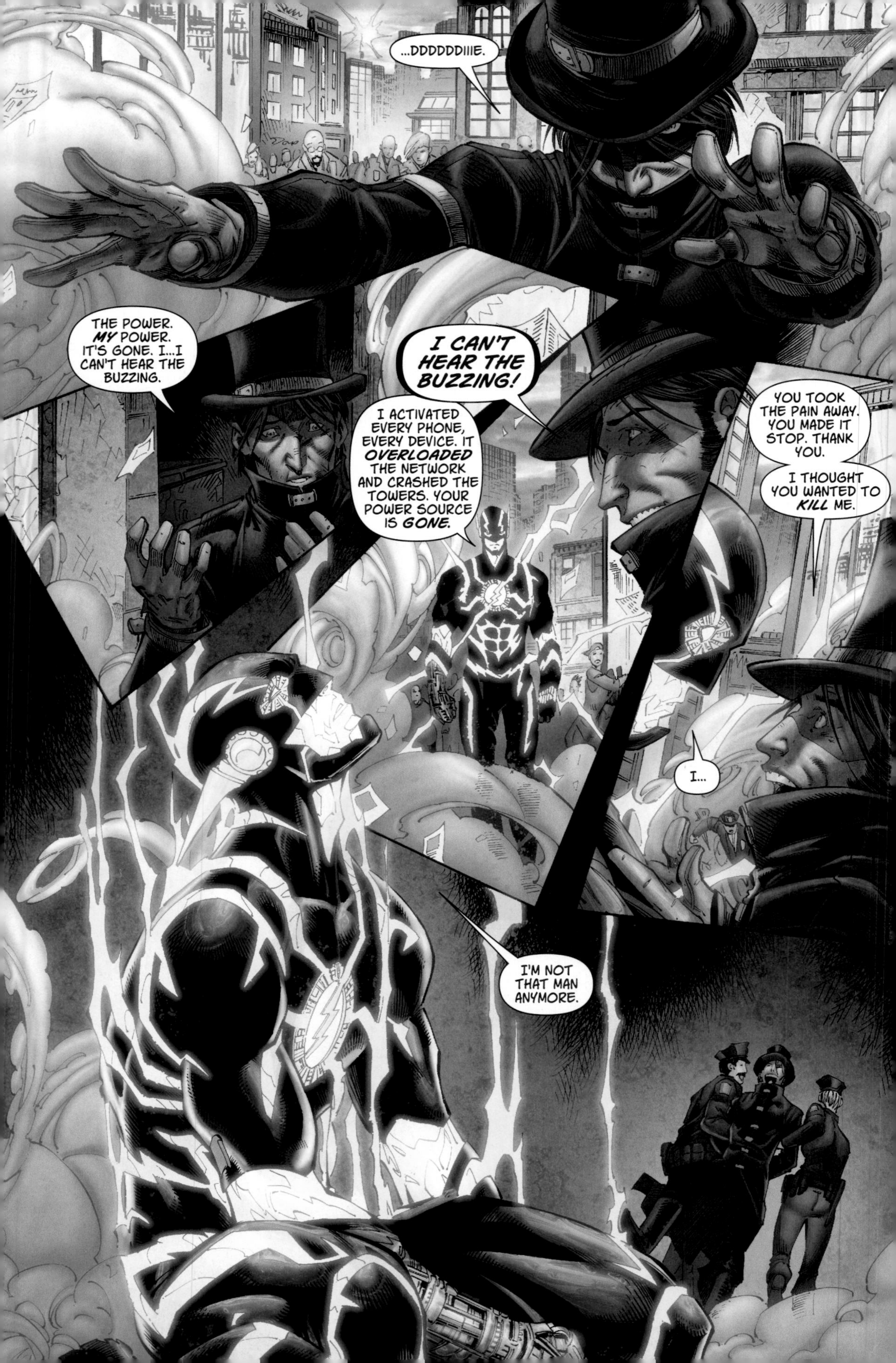
...DDDDDDIIIE.
THE POWER. MY POWER. IT'S GONE. I...I CAN'T HEAR THE BUZZING.
I CAN'T HEAR THE BUZZING!
I ACTIVATED EVERY PHONE, EVERY DEVICE. IT OVERLOADED THE NETWORK AND CRASHED THE TOWERS. YOUR POWER SOURCE IS GONE.
YOU TOOK THE PAIN AWAY. YOU MADE IT STOP. THANK YOU.
I THOUGHT YOU WANTED TO KILL ME.
I...
I'M NOT THAT MAN ANYMORE.

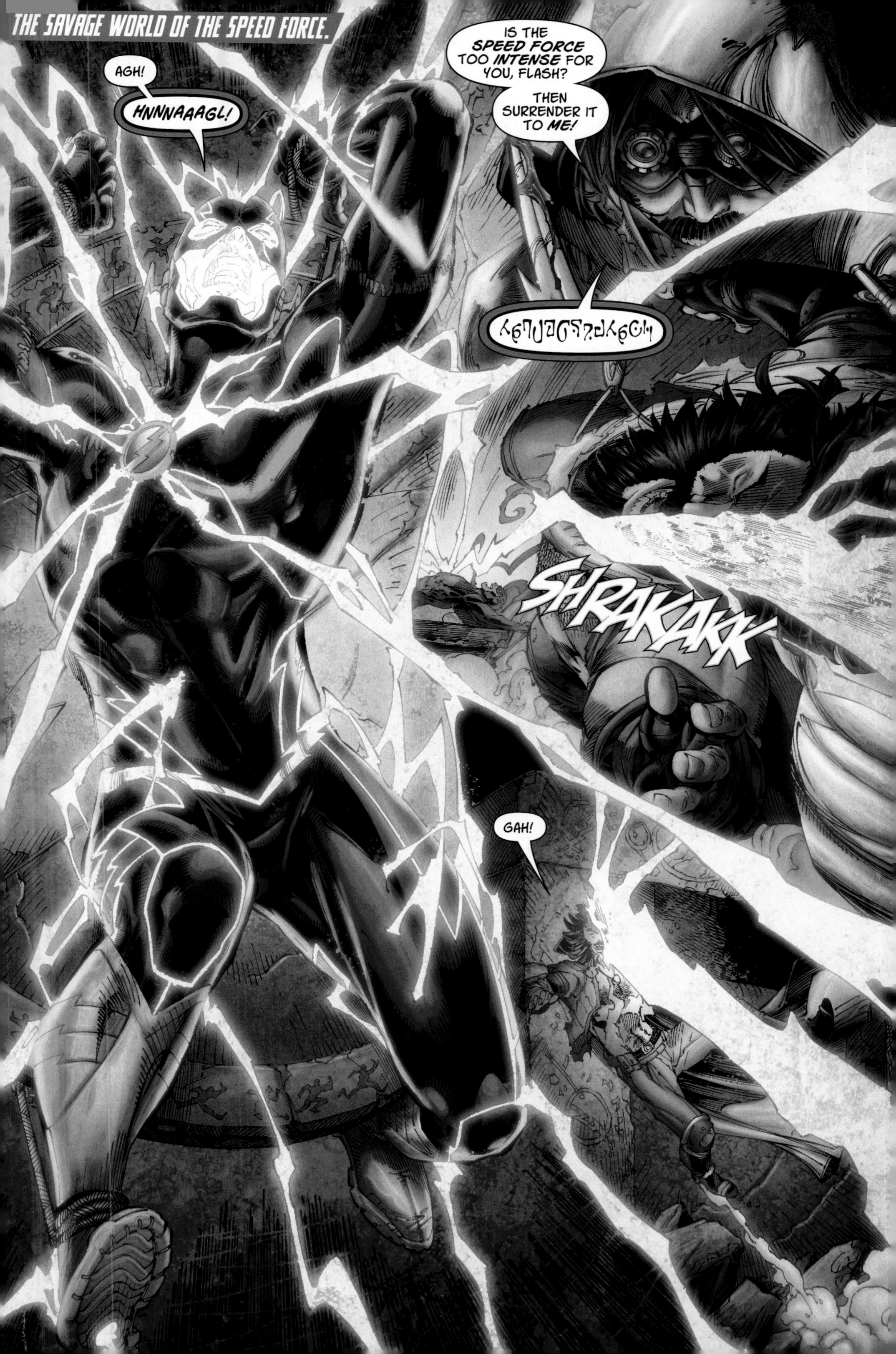
THE SAVAGE WORLD OF THE SPEED FORCE.
AGH!
HNNNAAAGL!
IS THE SPEED FORCE TOO INTENSE FOR YOU, FLASH?
THEN SURRENDER IT TO ME!
SHRAKAKK
GAH!

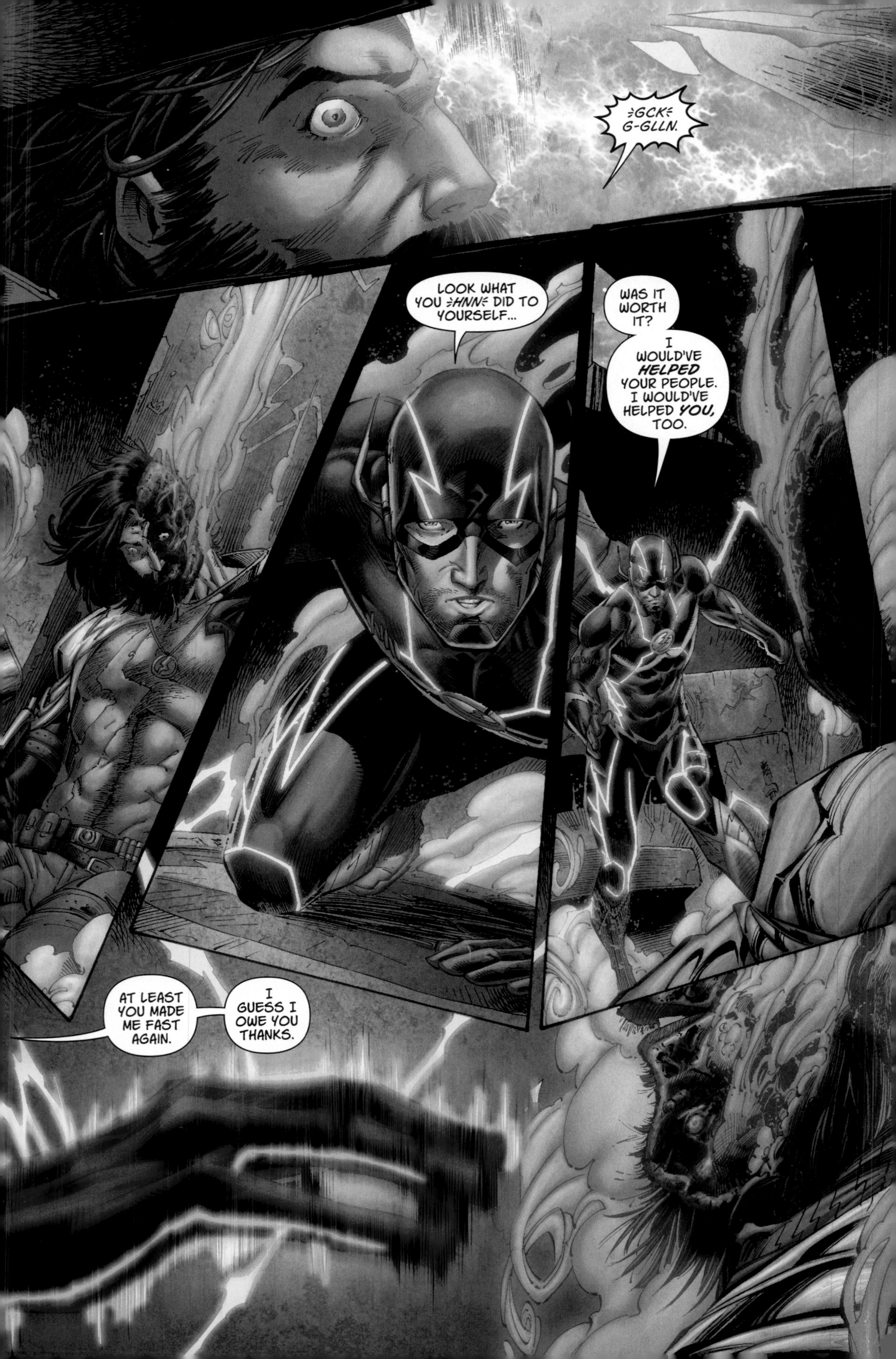

GCK G-GLLN.
LOOK WHAT YOU HNN DID TO YOURSELF...
WAS IT WORTH IT?
I WOULD'VE HELPED YOUR PEOPLE. I WOULD'VE HELPED YOU, TOO.
AT LEAST YOU MADE ME FAST AGAIN.
I GUESS I OWE YOU THANKS.

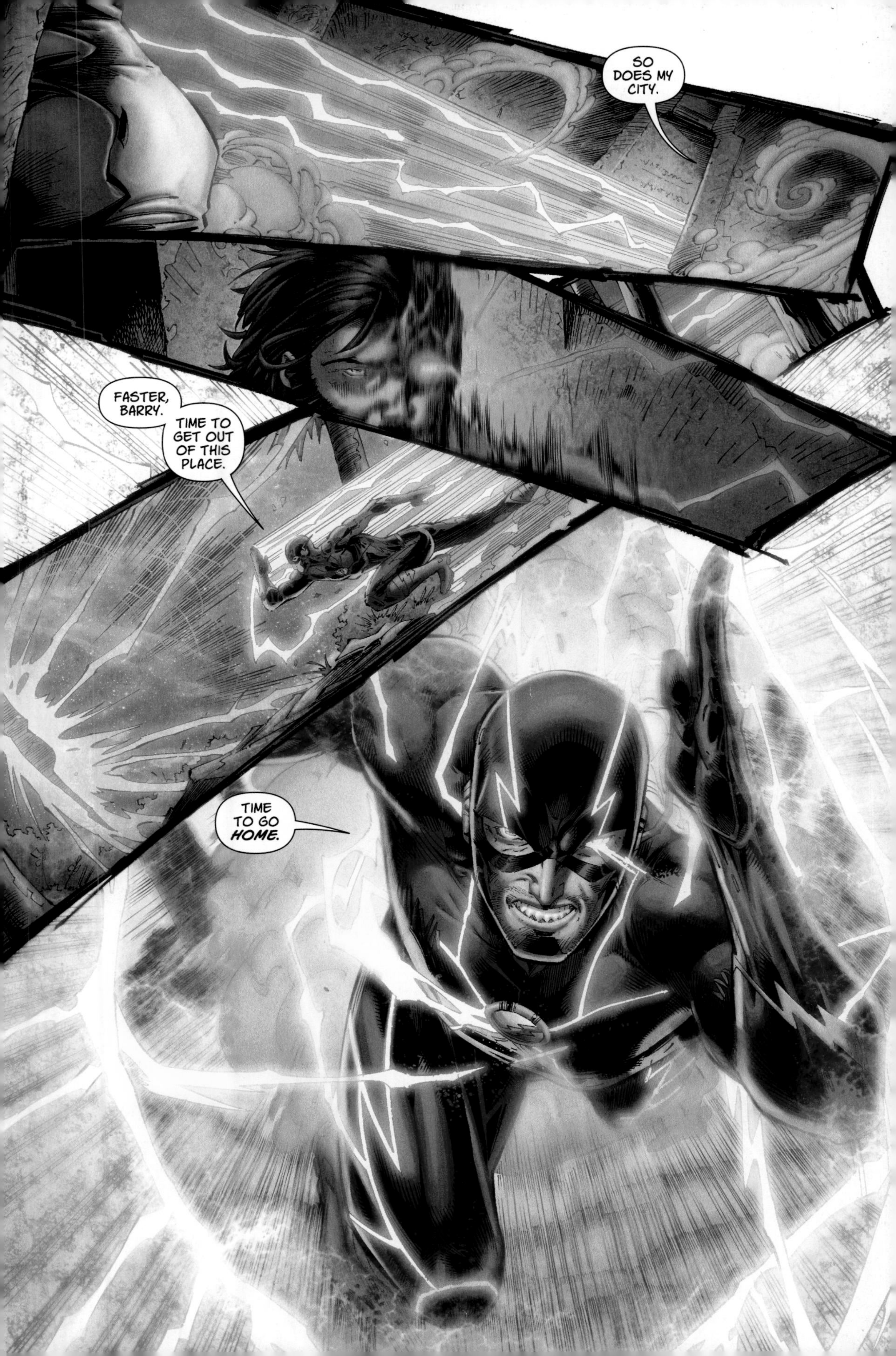
SO DOES MY CITY.
FASTER, BARRY.
TIME TO GET OUT OF THIS PLACE.
TIME TO GO HOME.

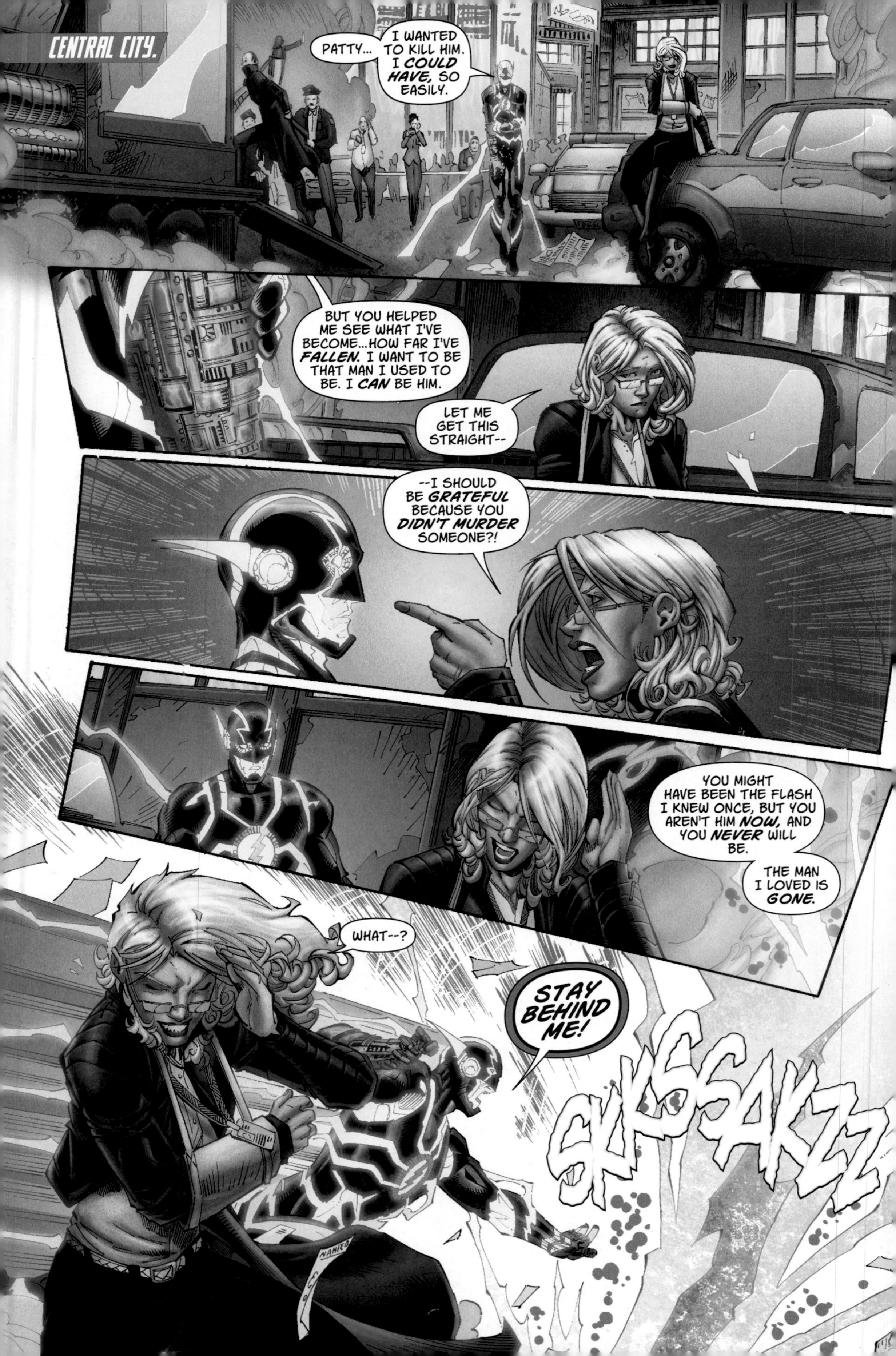
CENTRAL CITY.
PATTY...
I WANTED TO KILL HIM. I COULD HAVE, SO EASILY.
BUT YOU HELPED ME SEE WHAT I'VE BECOME...HOW FAR I'VE FALLEN. I WANT TO BE THAT MAN I USED TO BE. I CAN BE HIM.
LET ME GET THIS STRAIGHT--
--I SHOULD BE GRATEFUL BECAUSE YOU DIDN'T MURDER SOMEONE?!
YOU MIGHT HAVE BEEN THE FLASH I KNEW ONCE, BUT YOU AREN'T HIM NOW, AND YOU NEVER WILL BE.
THE MAN I LOVED IS GONE.
WHAT--?
STAY BEHIND ME!
SKKSSAKZZ

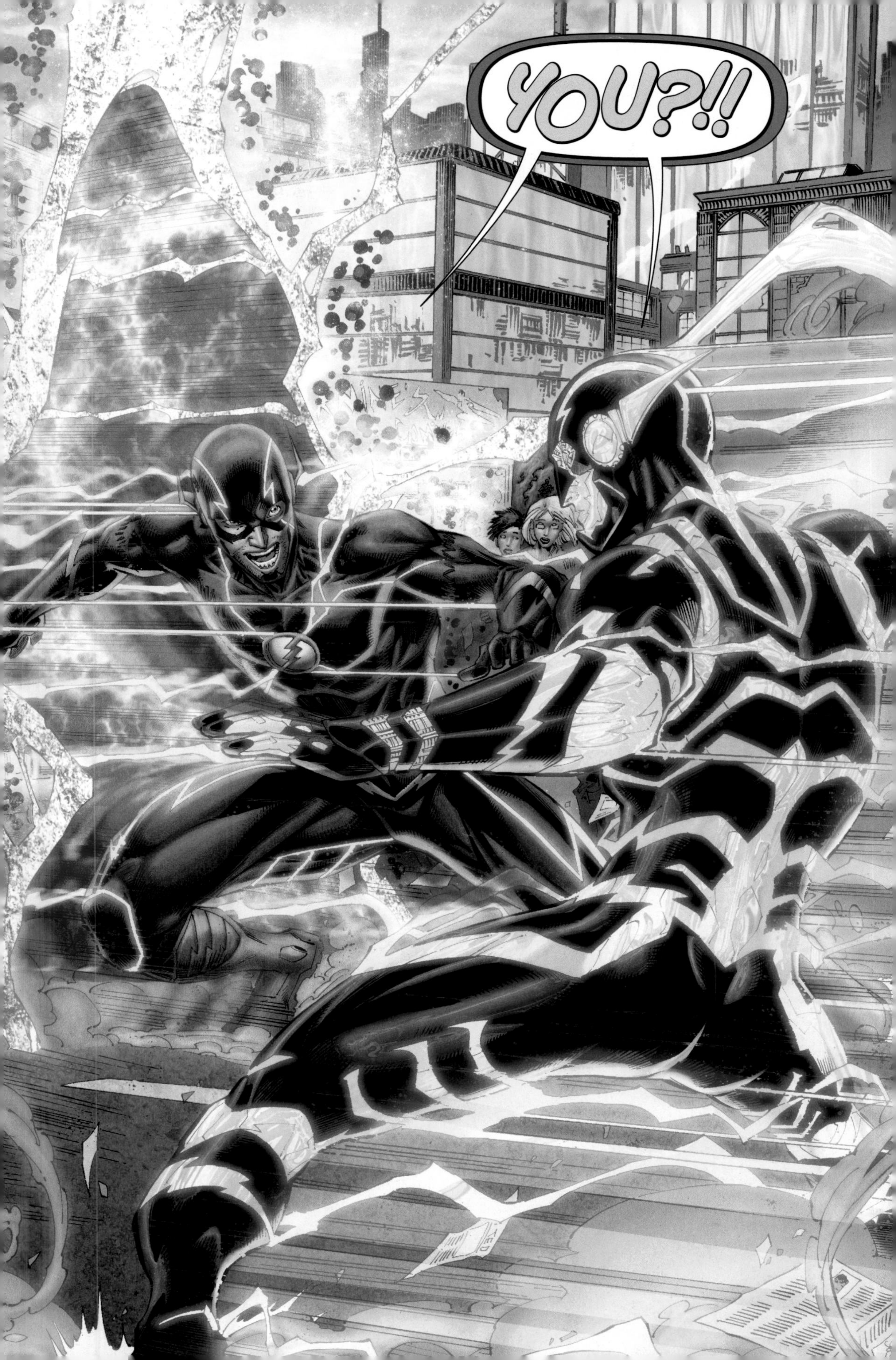
YOU?!!

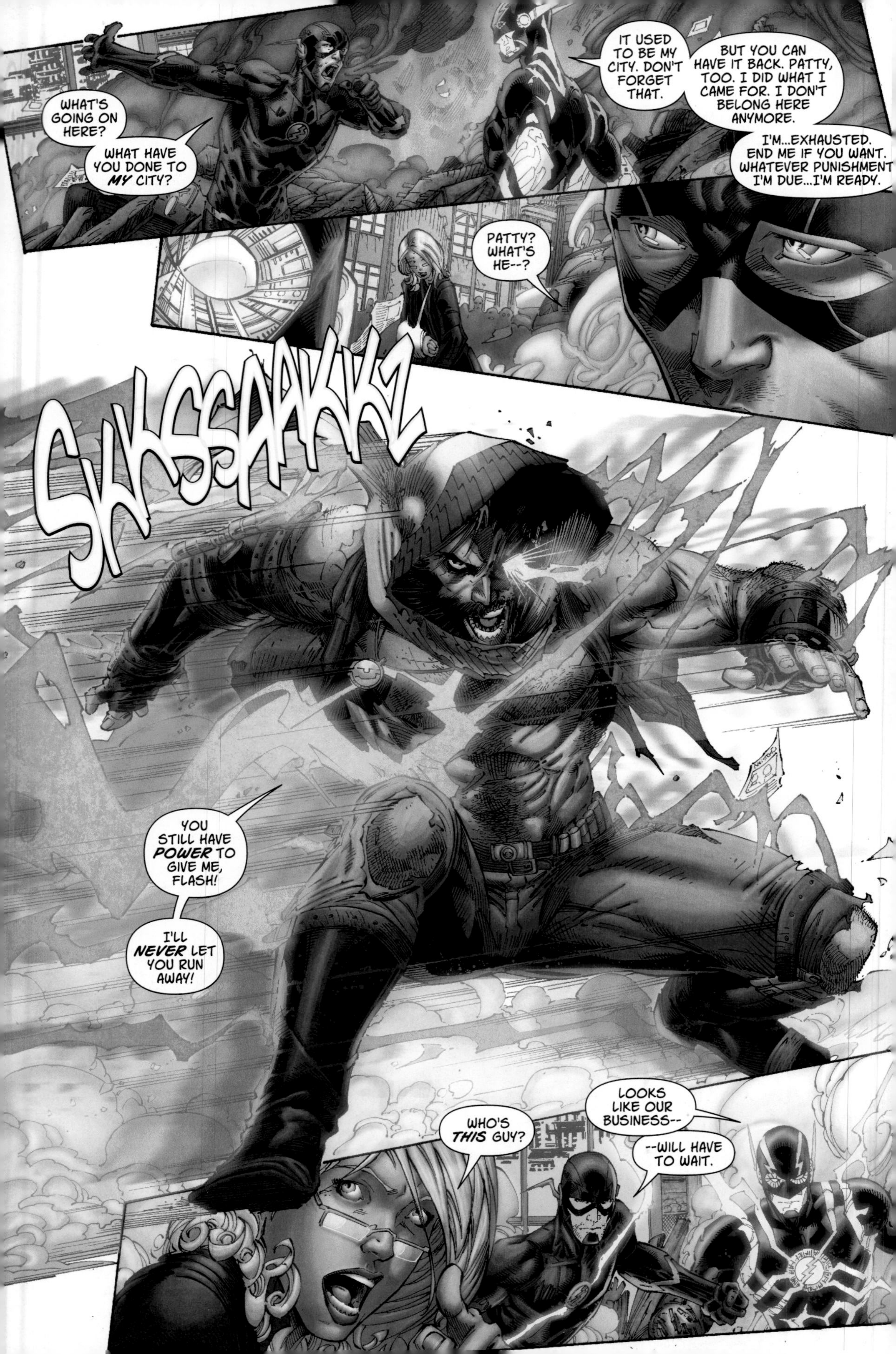
WHAT'S GOING ON HERE?
WHAT HAVE YOU DONE TO MY CITY?
IT USED TO BE MY CITY. DON'T FORGET THAT.
BUT YOU CAN HAVE IT BACK. PATTY, TOO. I DID WHAT I CAME FOR. I DON'T BELONG HERE ANYMORE.
I'M...EXHAUSTED. END ME IF YOU WANT. WHATEVER PUNISHMENT I'M DUE...I'M READY.
PATTY? WHAT'S HE--?
SKKSSAKKZ
YOU STILL HAVE POWER TO GIVE ME, FLASH!
I'LL NEVER LET YOU RUN AWAY!
WHO'S THIS GUY?
LOOKS LIKE OUR BUSINESS--
--WILL HAVE TO WAIT.

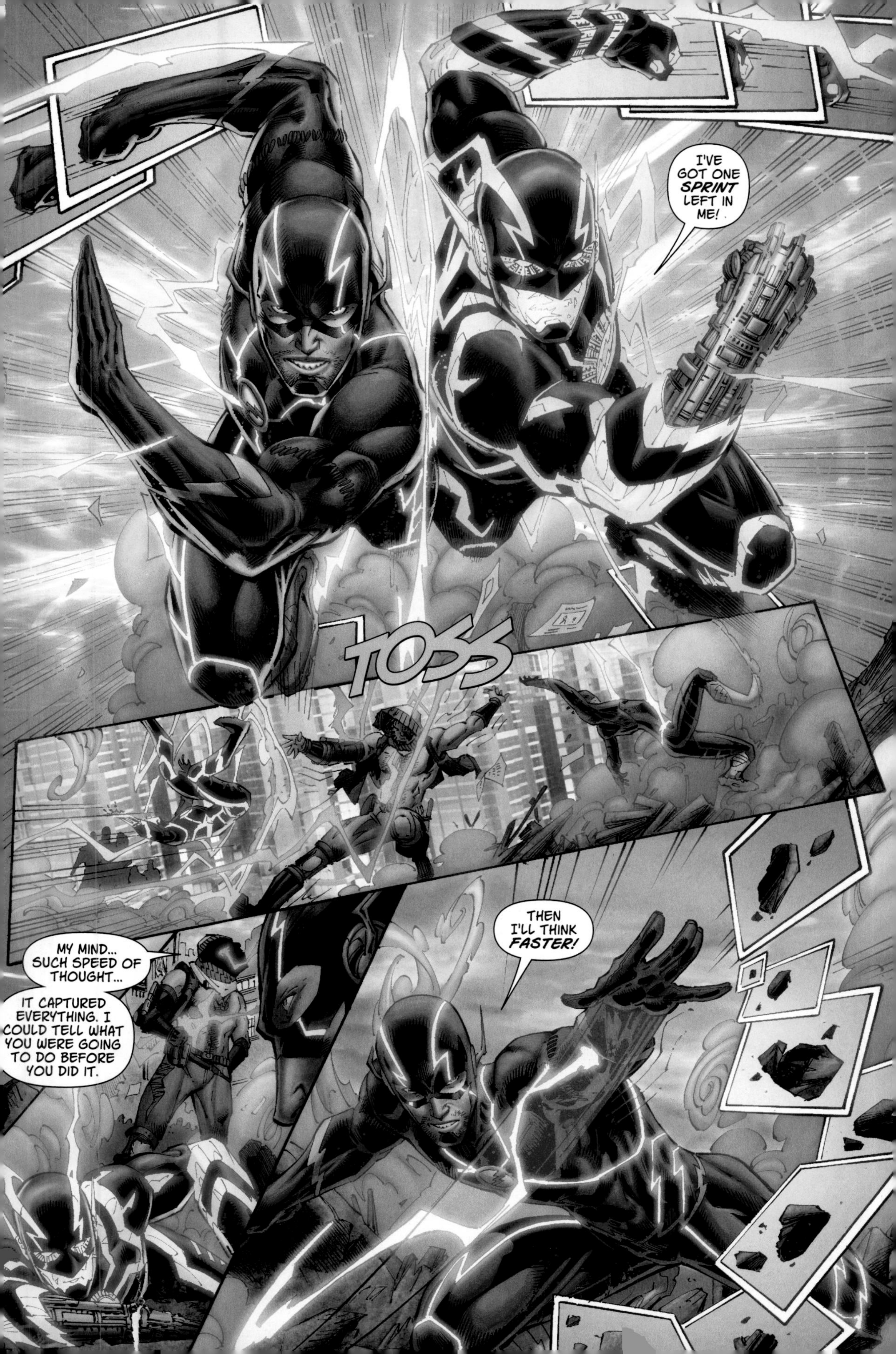
I'VE GOT ONE SPRINT LEFT IN ME!
TOSS
MY MIND... SUCH SPEED OF THOUGHT...
IT CAPTURED EVERYTHING. I COULD TELL WHAT YOU WERE GOING TO DO BEFORE YOU DID IT.
THEN I'LL THINK FASTER!

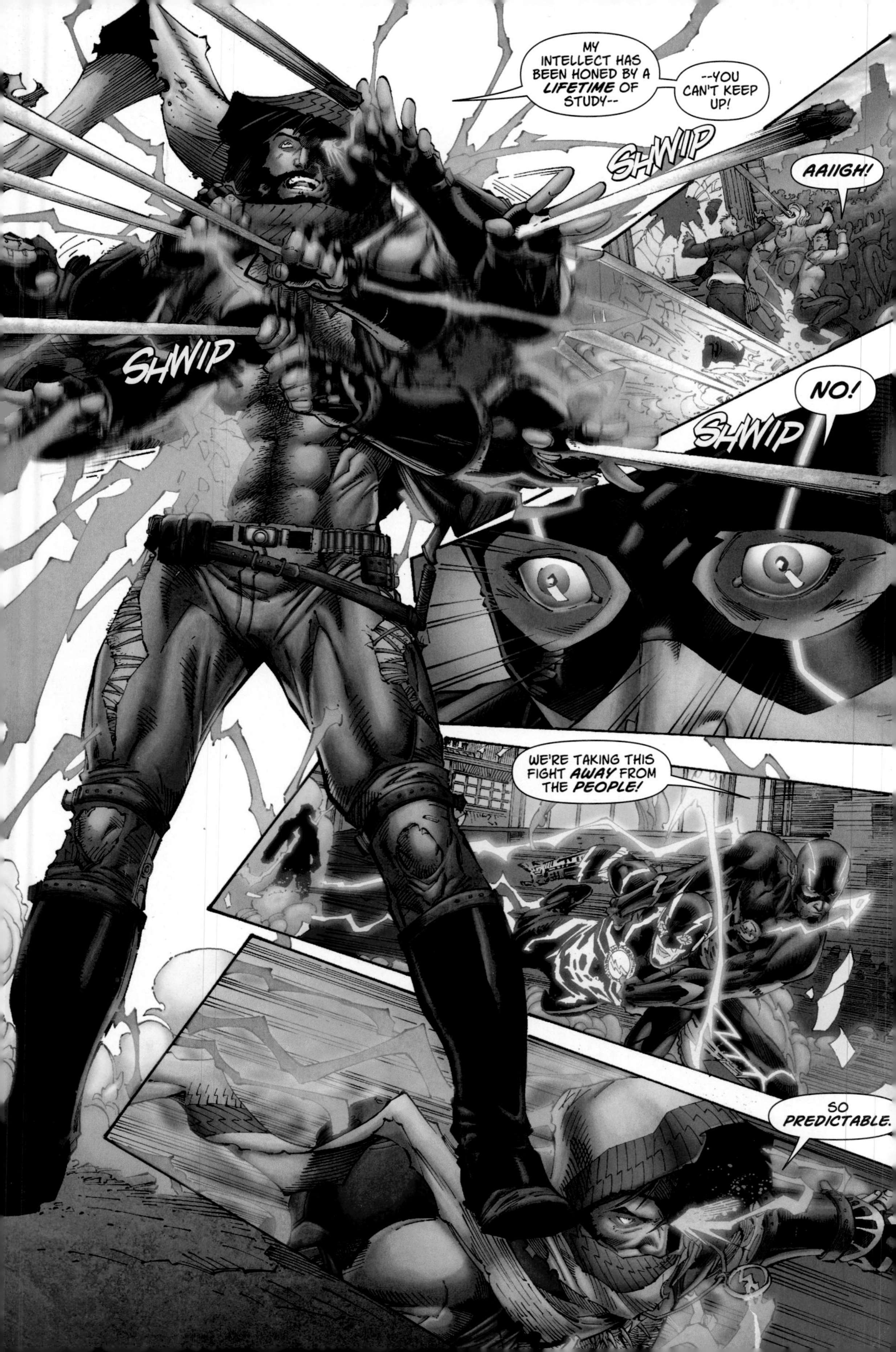
MY INTELLECT HAS BEEN HONED BY A LIFETIME OF STUDY--
--YOU CAN'T KEEP UP!
SHWIP
AAIIGH!
SHWIP
NO!
SHWIP
WE'RE TAKING THIS FIGHT AWAY FROM THE PEOPLE!
SO PREDICTABLE.

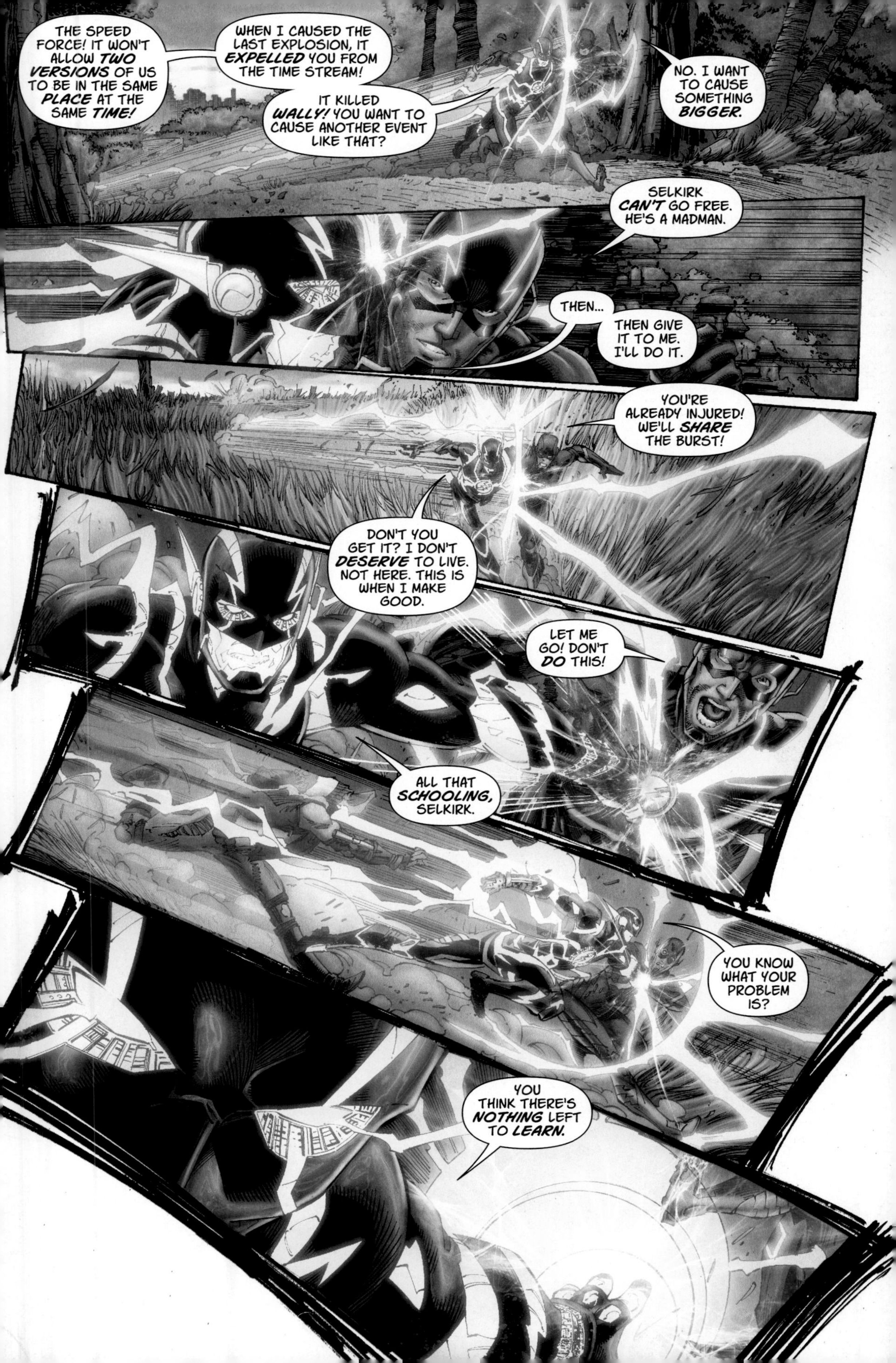
THE SPEED FORCE! IT WON'T ALLOW TWO VERSIONS OF US TO BE IN THE SAME PLACE AT THE SAME TIME!
WHEN I CAUSED THE LAST EXPLOSION, IT EXPELLED YOU FROM THE TIME STREAM!
IT KILLED WALLY! YOU WANT TO CAUSE ANOTHER EVENT LIKE THAT?
NO. I WANT TO CAUSE SOMETHING BIGGER.
SELKIRK CAN'T GO FREE. HE'S A MADMAN.
THEN...
THEN GIVE IT TO ME. I'LL DO IT.
YOU'RE ALREADY INJURED! WE'LL SHARE THE BURST!
DON'T YOU GET IT? I DON'T DESERVE TO LIVE. NOT HERE. THIS IS WHEN I MAKE GOOD.
LET ME GO! DON'T DO THIS!
ALL THAT SCHOOLING, SELKIRK.
YOU KNOW WHAT YOUR PROBLEM IS?
YOU THINK THERE'S NOTHING LEFT TO LEARN.

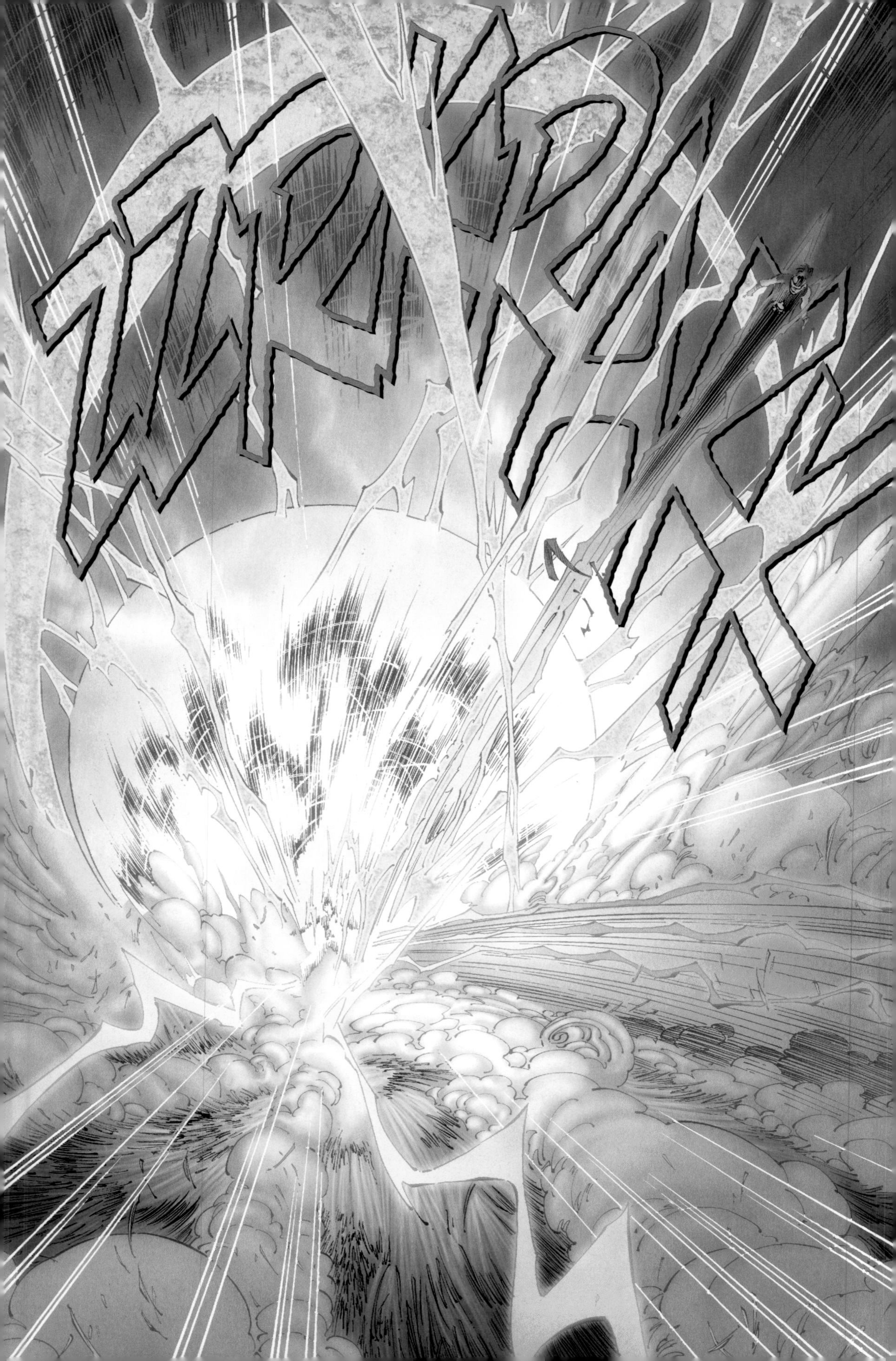

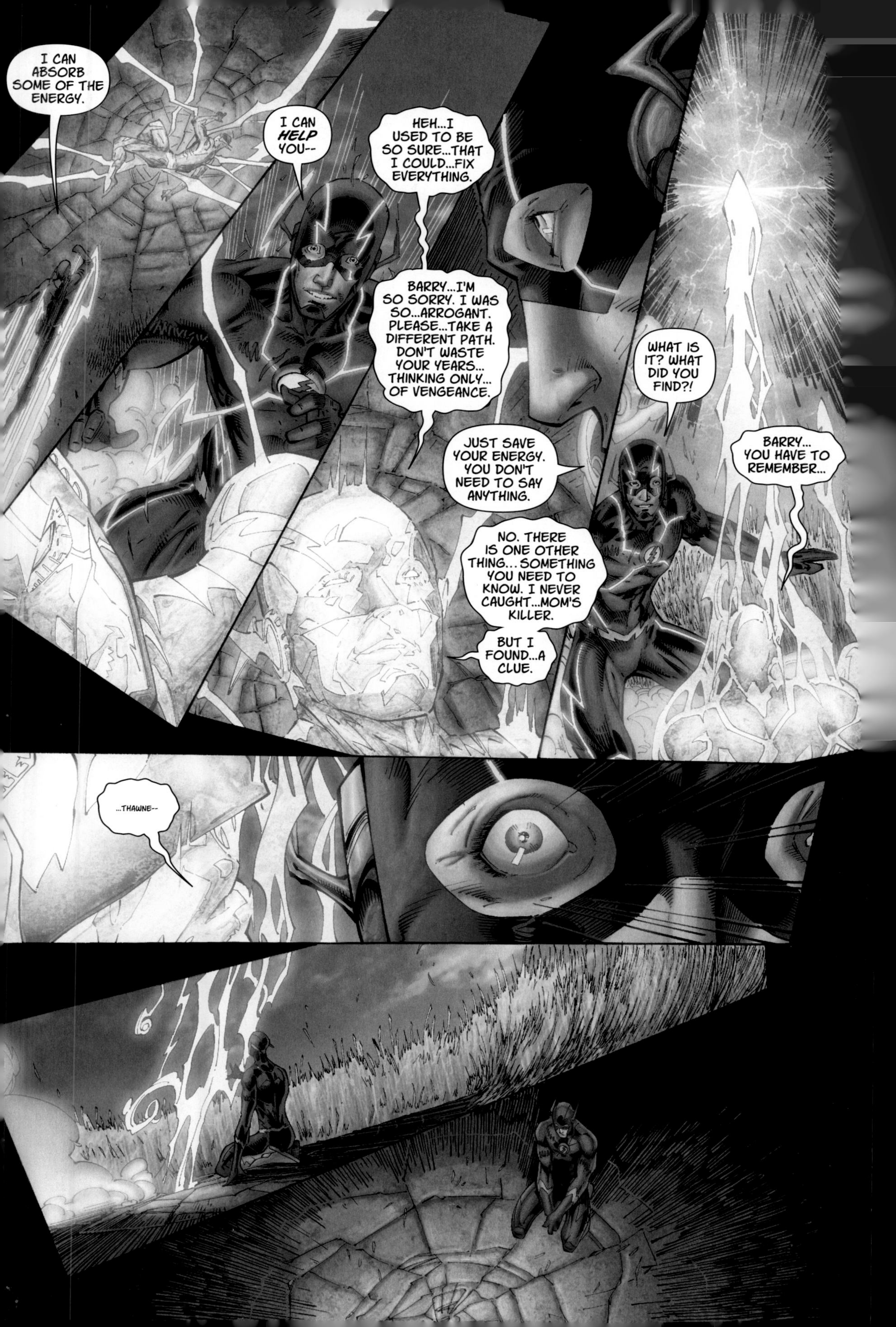

I CAN ABSORB SOME OF THE ENERGY.
I CAN *HELP* YOU--
HEH...I USED TO BE SO SURE...THAT I COULD...FIX EVERYTHING.
BARRY...I'M SO SORRY. I WAS SO...ARROGANT. PLEASE...TAKE A DIFFERENT PATH. DON'T WASTE YOUR YEARS... THINKING ONLY... OF VENGEANCE.
JUST SAVE YOUR ENERGY. YOU DON'T NEED TO SAY ANYTHING.
NO. THERE IS ONE OTHER THING... SOMETHING YOU NEED TO KNOW. I NEVER CAUGHT...MOM'S KILLER.
BUT I FOUND...A CLUE.
WHAT IS IT? WHAT DID YOU FIND?!
BARRY... YOU HAVE TO REMEMBER...
...THAWNE--

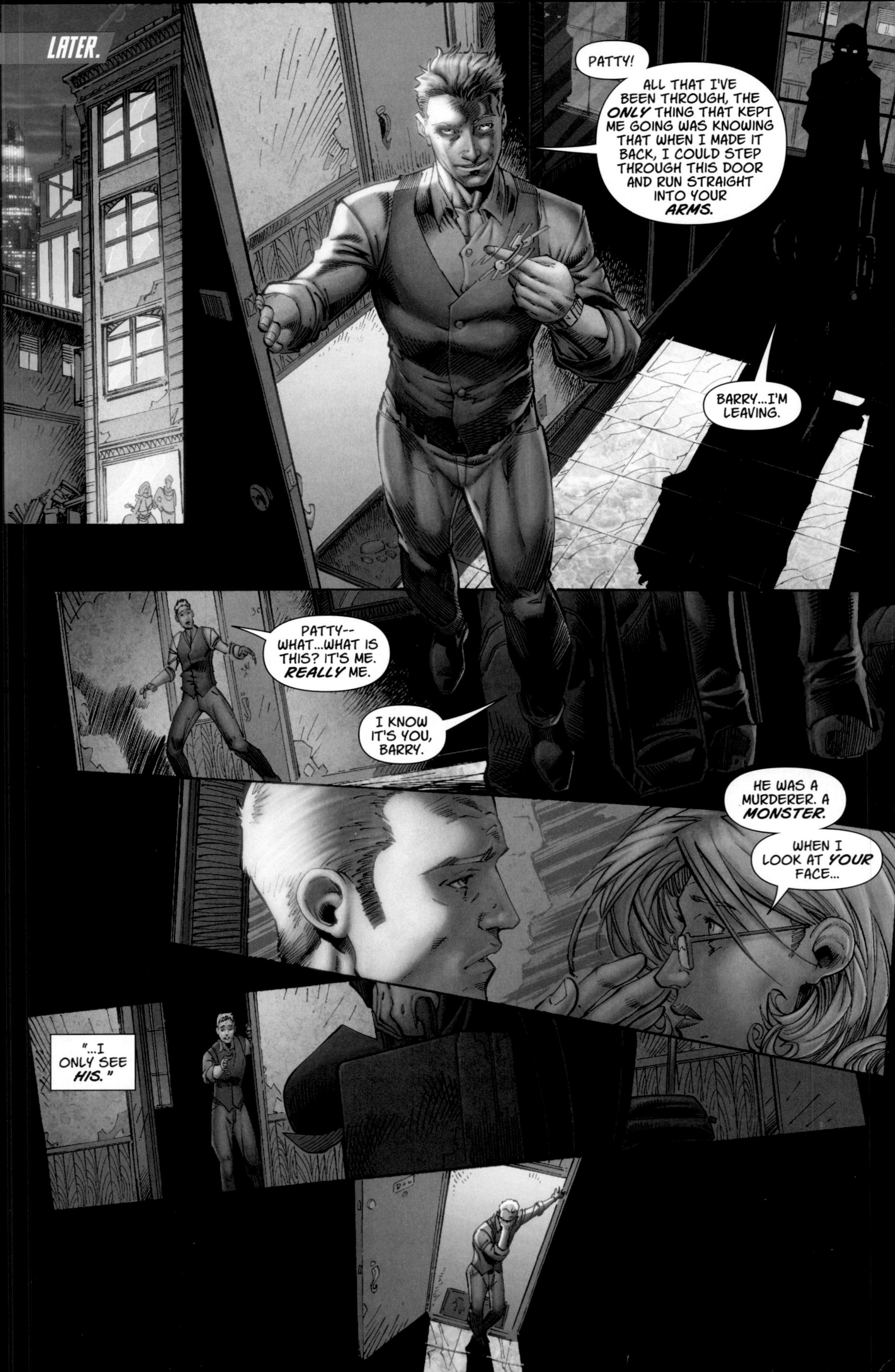
LATER.
PATTY!
ALL THAT I'VE BEEN THROUGH, THE ONLY THING THAT KEPT ME GOING WAS KNOWING THAT WHEN I MADE IT BACK, I COULD STEP THROUGH THIS DOOR AND RUN STRAIGHT INTO YOUR ARMS.
BARRY...I'M LEAVING.
PATTY-- WHAT...WHAT IS THIS? IT'S ME. REALLY ME.
I KNOW IT'S YOU, BARRY.
HE WAS A MURDERER. A MONSTER.
WHEN I LOOK AT YOUR FACE...
"...I ONLY SEE HIS."

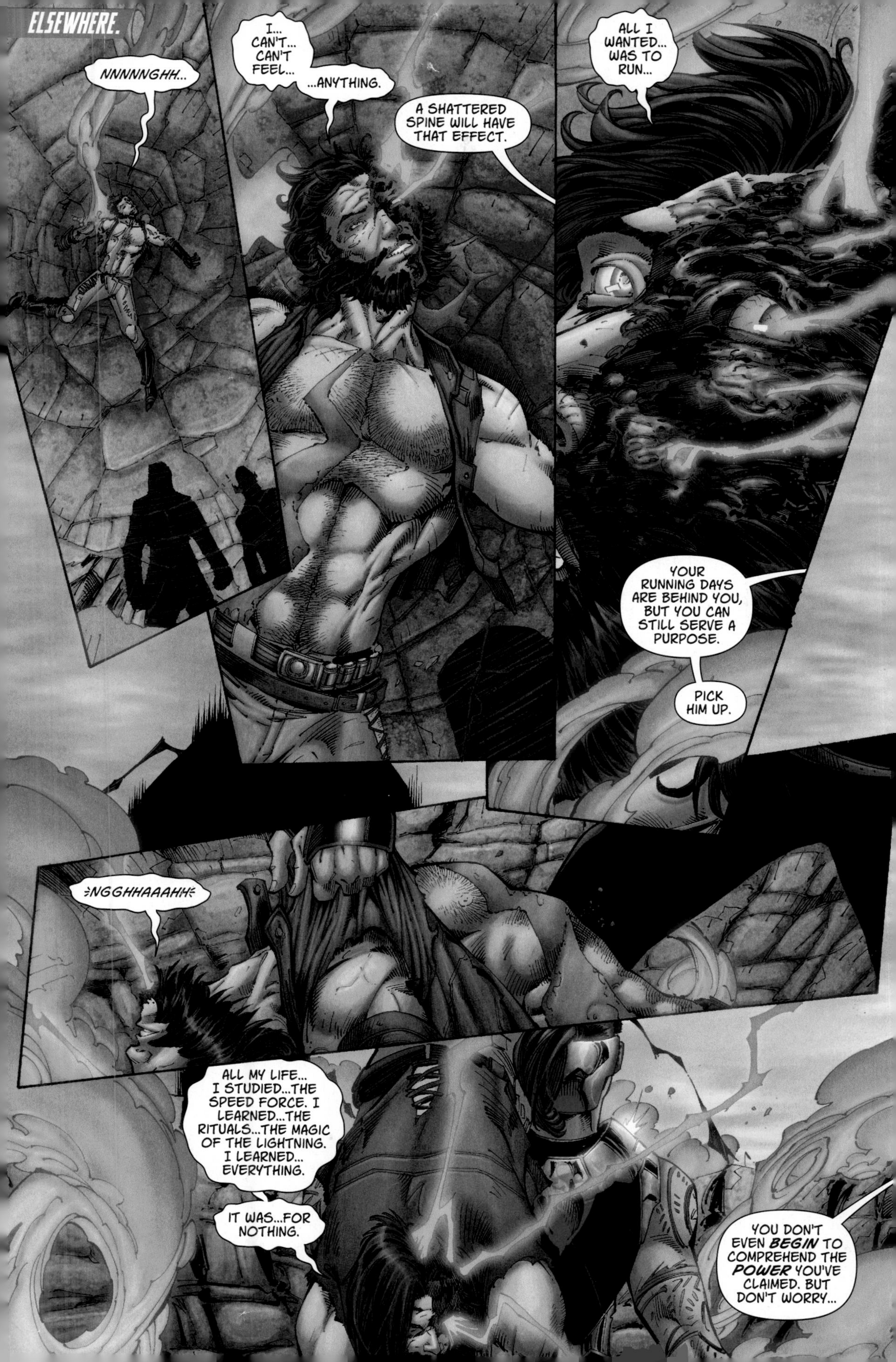
ELSEWHERE.
NNNNNGHH...
I... CAN'T... CAN'T FEEL...
...ANYTHING.
A SHATTERED SPINE WILL HAVE THAT EFFECT.
ALL I WANTED... WAS TO RUN...
YOUR RUNNING DAYS ARE BEHIND YOU, BUT YOU CAN STILL SERVE A PURPOSE.
PICK HIM UP.
NGGHHAAAHH
ALL MY LIFE... I STUDIED...THE SPEED FORCE. I LEARNED...THE RITUALS...THE MAGIC OF THE LIGHTNING. I LEARNED... EVERYTHING.
IT WAS...FOR NOTHING.
YOU DON'T EVEN BEGIN TO COMPREHEND THE POWER YOU'VE CLAIMED. BUT DON'T WORRY...

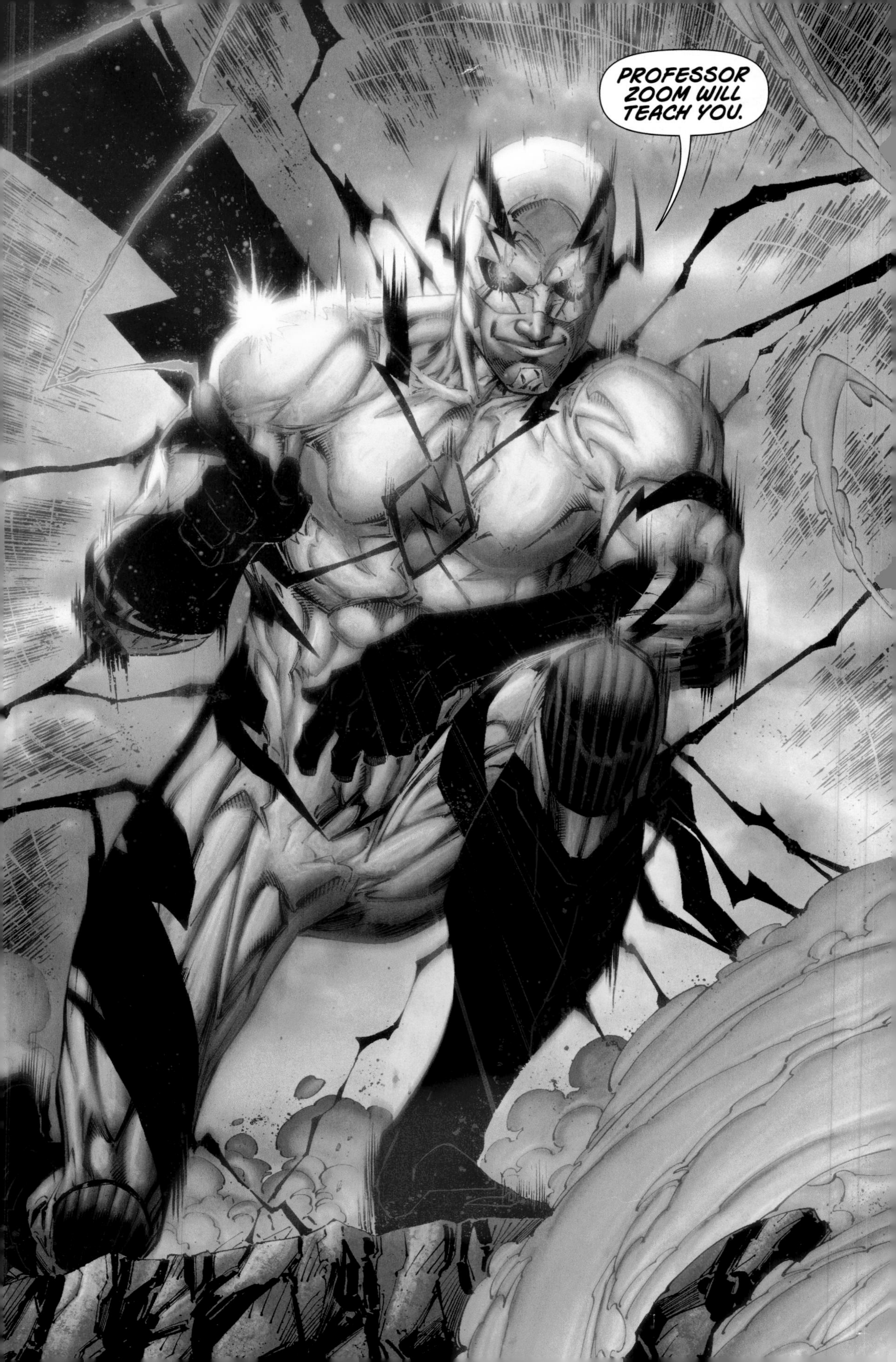
PROFESSOR ZOOM WILL TEACH YOU.

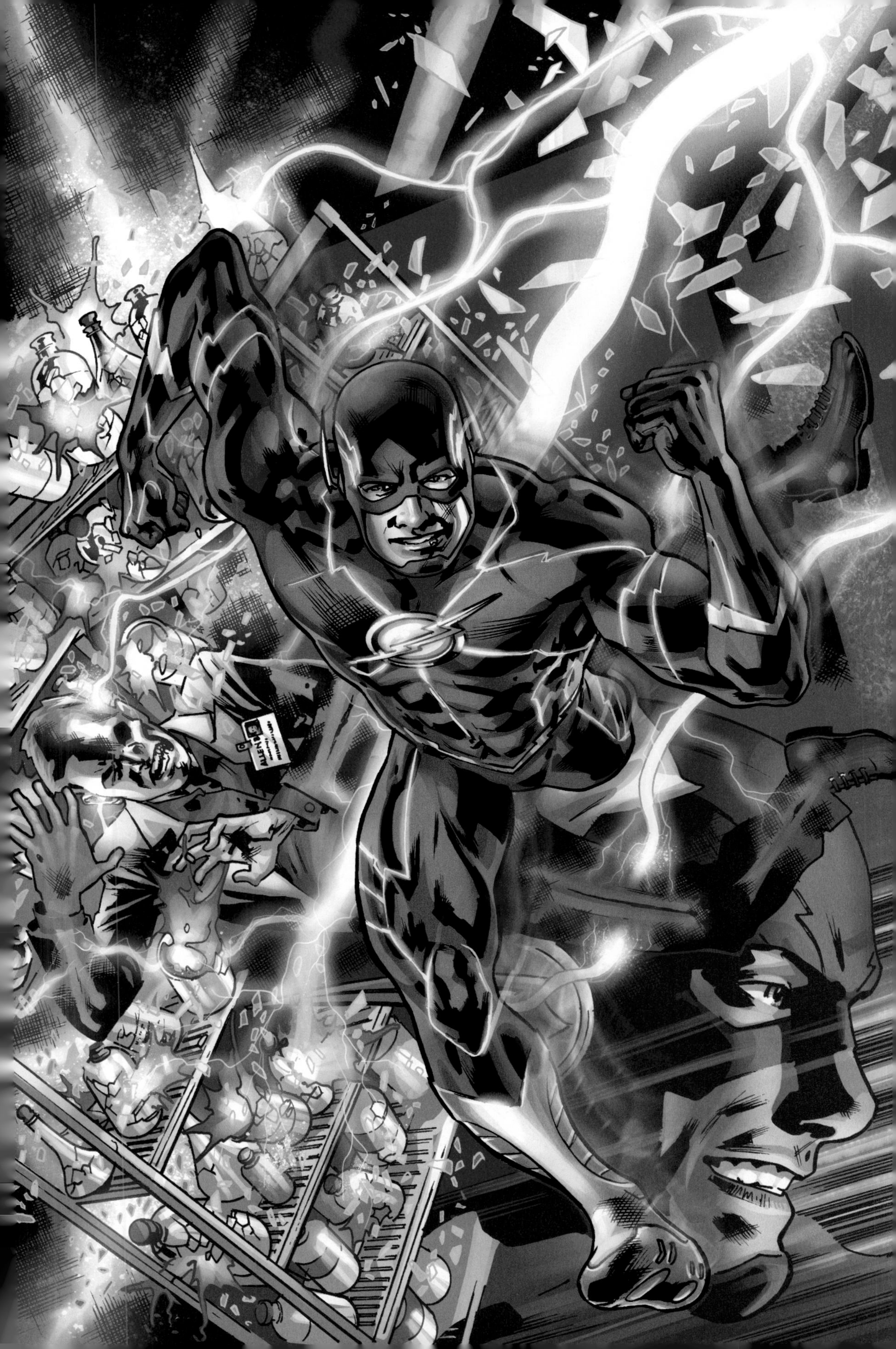
ALLEN

THE CHASE

ROBERT VENDITTI & VAN JENSEN writers **MIGUEL SEPULVEDA** penciller **SCOTT HANNA** inker **ANDREW DALHOUSE** colorist **TAYLOR ESPOSITO** letterer
cover by **BRYAN HITCH & ALEX SINCLAIR**

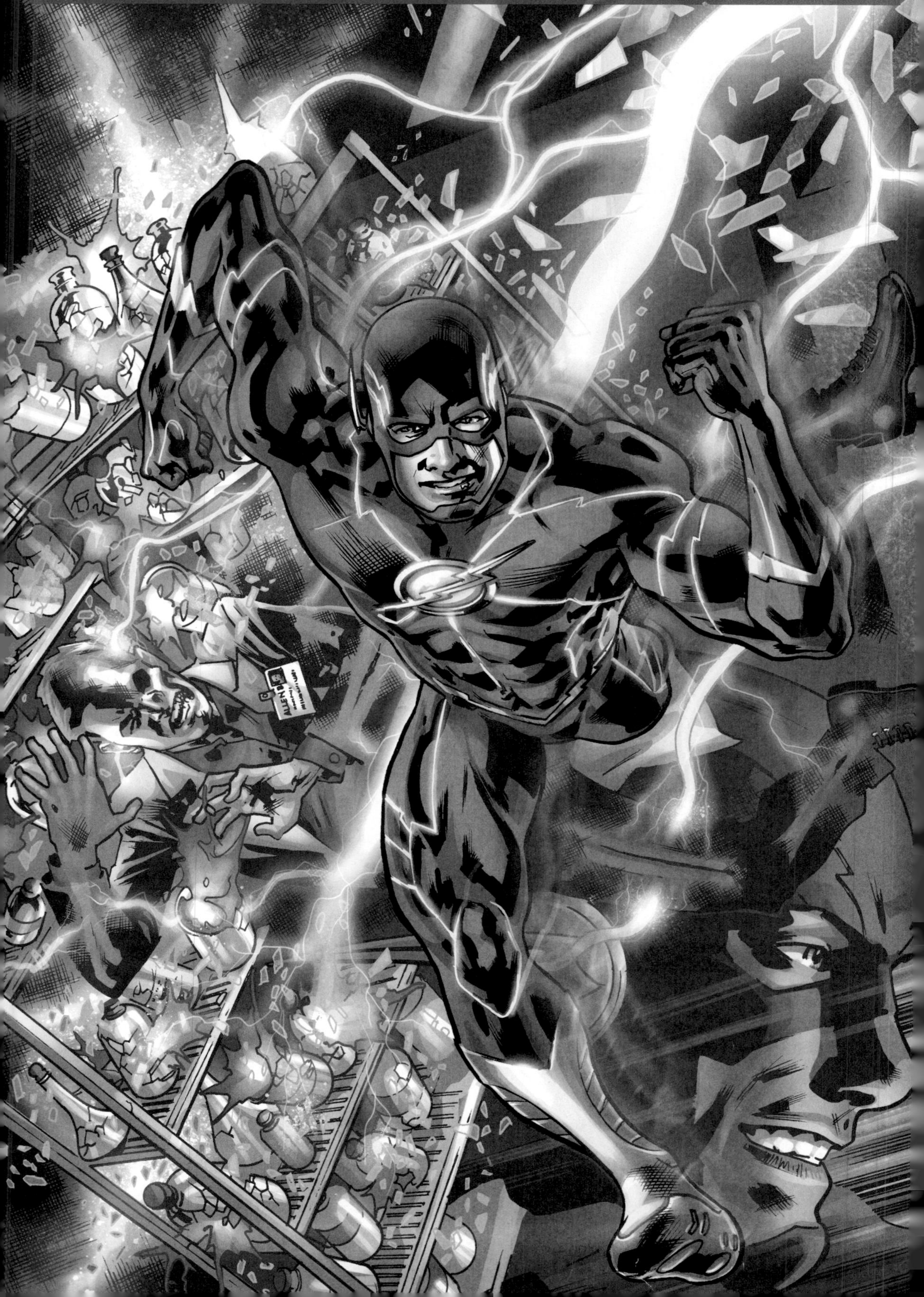

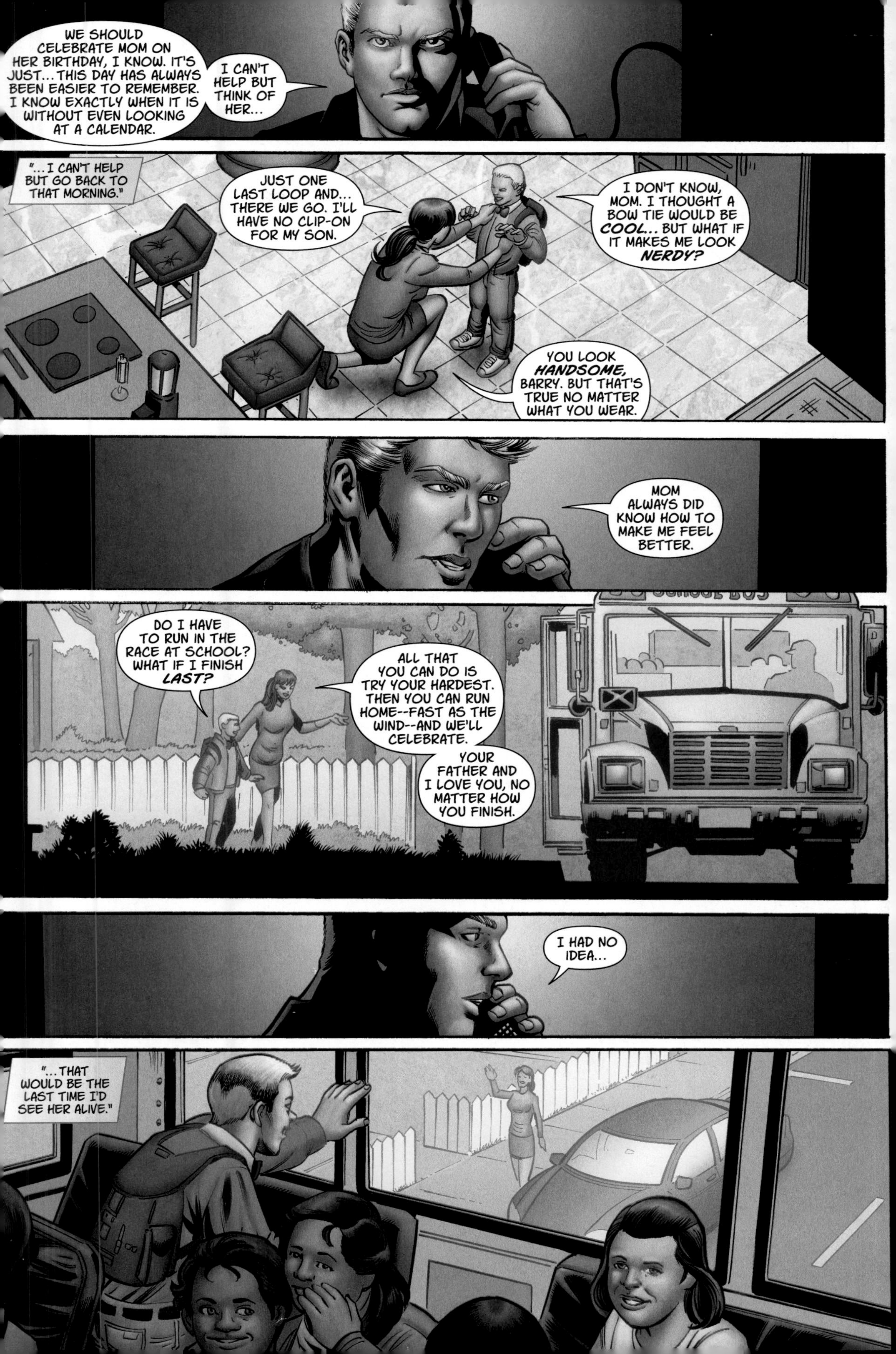
WE SHOULD CELEBRATE MOM ON HER BIRTHDAY, I KNOW. IT'S JUST... THIS DAY HAS ALWAYS BEEN EASIER TO REMEMBER. I KNOW EXACTLY WHEN IT IS WITHOUT EVEN LOOKING AT A CALENDAR.
I CAN'T HELP BUT THINK OF HER...
"...I CAN'T HELP BUT GO BACK TO THAT MORNING."
JUST ONE LAST LOOP AND... THERE WE GO. I'LL HAVE NO CLIP-ON FOR MY SON.
I DON'T KNOW, MOM. I THOUGHT A BOW TIE WOULD BE COOL... BUT WHAT IF IT MAKES ME LOOK NERDY?
YOU LOOK HANDSOME, BARRY. BUT THAT'S TRUE NO MATTER WHAT YOU WEAR.
MOM ALWAYS DID KNOW HOW TO MAKE ME FEEL BETTER.
DO I HAVE TO RUN IN THE RACE AT SCHOOL? WHAT IF I FINISH LAST?
ALL THAT YOU CAN DO IS TRY YOUR HARDEST. THEN YOU CAN RUN HOME--FAST AS THE WIND--AND WE'LL CELEBRATE.
YOUR FATHER AND I LOVE YOU, NO MATTER HOW YOU FINISH.
I HAD NO IDEA...
"...THAT WOULD BE THE LAST TIME I'D SEE HER ALIVE."

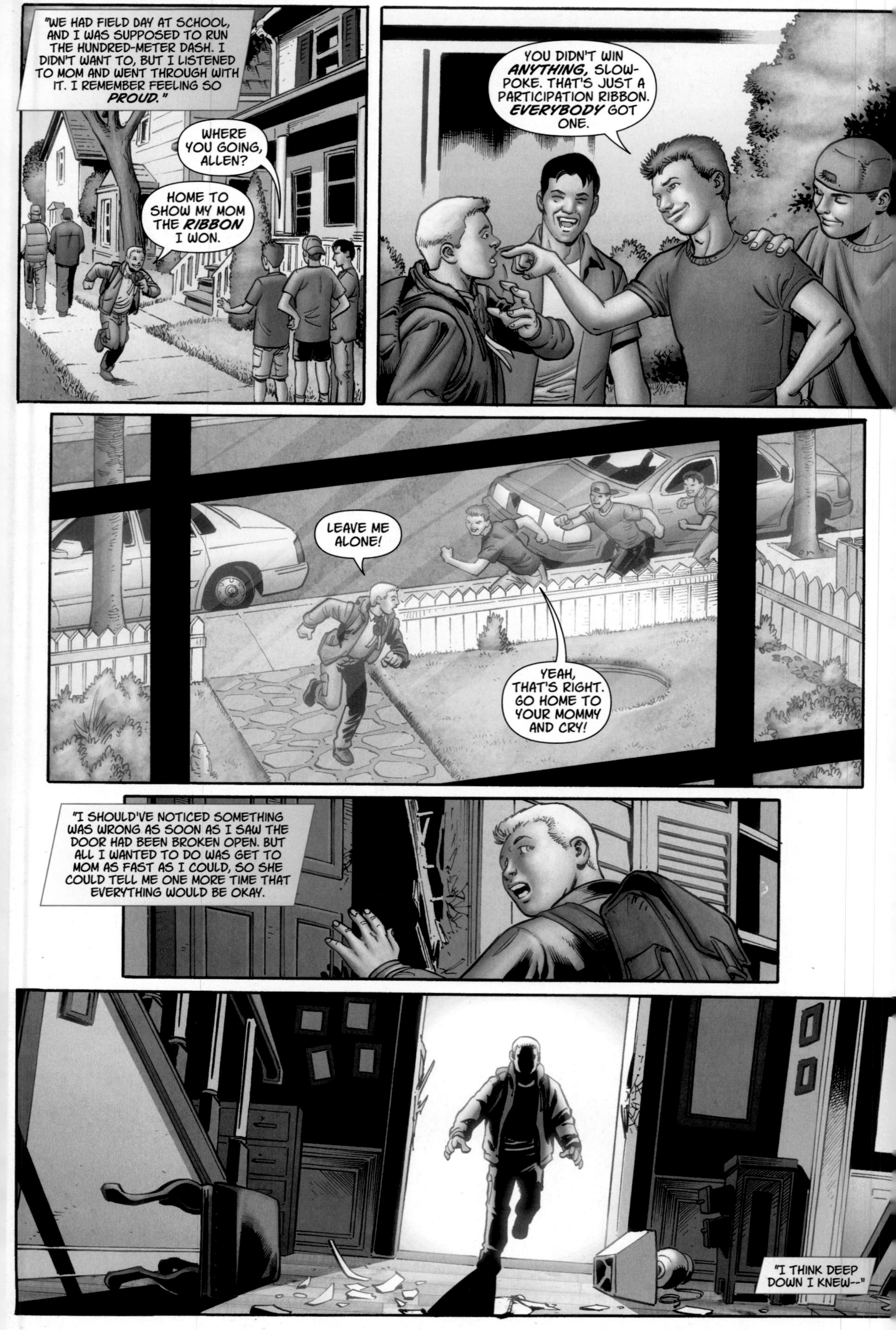
"WE HAD FIELD DAY AT SCHOOL, AND I WAS SUPPOSED TO RUN THE HUNDRED-METER DASH. I DIDN'T WANT TO, BUT I LISTENED TO MOM AND WENT THROUGH WITH IT. I REMEMBER FEELING SO PROUD."
WHERE YOU GOING, ALLEN?
HOME TO SHOW MY MOM THE RIBBON I WON.
YOU DIDN'T WIN ANYTHING, SLOW-POKE. THAT'S JUST A PARTICIPATION RIBBON. EVERYBODY GOT ONE.
LEAVE ME ALONE!
YEAH, THAT'S RIGHT. GO HOME TO YOUR MOMMY AND CRY!
"I SHOULD'VE NOTICED SOMETHING WAS WRONG AS SOON AS I SAW THE DOOR HAD BEEN BROKEN OPEN. BUT ALL I WANTED TO DO WAS GET TO MOM AS FAST AS I COULD, SO SHE COULD TELL ME ONE MORE TIME THAT EVERYTHING WOULD BE OKAY.
"I THINK DEEP DOWN I KNEW--"

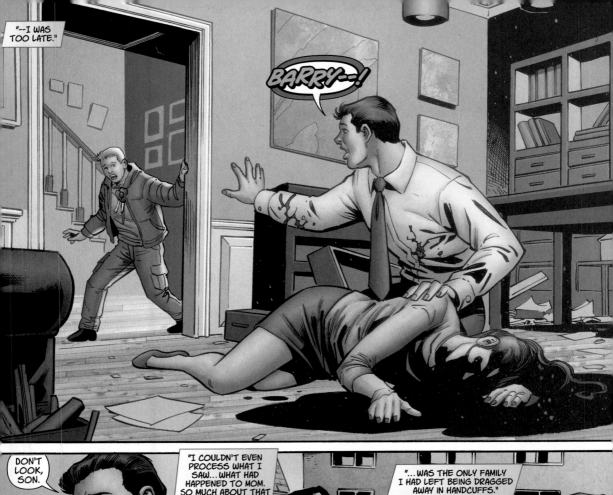

"--I WAS TOO LATE."

BARRY--!

DON'T LOOK, SON.

"I COULDN'T EVEN PROCESS WHAT I SAW... WHAT HAD HAPPENED TO MOM. SO MUCH ABOUT THAT DAY I REMEMBER PERFECTLY--

"--BUT I MUST HAVE BLACKED OUT, BECAUSE THE NEXT THING I REMEMBER...

"...WAS THE ONLY FAMILY I HAD LEFT BEING DRAGGED AWAY IN HANDCUFFS."

DAD!

YOU'RE UNDER ARREST FOR THE MURDER OF NORA ALLEN. ANYTHING YOU SAY...

WHERE ARE YOU TAKING HIM? WHAT HAPPENED?!

HOLD ON, KID. I'VE GOT YOU.

"THEY SAID IT WAS AN OPEN-AND-SHUT CASE, THAT NOT A SHRED OF EVIDENCE INDICATED SOMEONE ELSE KILLED HER. BUT I COULDN'T BELIEVE IT. I WOULDN'T.

"THE DOOR HAD BEEN BROKEN FROM THE OUTSIDE. BUT THERE WAS SOMETHING ELSE... SOMETHING I COULDN'T QUITE REMEMBER...

"I KNEW THE REAL KILLER WAS OUT THERE SOMEWHERE, AND I WOULDN'T REST UNTIL I FOUND HIM."

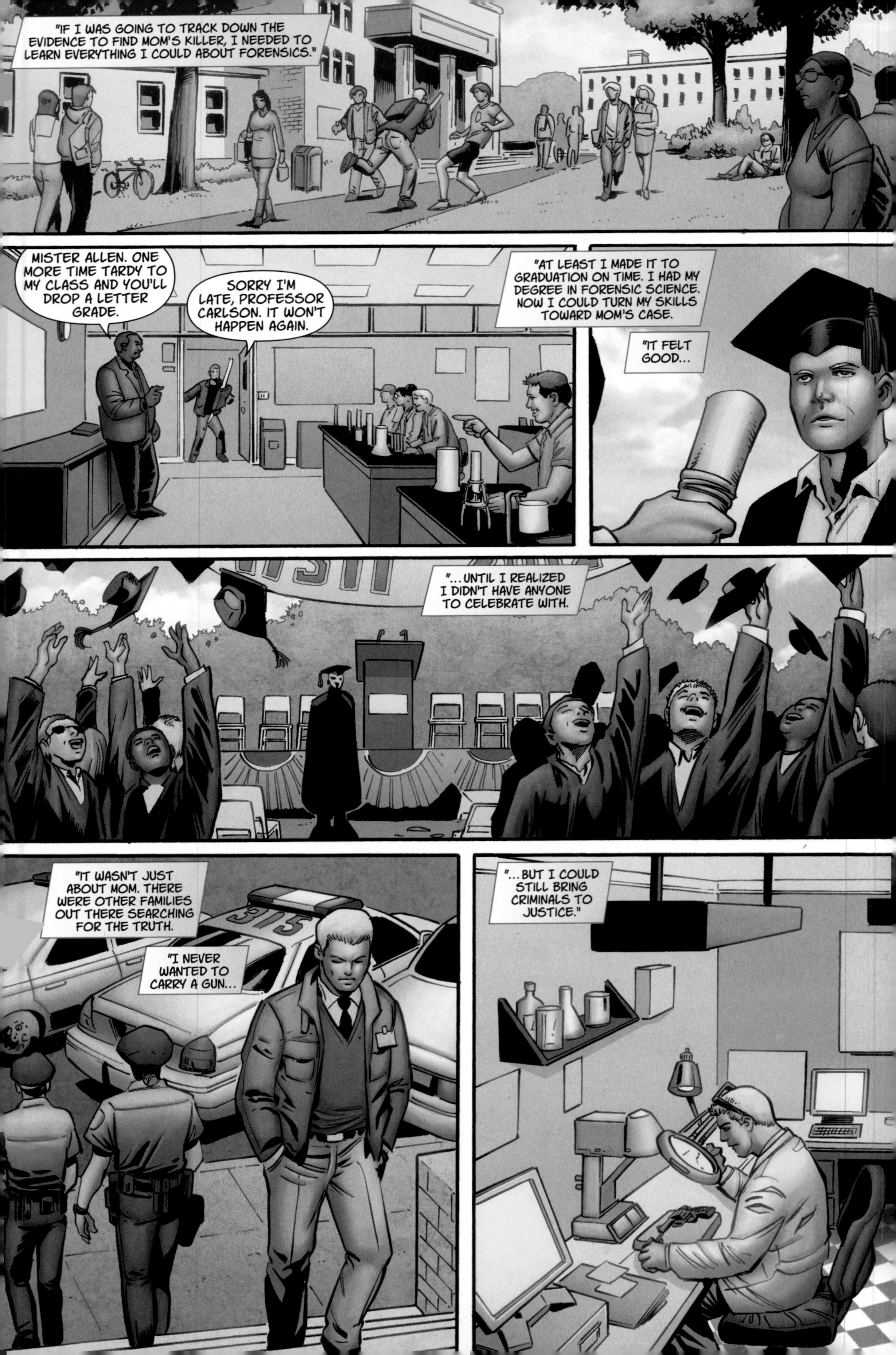
"IF I WAS GOING TO TRACK DOWN THE EVIDENCE TO FIND MOM'S KILLER, I NEEDED TO LEARN EVERYTHING I COULD ABOUT FORENSICS."
MISTER ALLEN. ONE MORE TIME TARDY TO MY CLASS AND YOU'LL DROP A LETTER GRADE.
SORRY I'M LATE, PROFESSOR CARLSON. IT WON'T HAPPEN AGAIN.
"AT LEAST I MADE IT TO GRADUATION ON TIME. I HAD MY DEGREE IN FORENSIC SCIENCE. NOW I COULD TURN MY SKILLS TOWARD MOM'S CASE.
"IT FELT GOOD...
"...UNTIL I REALIZED I DIDN'T HAVE ANYONE TO CELEBRATE WITH.
"IT WASN'T JUST ABOUT MOM. THERE WERE OTHER FAMILIES OUT THERE SEARCHING FOR THE TRUTH.
"I NEVER WANTED TO CARRY A GUN...
"...BUT I COULD STILL BRING CRIMINALS TO JUSTICE."

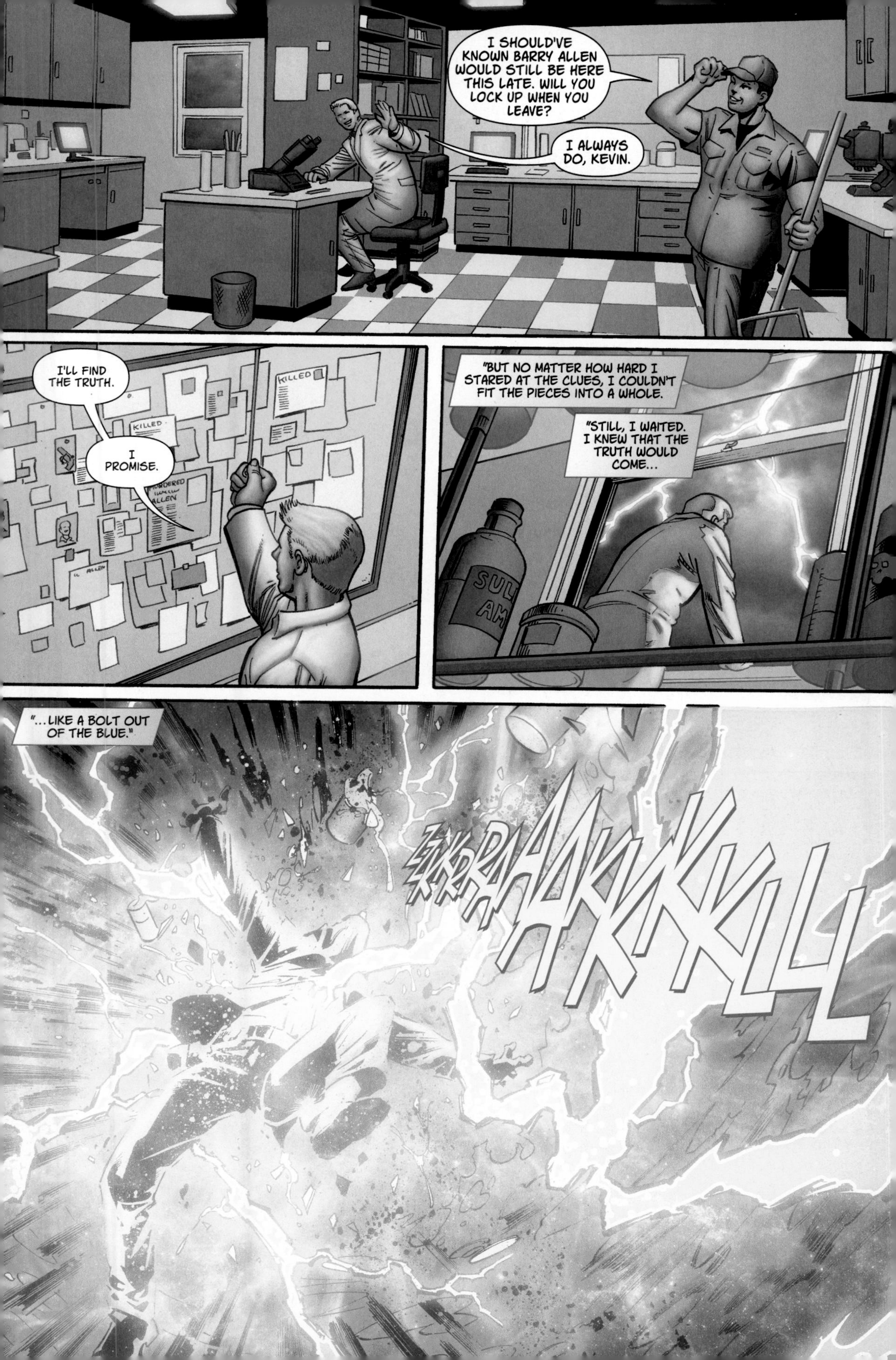

I SHOULD'VE KNOWN BARRY ALLEN WOULD STILL BE HERE THIS LATE. WILL YOU LOCK UP WHEN YOU LEAVE?
I ALWAYS DO, KEVIN.
I'LL FIND THE TRUTH.
I PROMISE.
"BUT NO MATTER HOW HARD I STARED AT THE CLUES, I COULDN'T FIT THE PIECES INTO A WHOLE.
"STILL, I WAITED. I KNEW THAT THE TRUTH WOULD COME...
"...LIKE A BOLT OUT OF THE BLUE."

I...I DON'T UNDERSTAND, MR. ALLEN. YOU CAME INTO THE E.R. WITH ELECTRICAL AND CHEMICAL BURNS ACROSS MOST OF YOUR BODY, BUT THEY'VE *ALREADY* HEALED. YOU DON'T EVEN HAVE ANY *SCARS*.

SO... CAN I GET BACK TO WORK?

GO AHEAD. BUT PLEASE BE CAREFUL--

"--LIGHTNING STRIKES CAN CAUSE SOME *UNEXPECTED* SIDE EFFECTS."

"...TO JUST RUN AS FAST AS YOU CAN."

I'M IN... INDIA--?

"AFTER MOM DIED, I HAD TO GROW UP FAST. I MISSED OUT ON BEING A KID, NOT HAVING ANY WORRIES..."

"BUT THAT'S THE THING ABOUT GROWING UP. YOU CAN'T JUST HAVE FUN. YOU LEARN NEW THINGS, DEVELOP NEW...ABILITIES..."

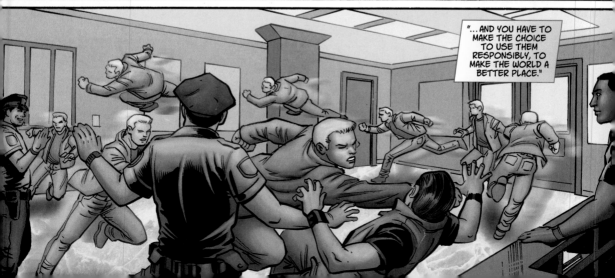

"...AND YOU HAVE TO MAKE THE CHOICE TO USE THEM RESPONSIBLY, TO MAKE THE WORLD A BETTER PLACE."

TALKING ABOUT IT OUT LOUD MAKES ME REALIZE...I DIDN'T DECIDE TO FIGHT CRIME JUST BECAUSE OF MOM.

IT WAS BECAUSE OF WHAT A LIFE OF SERVICE MEANS TO THE *GREATER GOOD.*

"LOOK AT A POLICE OFFICER, AND WHAT ARE THE FIRST THINGS YOU NOTICE?

"THE BADGE.

"THE UNIFORM.

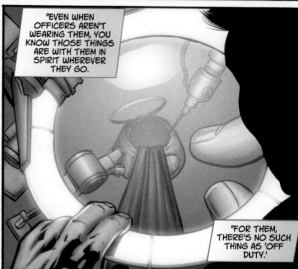

"EVEN WHEN OFFICERS AREN'T WEARING THEM, YOU KNOW THOSE THINGS ARE WITH THEM IN SPIRIT WHEREVER THEY GO.

"FOR THEM, THERE'S NO SUCH THING AS 'OFF DUTY.'

"AND WHEN THEY'RE *ON* DUTY--"

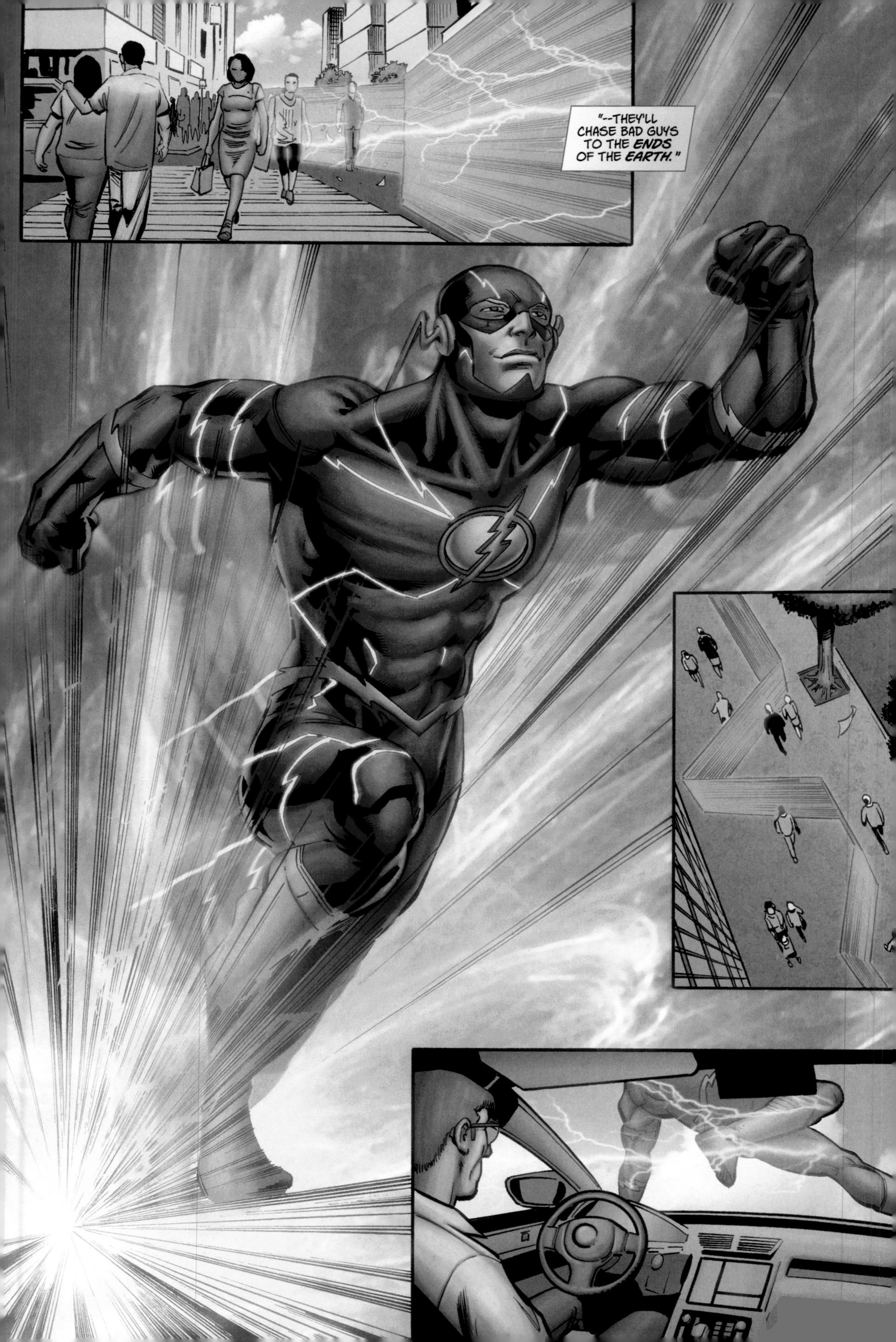
"--THEY'LL CHASE BAD GUYS TO THE *ENDS* OF THE *EARTH*."

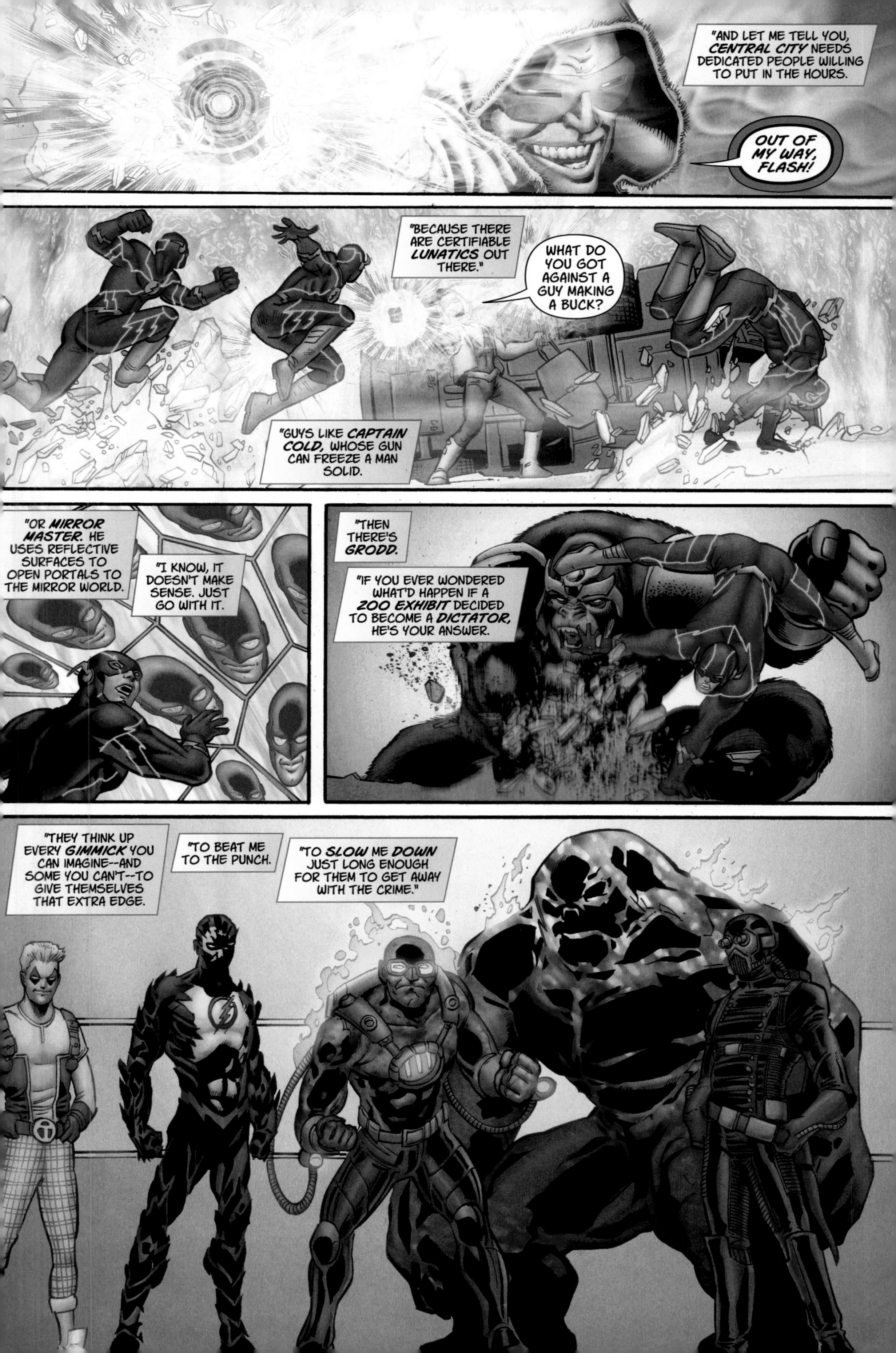
"AND LET ME TELL YOU, CENTRAL CITY NEEDS DEDICATED PEOPLE WILLING TO PUT IN THE HOURS.
OUT OF MY WAY, FLASH!
"BECAUSE THERE ARE CERTIFIABLE LUNATICS OUT THERE."
WHAT DO YOU GOT AGAINST A GUY MAKING A BUCK?
"GUYS LIKE CAPTAIN COLD, WHOSE GUN CAN FREEZE A MAN SOLID.
"OR MIRROR MASTER. HE USES REFLECTIVE SURFACES TO OPEN PORTALS TO THE MIRROR WORLD.
"I KNOW, IT DOESN'T MAKE SENSE. JUST GO WITH IT.
"THEN THERE'S GRODD.
"IF YOU EVER WONDERED WHAT'D HAPPEN IF A ZOO EXHIBIT DECIDED TO BECOME A DICTATOR, HE'S YOUR ANSWER.
"THEY THINK UP EVERY GIMMICK YOU CAN IMAGINE--AND SOME YOU CAN'T--TO GIVE THEMSELVES THAT EXTRA EDGE.
"TO BEAT ME TO THE PUNCH.
"TO SLOW ME DOWN JUST LONG ENOUGH FOR THEM TO GET AWAY WITH THE CRIME."

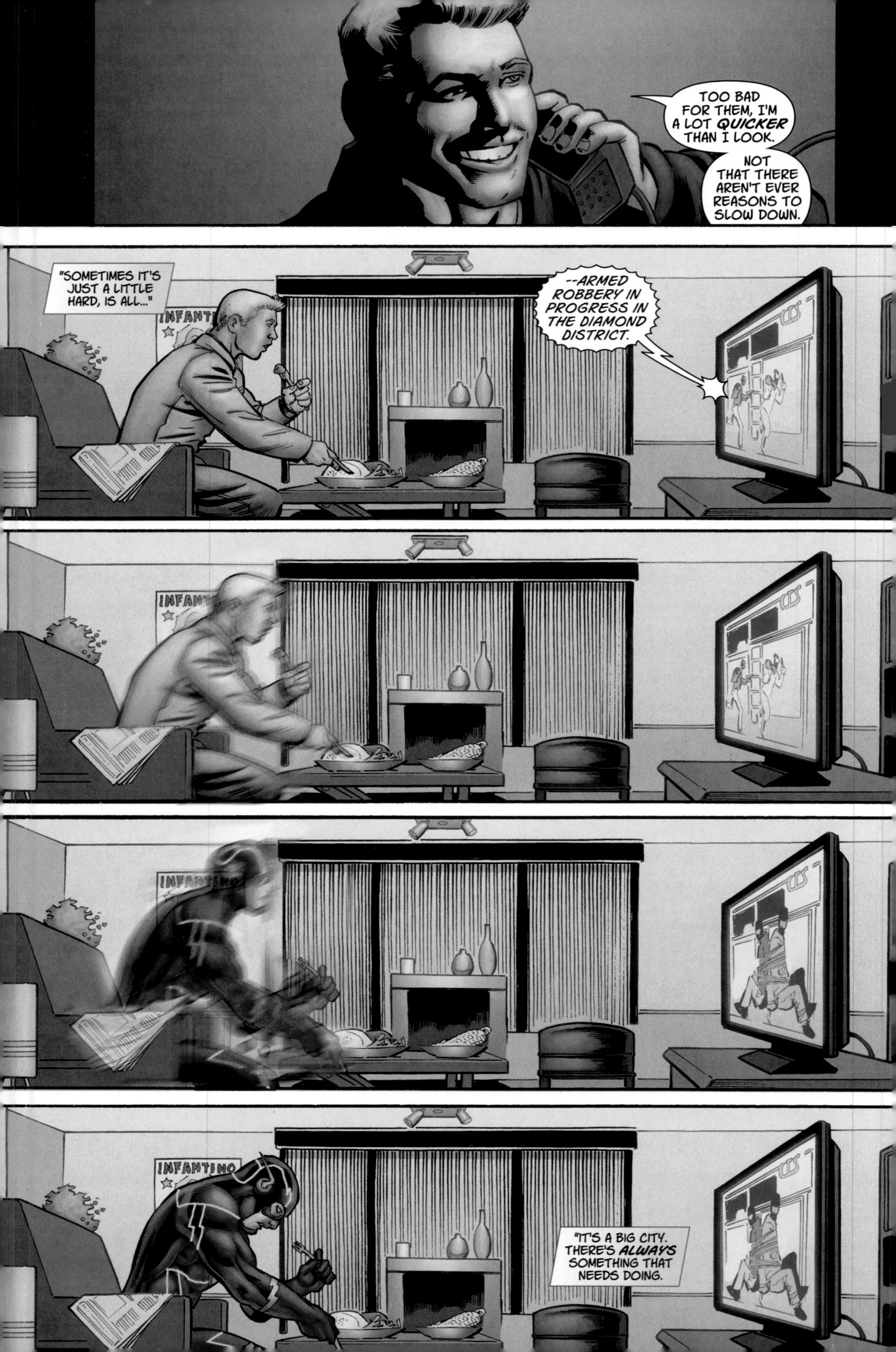
TOO BAD FOR THEM, I'M A LOT *QUICKER* THAN I LOOK.
NOT THAT THERE AREN'T EVER REASONS TO SLOW DOWN.
"SOMETIMES IT'S JUST A LITTLE HARD, IS ALL..."
--ARMED ROBBERY IN PROGRESS IN THE DIAMOND DISTRICT.
INFANTINO
"IT'S A BIG CITY. THERE'S *ALWAYS* SOMETHING THAT NEEDS DOING.

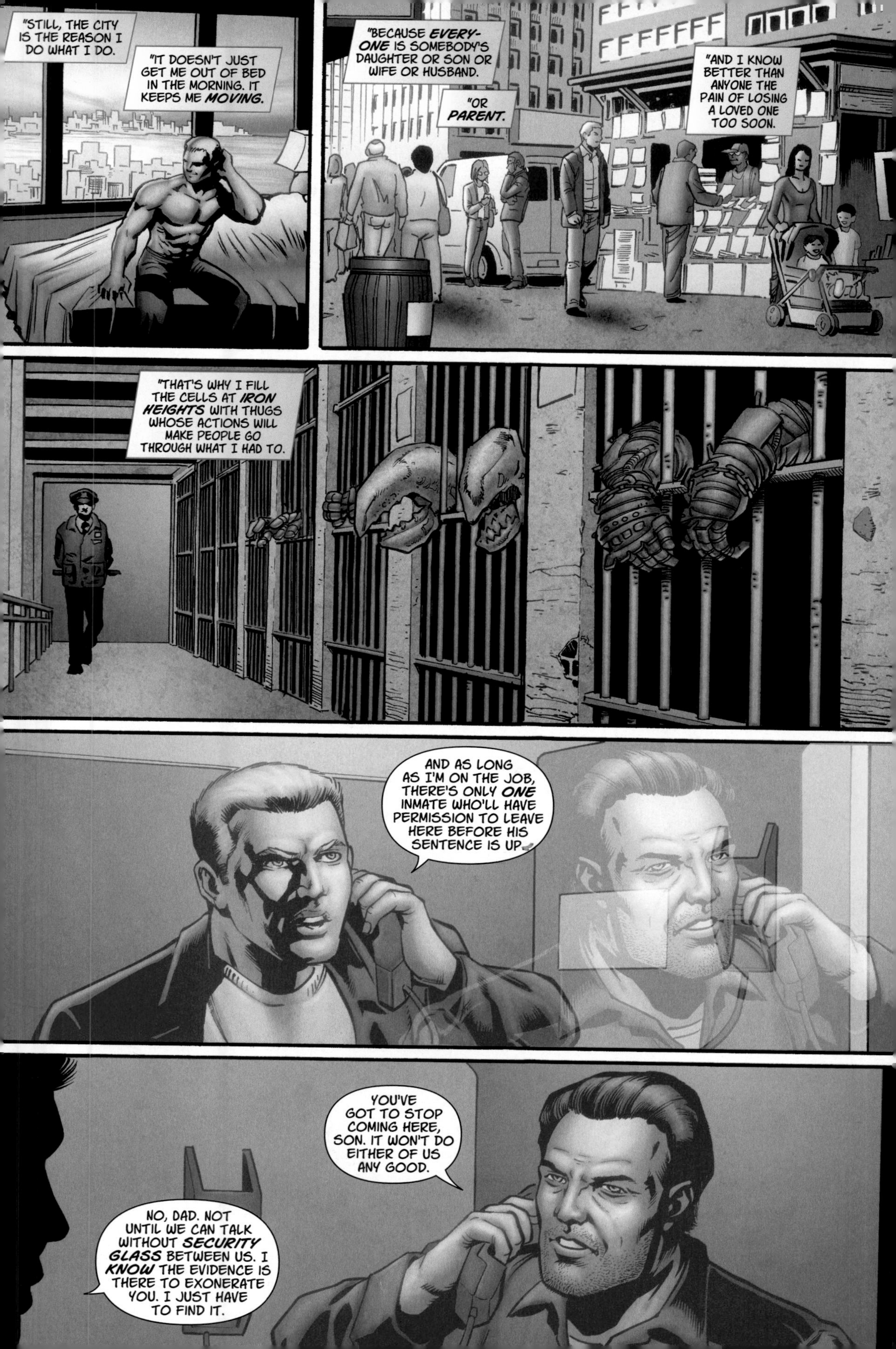
"STILL, THE CITY IS THE REASON I DO WHAT I DO.
"IT DOESN'T JUST GET ME OUT OF BED IN THE MORNING. IT KEEPS ME MOVING.
"BECAUSE EVERY-ONE IS SOMEBODY'S DAUGHTER OR SON OR WIFE OR HUSBAND.
"OR PARENT.
"AND I KNOW BETTER THAN ANYONE THE PAIN OF LOSING A LOVED ONE TOO SOON.
FFFFFFF
"THAT'S WHY I FILL THE CELLS AT IRON HEIGHTS WITH THUGS WHOSE ACTIONS WILL MAKE PEOPLE GO THROUGH WHAT I HAD TO.
AND AS LONG AS I'M ON THE JOB, THERE'S ONLY ONE INMATE WHO'LL HAVE PERMISSION TO LEAVE HERE BEFORE HIS SENTENCE IS UP.
YOU'VE GOT TO STOP COMING HERE, SON. IT WON'T DO EITHER OF US ANY GOOD.
NO, DAD. NOT UNTIL WE CAN TALK WITHOUT SECURITY GLASS BETWEEN US. I KNOW THE EVIDENCE IS THERE TO EXONERATE YOU. I JUST HAVE TO FIND IT.

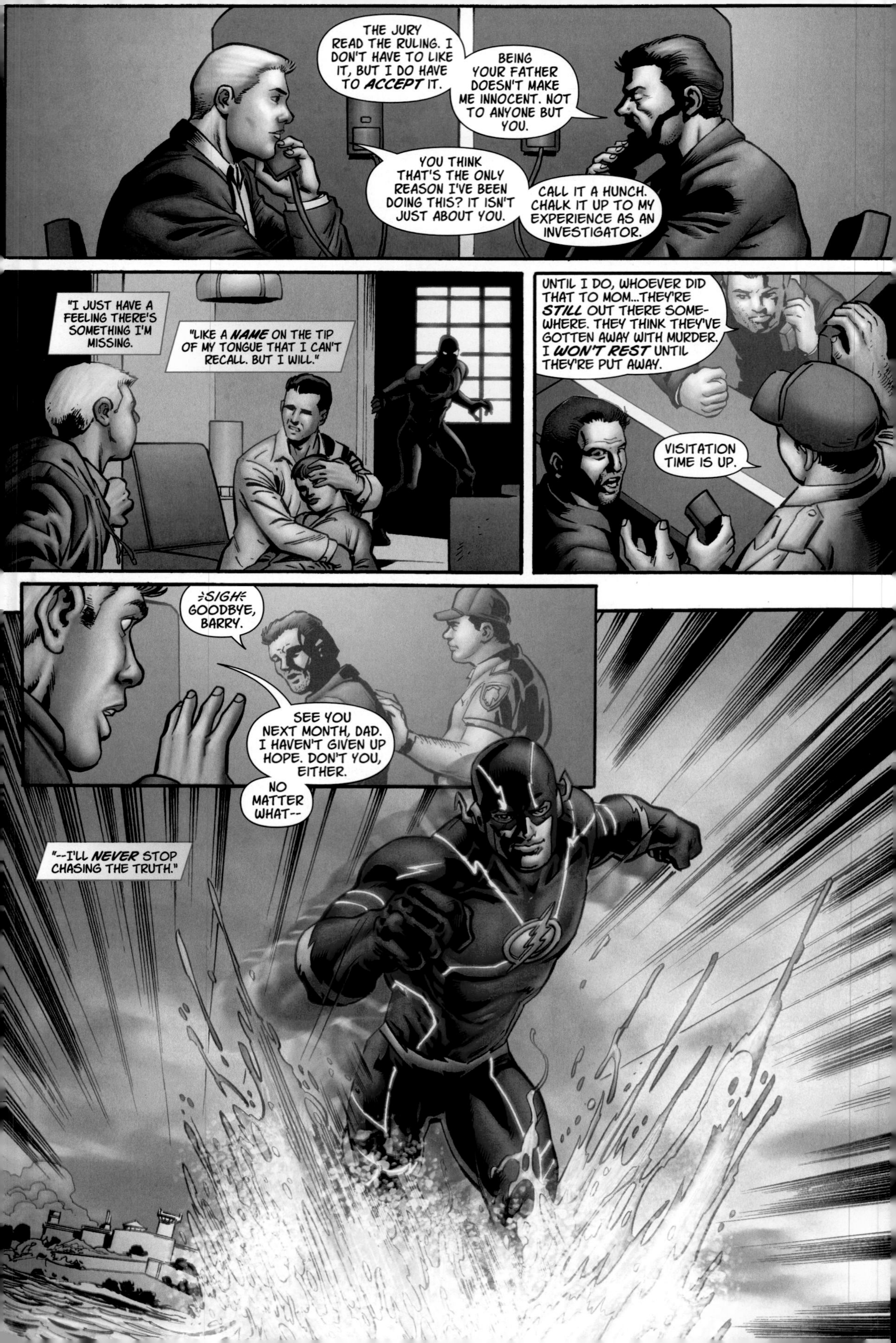

THE JURY READ THE RULING. I DON'T HAVE TO LIKE IT, BUT I DO HAVE TO ACCEPT IT.
BEING YOUR FATHER DOESN'T MAKE ME INNOCENT. NOT TO ANYONE BUT YOU.
YOU THINK THAT'S THE ONLY REASON I'VE BEEN DOING THIS? IT ISN'T JUST ABOUT YOU.
CALL IT A HUNCH. CHALK IT UP TO MY EXPERIENCE AS AN INVESTIGATOR.
"I JUST HAVE A FEELING THERE'S SOMETHING I'M MISSING.
"LIKE A NAME ON THE TIP OF MY TONGUE THAT I CAN'T RECALL. BUT I WILL."
UNTIL I DO, WHOEVER DID THAT TO MOM...THEY'RE STILL OUT THERE SOME-WHERE. THEY THINK THEY'VE GOTTEN AWAY WITH MURDER. I WON'T REST UNTIL THEY'RE PUT AWAY.
VISITATION TIME IS UP.
SIGH GOODBYE, BARRY.
SEE YOU NEXT MONTH, DAD. I HAVEN'T GIVEN UP HOPE. DON'T YOU, EITHER.
NO MATTER WHAT--
"--I'LL NEVER STOP CHASING THE TRUTH."

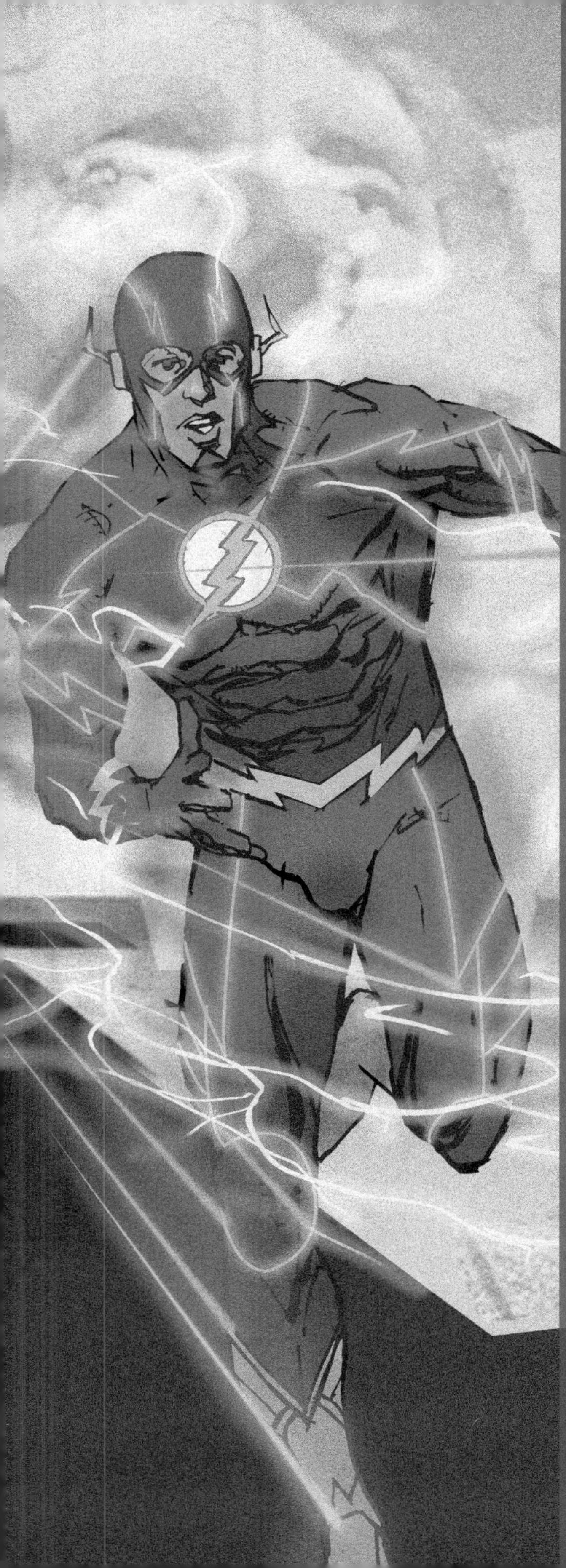

VARIANT COVER GALLERY

THE FLASH #36
LEGO VARIANT

THE FLASH #37
VARIANT BY
DARWYN COOKE

THE FLASH #38
THE FLASH 75TH ANNIVERSARY
VARIANT BY
HOWARD PORTER & HI-FI
AFTER CARMINE INFANTINO
& MURPHY ANDERSON

THE FLASH #39
HARLEY QUINN VARIANT BY
AMANDA CONNER
& PAUL MOUNTS

THE FLASH #40
NORTH BY NORTHWEST
MOVIE POSTER VARIANT BY
BILL SIENKIEWICZ

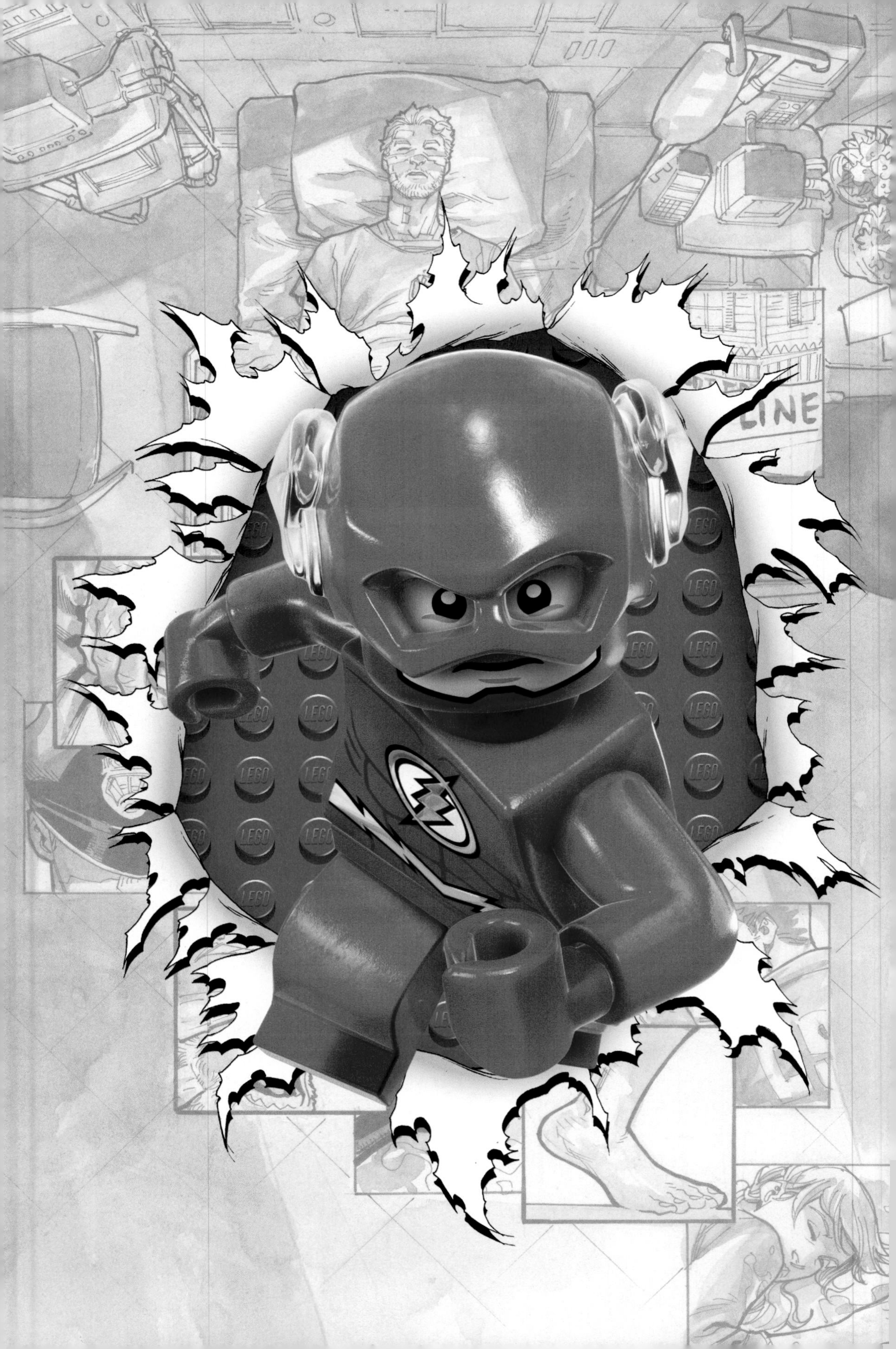
LINE
LEGO

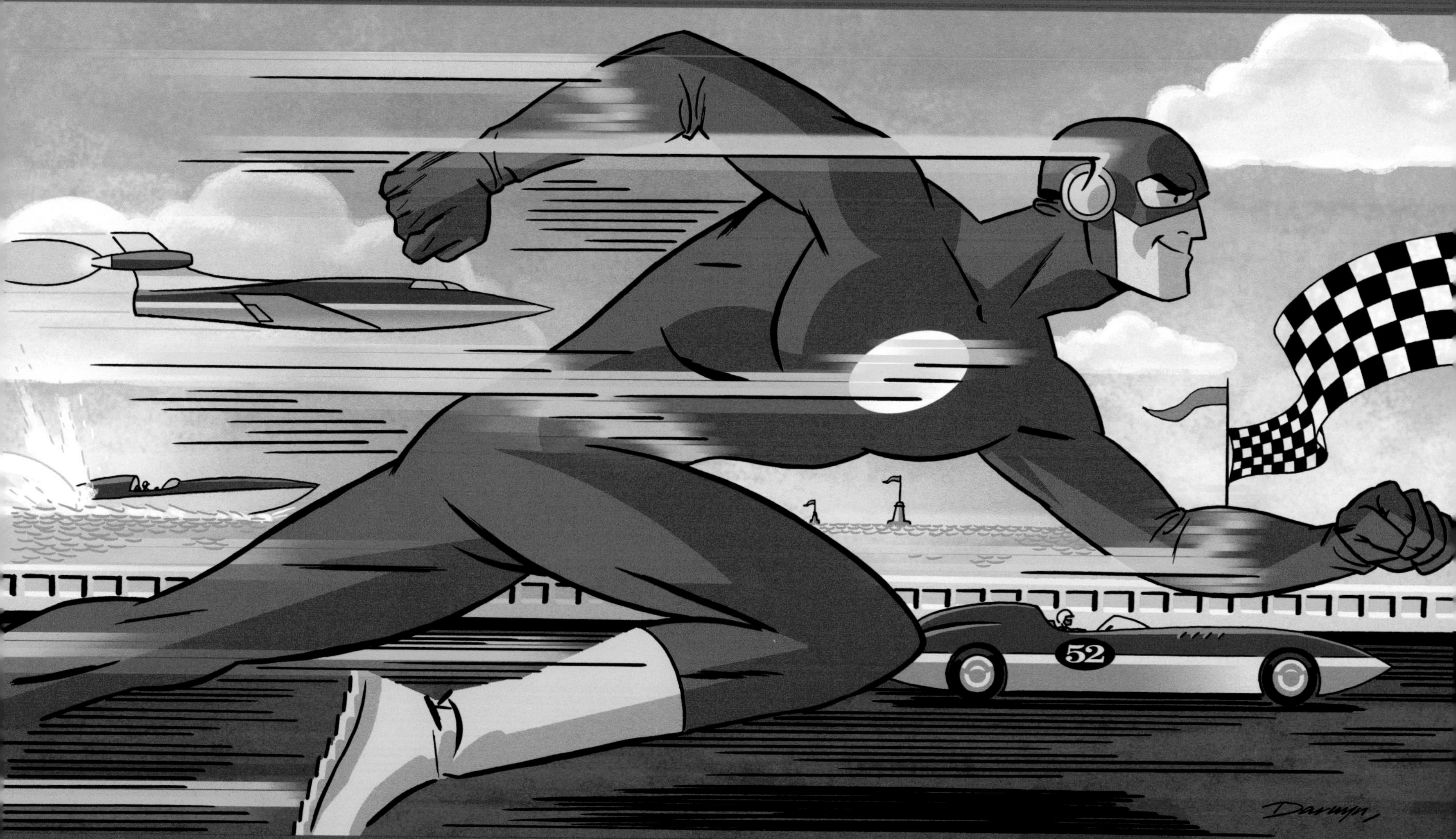
52
Darwyn

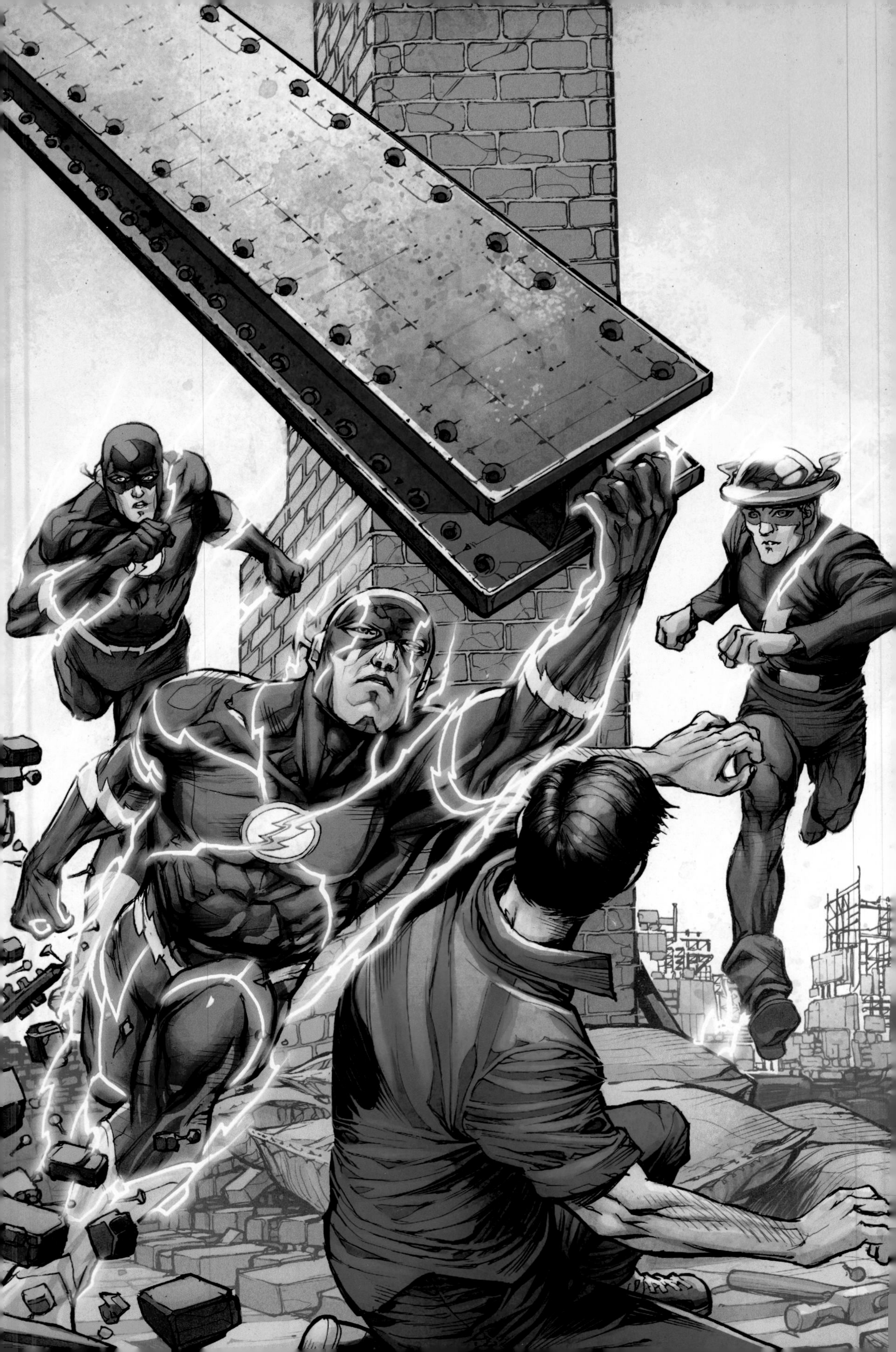

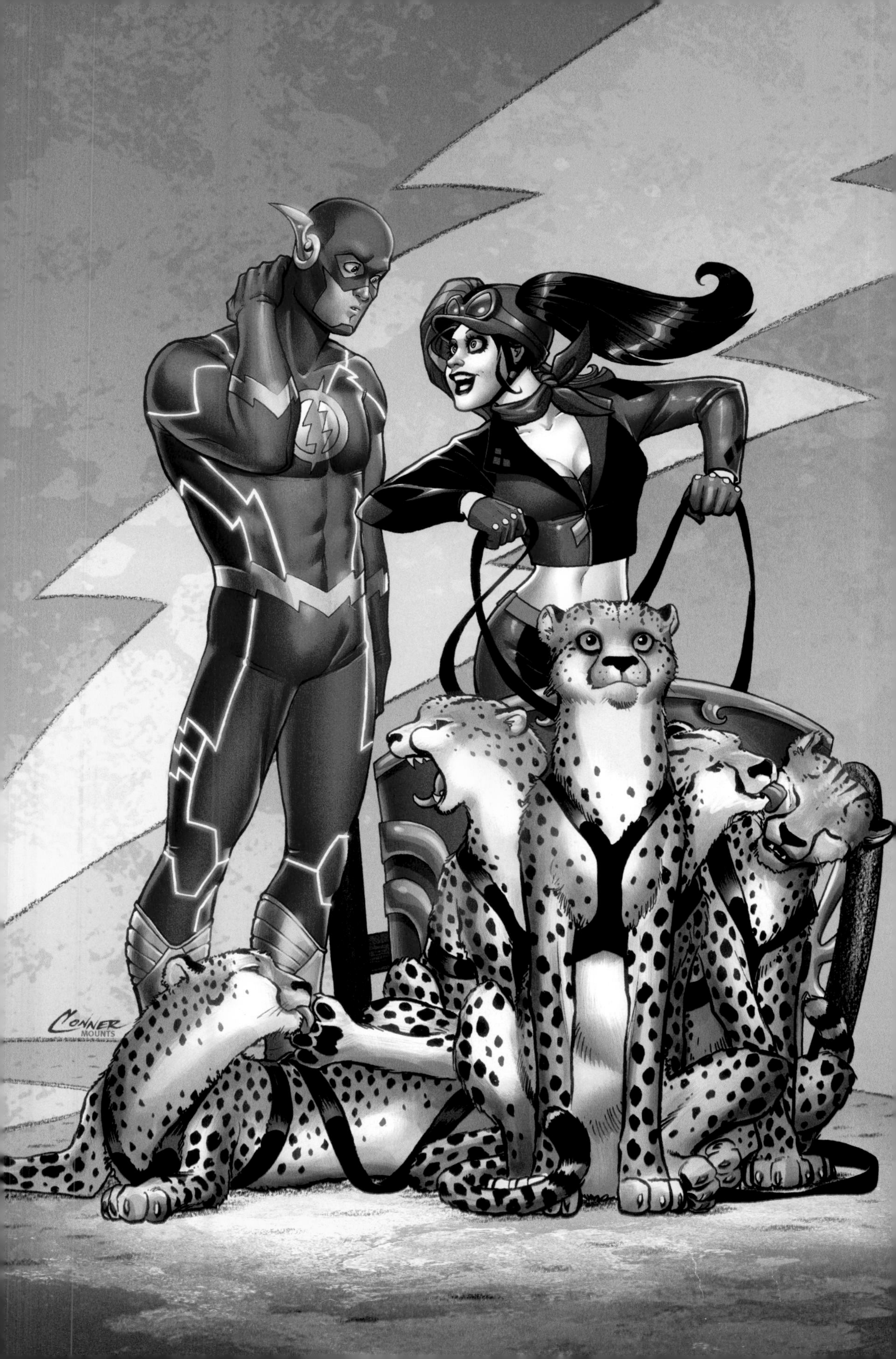
CONNER
MOUNTS

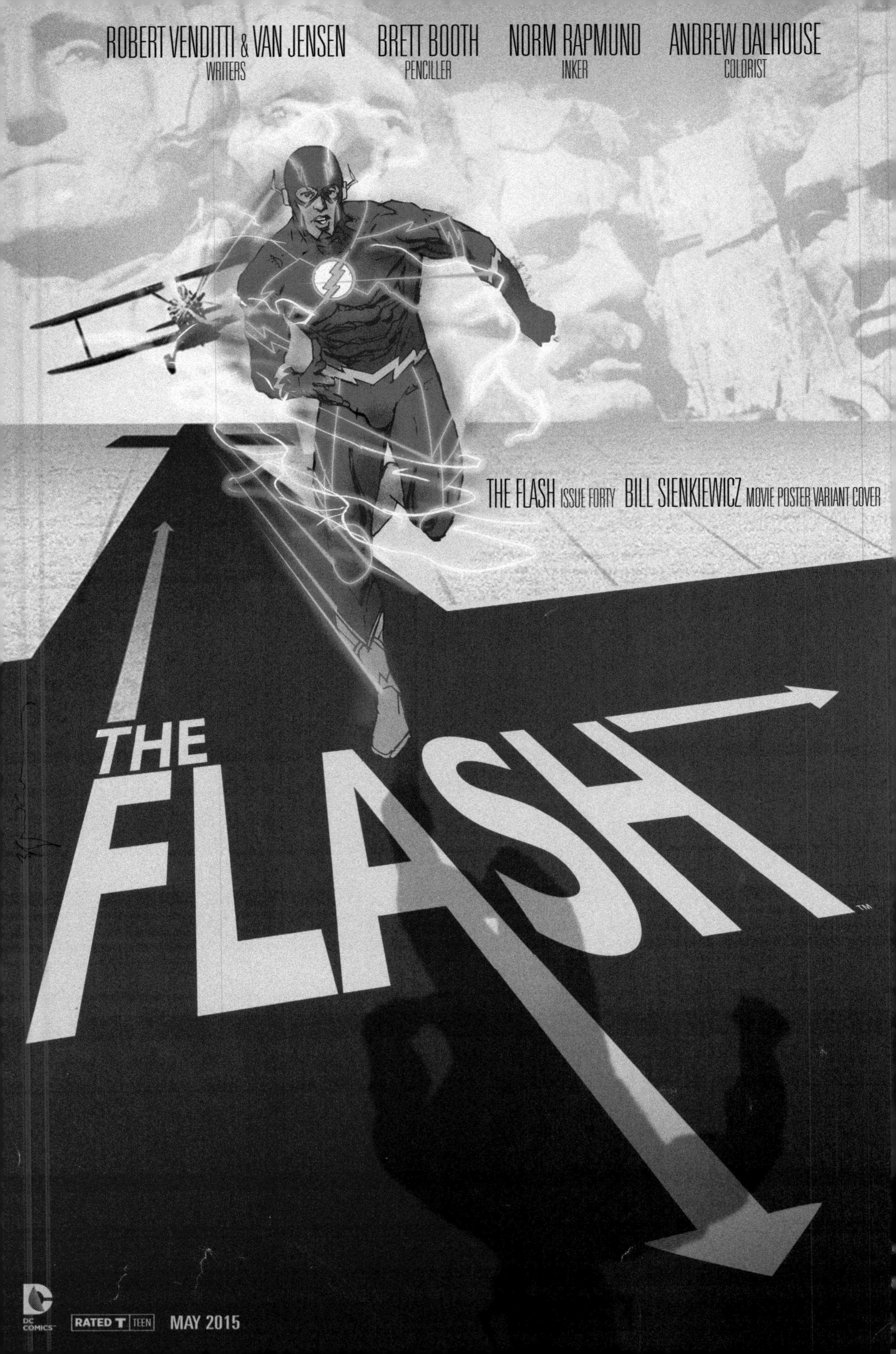
ROBERT VENDITTI & VAN JENSEN
WRITERS
BRETT BOOTH
PENCILLER
NORM RAPMUND
INKER
ANDREW DALHOUSE
COLORIST
THE FLASH ISSUE FORTY BILL SIENKIEWICZ MOVIE POSTER VARIANT COVER
THE FLASH™
DC COMICS
RATED T TEEN
MAY 2015

NAPALM CHARACTER SKETCH BY
BRETT BOOTH

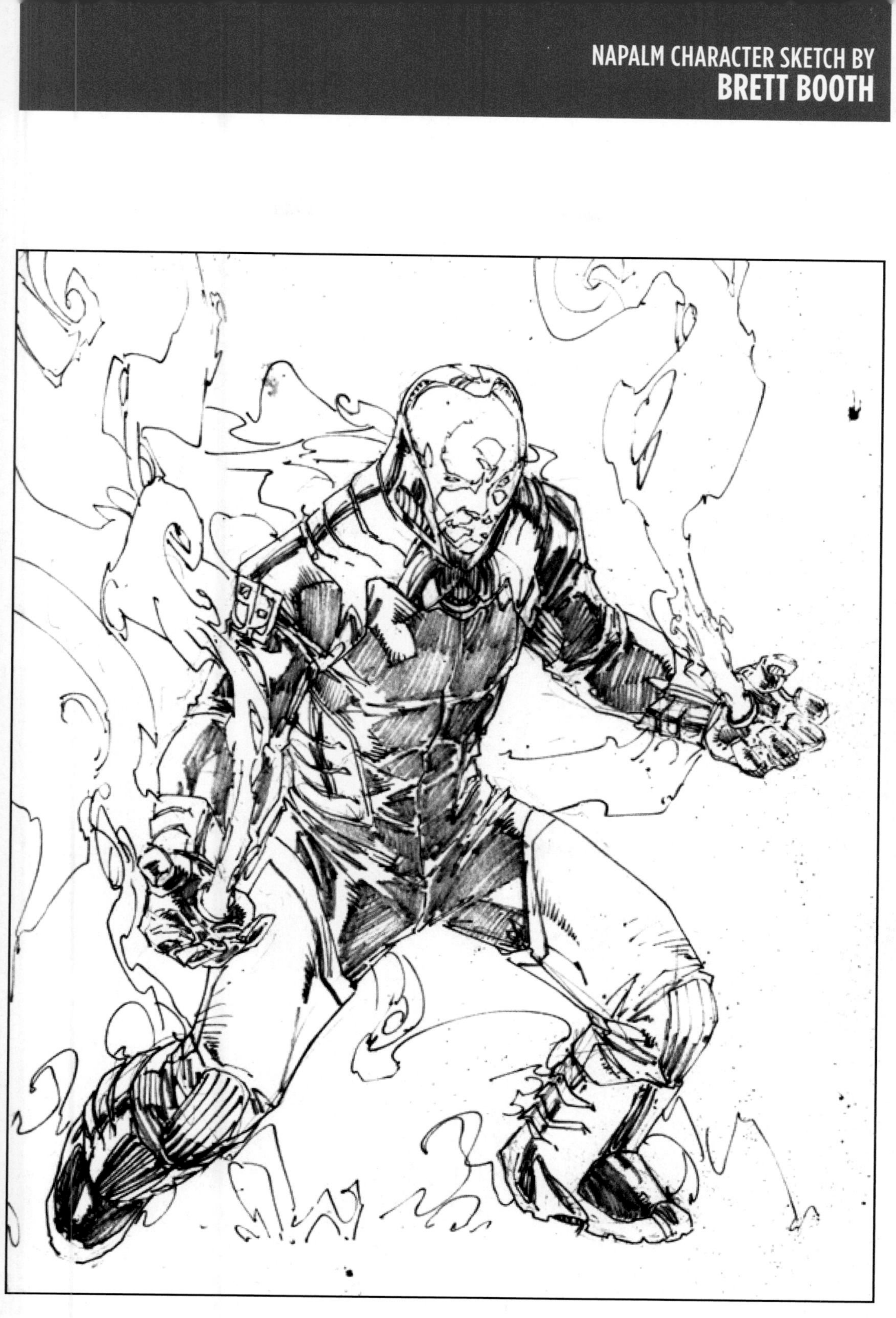

THE FLASH #36
COVER ROUGH LAYOUTS TO PENCILS TO FINAL

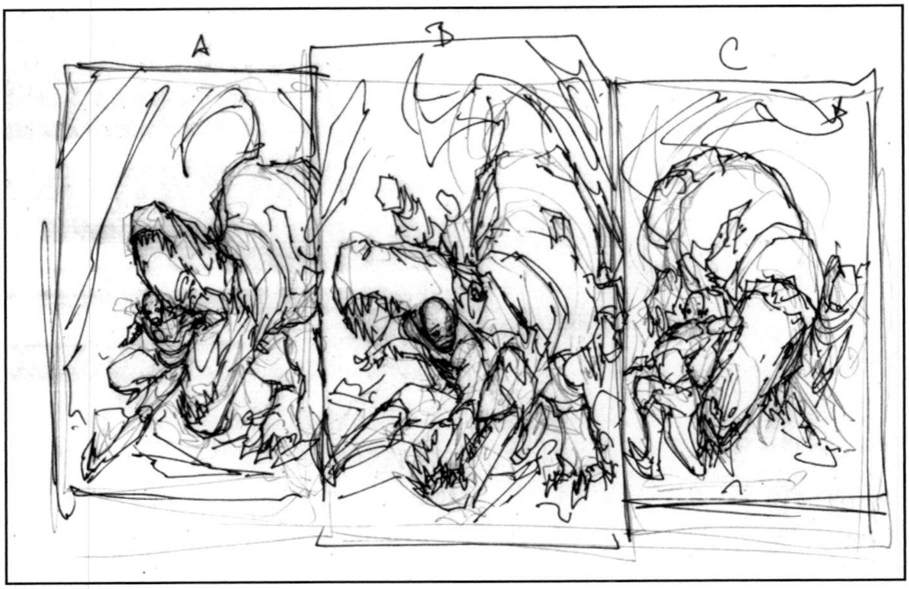
A
B
C

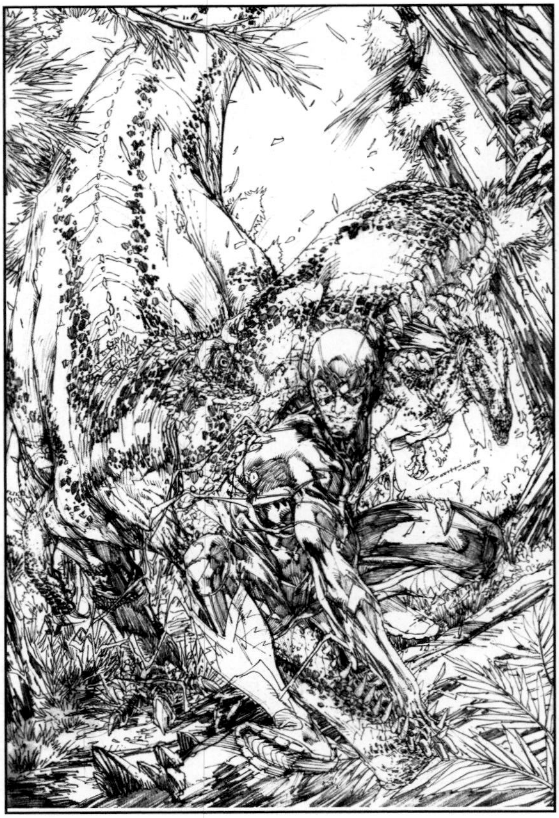

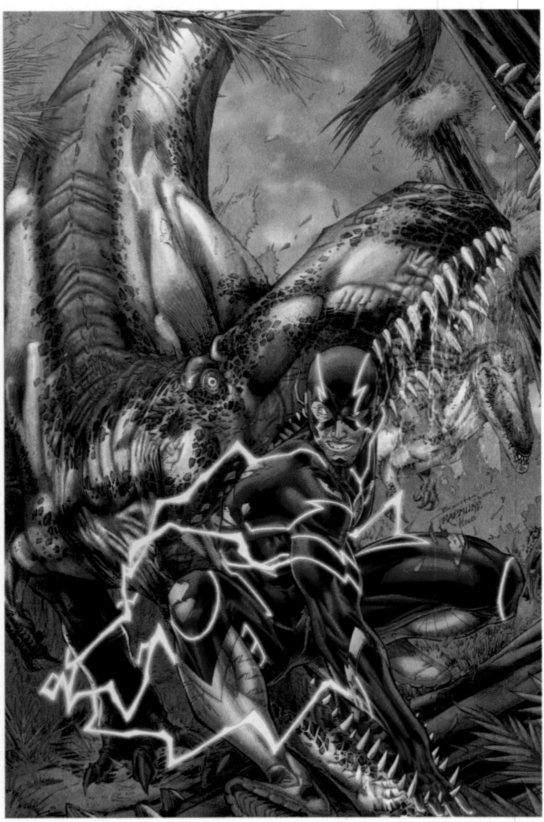

THE FLASH #38
COVER ROUGH LAYOUTS TO PENCILS TO FINAL

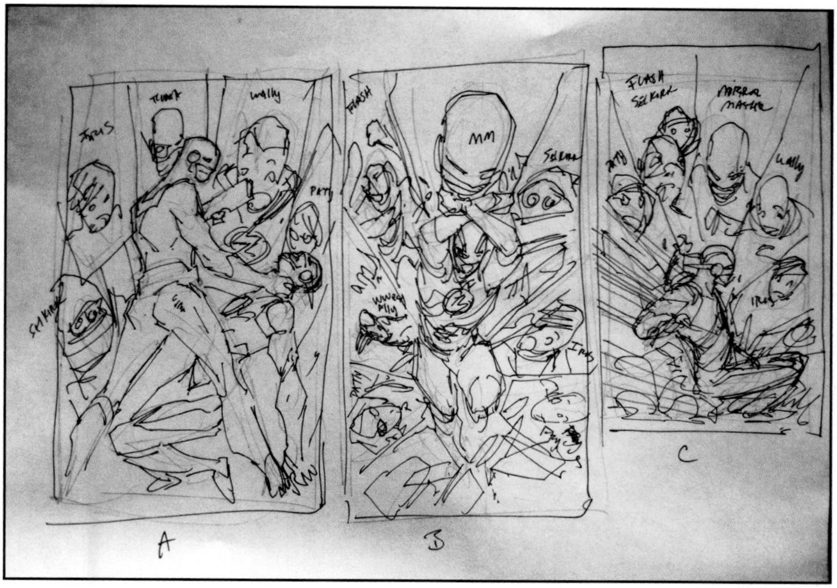

FLASH
MM
wally
A
B
C

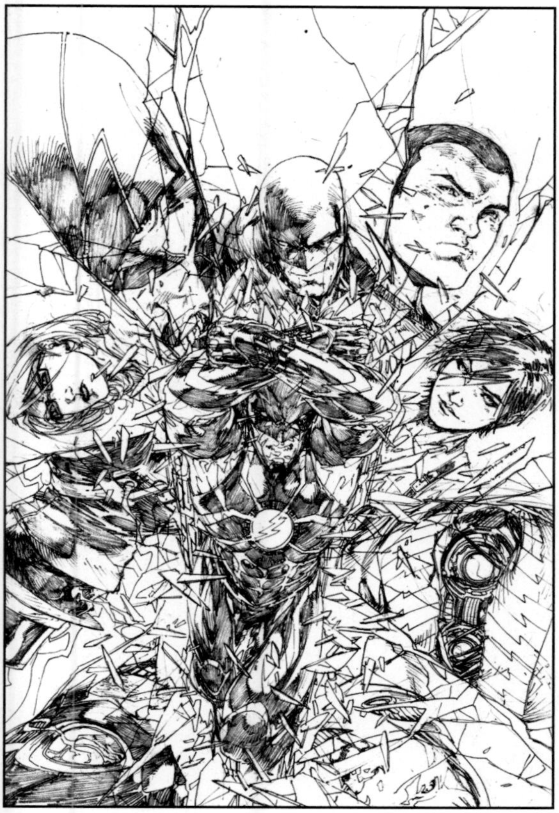

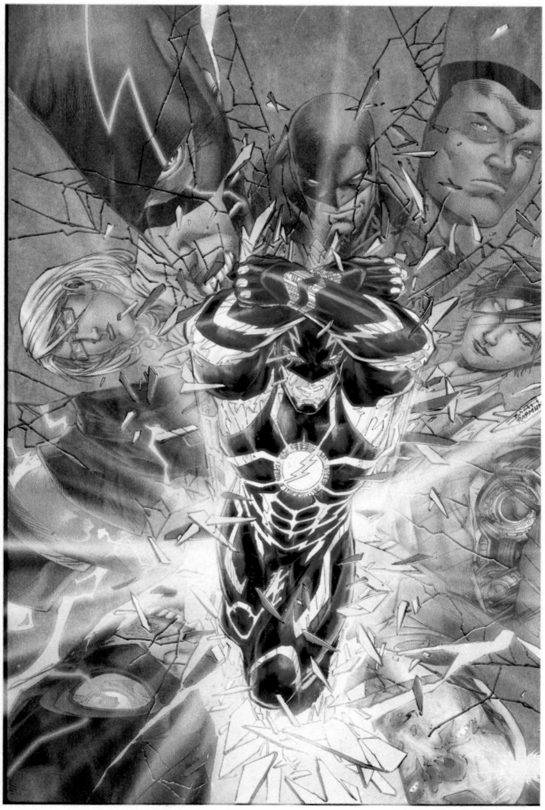

DC COMICS™

START AT THE BEGINNING!

THE FLASH
VOLUME 1: MOVE FORWARD

THE FLASH VOL. 2: ROGUES REVOLUTION

THE FLASH VOL. 3: GORILLA WARFARE

JUSTICE LEAGUE VOL. 1: ORIGIN

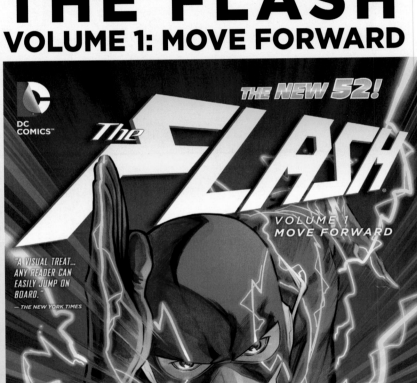

FRANCIS MANAPUL **BRIAN BUCCELLATO**